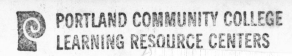

This volume is sponsored by
the Center for Chinese Studies
University of California, Berkeley

The Center for Chinese Studies
at the University of California, Berkeley, supported by
the East Asian Institute (University of California, Berkeley)
and the State of California, is the unifying organization for
social science and interdisciplinary research on modern China.

A Madman of Ch'u

To obey, but to resist.
There is the whole secret.

Alain

A Madman of Ch'u

The Chinese Myth of Loyalty and Dissent

Laurence A. Schneider

University of California Press
Berkeley, Los Angeles, London

University of California Press
Berkeley and Los Angeles, California
University of California Press, Ltd. London, England
© 1980 by The Regents of the University of California
ISBN 0-520-03685-9
Library of Congress Catalog Card Number: 78-54800
Printed in the United States of America

1 2 3 4 5 6 7 8 9

For my son Aaron,
born on Tuan Wu,
the Fifth of the Fifth.

Contents

List of Maps

Acknowledgments

I WOULD like Professor Wolfram Eberhard to consider this book as an expression of my esteem on the occasion of his retirement from a long, distinguished, and productive career of teaching. His own imaginative research provided me with a foundation for my venture into mythography and local culture. With his usual enthusiasm and insight, he personally encouraged me to pursue this unconventional line of inquiry into Chinese culture. I wish him *wan sui*!

My good friend Martin Plax and I outdid the Peripatetics as we discussed each phase of this study on the streets of north Buffalo and Shaker Heights. He is a superb listener and generously shared his insights into Western political philosophy.

Arif Dirlik read the entire first draft and provided me with encouragement and invaluable criticism at a critical time. David Knechtges most generously read and criticized chapter one. His expertise has been indispensable. Chapter two was read and criticized by Richard Davis and Professor James T. C. Liu. Susan Alitto, Stephen Salamone and Shelah Leader read portions of the manuscript and made important editorial suggestions, which I have followed. And my special thanks to John S. Service for his sensitive editorial scrutiny of the entire text.

Research for this study was partially carried out under fellowships from the State University of New York Research Foundation and the Joint Committee on Contemporary China of the Social Science Research Council.

Grateful acknowledgment is extended to David Knechtges for permission to quote from "Two Han Dynasty *Fu* on Ch'ü Yüan," published in *Parerga*, no. 1, Seattle: Far Eastern and Russian Institute, 1968; to George Allen and Unwin Ltd. for quotations from Arthur Waley's *Poetry and Career of Li Po*, 1950, *The Analects of Confucius*, 1938, and *The Nine Songs*, 1955; to the Cleveland Museum of Art to quote from a translation by Wai-kam Ho in Sherman Lee and W. K. Ho, *Chinese Art Under the Mongols*, 1968; to the Metropolitan Museum of Art for a quotation from Wen Fong, *Sung and Yuan Paintings*, 1973; to the University of Arizona Press for a quotation from *K'ang Yu-wei*, J. P. Lo, editor, Association for Asian Studies Monograph No. XXIII, Tucson, copyright 1967; to Oxford University Press for quotations of translations from David Hawkes, *Ch'u Tz'u: The Songs of the South*, copyright Oxford University Press, 1959, and from James R. Hightower, *The Poetry of T'ao Ch'ien*, copyright Oxford University Press, 1970.

Illustrations were prepared for publication by the expert and devoted photography staff of the Educational Communications Center of the State University of New York at Buffalo. No technical problem was too difficult for them.

My thanks to University of California Press for deviating from its usual publishing format and permitting notes to be placed at the back of the book. Warm appreciation is expressed to Phyllis Killen and Philip Lilienthal of the University of California Press for their encouragement.

Chen Shih-hsiang (1912–1971), who taught me to read and love Chinese poetry, would have understood my delight in preparing for this study and in writing it.

                                                                    L. S.

Buffalo, New York

Introduction

THIS is a study in Chinese political mythology. Its protagonist is the ancient official and poet, Ch'ü Yüan (338–278 B.C.) —high minister of the great southern kingdom of Ch'u, exemplar of political loyalty, paragon of public dedication. Its central subjects are the place of individuality in politics and the relationship of personal sentiment to public duty; the possibility of dissent for the loyal and the necessity of revolt for the committed.

Like the Yangtze River coursing its way across the breadth of China, the mythology of Ch'ü Yüan weaves its way through Chinese history from classical times in the second century B.C. to the present. And as the Yangtze Valley marks the boundary of southern culture in China, the Ch'ü Yüan mythology—in which the river plays its role—evokes southern ways in politics and art. The mythology's scope not only encompasses a grand stretch of historical time and cultural space, but also involves us in considerations of China's "great" and "little" traditions. The lore of Ch'ü Yüan spans oral and literary, regional and cosmopolitan cultures. Moreover it is possible to document this comprehensive mythology with considerable and reliable detail, which provides an unusual oppor-

1

tunity to understand certain perennial problems in Chinese civilization on the basis of Chinese cultural forms. The longevity of the mythology and the richness of its lore, in addition, provide a means for exploring questions about continuity and change within specific areas of Chinese culture, such as the ways in which the official class and intellectuals have identified themselves throughout Chinese history.

My motivating interest has been to understand what the lore of Ch'ü Yüan in the twentieth century tells us about the new Chinese intelligentsia, especially their tortured sense of public commitment and political purpose. To place this twentieth-century lore in the context of the entire Ch'ü Yüan tradition and to deepen our understanding of premodern problems, my study begins with a detailed analysis of the classical foundations of the myth in the Han dynasty (206 B.C.–A.D. 220). I turn next to the myth's evolution between the Han and the twentieth century, and then examine transformations in the myth during the Republican period (1911–1949). The latter will shed light on the special concerns and problems of modern intellectuals who self-consciously tried to arrive at a collective new identity using traditional cultural forms.

Although folk traditions begin to surround Ch'ü Yüan from around the sixth century A.D., I do not discuss them until after I have begun my analysis of the lore in the twentieth century. I do this to provide the reader with a coherent description and analysis of Ch'ü Yüan in the literary traditions of the intelligentsia. I also follow this scheme because the folk traditions surrounding Ch'ü Yüan become an intimate part of the modern intelligentsia's self-conscious struggle with their new identity, especially after 1949. The final consideration of this study is the extraordinary resurgence of the Ch'ü Yüan mythology in the People's Republic and the transformations of it which have been guided by the pressures of populism, historical materialism, and the doctrine of continuing revolution.

Ch'ü Yüan

There are only a few details to the earliest and most basic story of the minister of Ch'u who is at the center of the

mythology. Ch'ü Yüan served as one of the highest officials at
the king's court. The epoch in which he lived is known as the
period of Warring States (403–221 B.C.), a fractious time of
bloody rivalries among expanding states, each trying to engulf
the others. Vestiges of China's old, feudalistic political
economy were fast dissolving in aggressive efforts toward political centralization and the consolidation of all kingdoms into
one. The sprouts of bureaucracy began to show among the
debris of the old aristocratic order, and the standards of "government by talent and virtue" were called for.

   In the earliest strata of his story, Ch'ü Yüan is depicted as a
man of his times to the extent that he advocated the consolidation of the states under the aegis of his own kingdom, and
supported the values of government by virtue and talent. But
his story soon describes his fate in a timeless paradigm that has
made it possible for Chinese politicians to empathize with him
down through the ages. At court, Ch'ü Yüan's power and his
access to the king were envied by a clique, some of whose
members were traitors. Using the weapon of slander, the
clique dislodged Ch'ü Yüan from the king's good graces and
had him removed from the court. Then, because of Ch'ü
Yüan's persistent and dramatic self-defense, they had the king
banish him to the primitive riverine countryside of southern
Ch'u. Out of loyalty to both king and country, and self-
assurance of his "purity" and the correctness of his ideas, Ch'ü
Yüan continually tried to remonstrate with the court and to
express publicly his uncompromising ideals. Though he knew
the court had acted unjustly toward him, he refused to flee his
country and seek safety and personal success at the court of
some other kingdom. Such flight was common in his day and
had precedents in the itinerant careers of sages like Confucius
himself. Finally, the king of Ch'u is betrayed from within the
clique that attacked Ch'ü Yüan. When the king is duped and
murdered by a rival state, it is the beginning of the end for
Ch'u, which is soon invaded and annexed. The ignominious
end of his sovereign and the destruction of the capital city are
too much for Ch'ü Yüan to bear. He ends his life by drowning
himself in the Milo River.

Vital to the story of Ch'ü Yüan is his poetry, which is understood to be the product of his banishment. It was his medium
for remonstrating with his king and for expressing his self-
defense and personal grief. The most famous of these poems,
the *Li Sao* (Encountering sorrow), has conventionally been
considered a kind of elaborate suicide note in which the
banished official stated his case and resolved to sacrifice his life
in the hope of awakening his age to the truth. This long poem,
relying on allegory and rich, colorful symbolism, sets out the
basic themes and the somber, melancholy moods of the later
lore of Ch'ü Yüan. Flamboyantly self-righteous and self-
pitying, the poem evokes the individuality, independence of
mind, and isolation of the public figure whom time and fate
have cursed with a benighted sovereign. It laments the disjunction between moral insight and power and the dangers always
inherent in political commitment.

Most regard the body of poetry attributed to Ch'ü Yüan as
the first in China with an identifiable author, and, more or
less, the first poetry (perhaps the first Chinese literature altogether) to convey a full sense of personality and individual
sentiment. It is, in effect, the beginning of the lyrical tradition
in China, and for our purposes here, it is significant that
China's first poet and this lyrical tradition have their point of
departure in a political context. The literature we shall explore
will continuously speak to the implications of this junction of
politics and art and the relationship between private sentiment
and public obligation.

Ch'ü Yüan's poetry is also taken as evidence of a larger
cultural style: its concern with self and sentiment, its fantas-
tic imagery and language, its idealism, passion, and imagination all add up to an expression of southern culture. In the
development of the Ch'ü Yüan tradition, considerations of
the poet sometimes become secondary to considerations
of the South. Eventually, Ch'ü Yüan becomes an archetypal
southerner.

The basic structures of Ch'ü Yüan lore established over the
course of the Han dynasty are both a symptom of his popularity in those times and a source of his later fame as well. In the
second century B.C., a sympathetic biography was written for

him in a pioneer historical work of unequalled importance in Chinese letters. In the second century A.D., the poetry attributed to Ch'ü Yüan was anthologized along with the works of other southern poets in the *Ch'u Tz'u* (Poems of Ch'u). Shortly thereafter, the first gloss and commentary on Ch'ü Yüan's poetry appeared. These literary works define the scope of the classical Ch'ü Yüan lore. They are important not merely because they comprise a stage in the growth of the overall mythology, but also because they have remained in prominence into modern times and have been the points of departure for most who have contributed to the lore of Ch'ü Yüan.

The *Ch'u Tz'u* anthology has been the formal medium through which Ch'ü Yüan's poetry has been preserved for the ages. Its themes and style imitate that of the *Li Sao*, and its overall tone and message are basic to the myth of loyalty and dissent. In it, Ch'ü Yüan is celebrated and sometimes used as a persona through whom the Han poets express their resentful feelings about contemporary political problems. They primarily address themselves to the basic themes of the *Li Sao* and Ch'ü Yüan's classic biography: the seemingly inevitable disasters that await the virtuous, talented, and conscientious public servant; the limitations human mortality places even upon the ambitions of the righteous; the pitfalls set by the greedy, the sycophants, the jealous. The more worthy the official, the poetry implies, the greater his chances for frustration or betrayal, for a ruined career, exile, despair, and death.

The most seminal legacy of the classical lore of Ch'ü Yüan can best be epitomized as a kind of Prometheanism. Later generations, with increasing emphasis, perceived it as a legitimization of a challenge to authority on the grounds of a higher and more complete authority: Ch'ü Yüan's challenge, far from being nihilistic, was an affirmation of universal value; his self-righteousness was motivated not by self-interest but by altruism for the good of the people of his kingdom. Suffering the ordeal of banishment and facing death, he still remained loyal to an idea of authority and steadfast to his ideals.[1]

Another way of summarizing this classical legacy is to jux-

tapose Confucius and Ch'ü Yüan. Early commentators on
Ch'ü Yüan's poetry tried to co-opt Ch'ü Yüan into the Han
Confucian tradition, even though neither Confucius nor any
of the major Confucian exemplars appear in his poetry. The
characterization of Ch'ü Yüan as properly Confucian was
largely based on his deference to the values of the Golden
Age and the ancient sage-kings. Beyond that, it requires a
good deal of forced interpretation to Confucianize Ch'ü
Yüan's poetry. The lore of Confucius does overlap with that
of Ch'ü Yüan where it depicts Confucius as an "uncrowned
king"—the frustrated official whose superior talent and
knowledge of the Right Way in government went unused for
lack of recognition by his king. Then, however, their respective lore moves in two polar directions. Using the ancient
Greek terms, we could say that the lore of Confucius is informed by the notion of sophrosyne or moderation, and that
of Ch'ü Yüan is informed by hubris or excess. Perhaps the
key word here should be passion. Ch'ü Yüan's poetry and his
behavior are passionate while the writings and actions of
Confucius suggest restraint and reason; where Ch'ü Yüan is
appreciated (or criticized) for his preoccupation with self and
sentiment, Confucius is respected for his devotion to social
hierarchy and rational discourse. In the end; when Confucius retreats from his native state and quietly engages in
discourse with his students, Ch'ü Yüan raves wildly at the
world, then throws himself into the Milo's depths.

The Folk Tradition

Within a century after the compilation of the *Ch'u Tz'u*,
Ch'ü Yüan began to be associated with folk customs. By the
sixth century A.D., he had become the center of a complex of
festivals and rites. On the day of the summer solstice, the
fifth day of the fifth month, the drowning of Ch'ü Yüan is
memorialized with water festivals that sometimes feature
Dragon Boat races or a ritual reenactment of the search for
Ch'ü Yüan's drowned body and the recalling of his soul. This
is a uniquely southern phenomenon which evolved out of
local cults and customs, interwoven with each other and il-

lustrating the interaction of various southern subcultures. The celebrations of the "Fifth of the Fifth" served to bring Ch'ü Yüan out of the confines of the official literary culture and to make him into a folk rice-god, the focal point of one of China's most important calendar festivals. In the mid-Yangtze Valley, Ch'ü Yüan and the summer solstice rites became central to the "ceremonialism of rice transplantation" and inseparable from perennial concerns for an abundant harvest. This folk tradition interacts with the classical lore of Ch'ü Yüan, complementing it and providing it a broader medium for transmission to modern times. In the twentieth century, the folk tradition facilitated the transformation of Ch'ü Yüan into a model for radical populist intellectuals.

Ch'ü Yüan in the Post-Classical Literary Tradition

From the seventh to the seventeenth century, the classical Confucian concerns with Ch'ü Yüan's loyalty—his devotion to king and country—gradually disappear or petrify into routine clichés. In their place, there develops in a variety of media (poetry, painting, drama) a special concern for Ch'ü Yüan as an exemplar of ethical authenticity. What concerns succeeding generations is Ch'ü Yüan's lone independence of mind, his unwillingness to compromise his values, his daring to stand up against authority for "the right," and his willingness to put his life on the line.

Revolving about these themes in the post-classical lore are a number of others which help to clarify what Ch'ü Yüan was coming to represent. There is, for example, a prominent development of the exile theme in poetry—a kind of ritualized identification with Ch'ü Yüan's banishment to the southern wilds. This theme plays on the sentimental, self-pitying aspects of the lore. Additionally, I will emphasize the special attitude in the lore toward public obligation and commitment by contrasting Ch'ü Yüan to other famous poet-officials, and to the hermits, eccentrics, and dropouts with whom he has incorrectly been equated. Related to this there is the question of the poet or artist's role in society, or its complement—the relationship of politics and art. In brief, the post-classical literature characterizes a tradition that became a source of inner strength for going against the existing order: a tradition which provided an autonomous source for individual conscience.

The Twentieth Century

The modern intelligentsia seized upon the Ch'ü Yüan lore to formulate their role as leaders of radical change throughout Chinese culture. China's "romantic generation" of the 1920s and 1930s, for example, saw Ch'ü Yüan's plight as their own: the moral individual pitted against an immoral society; his existence in a topsy-turvy world that demanded the leadership only artistic sensibilities could give; the necessity of liberating individual passions and talents from conventional restraints in order to energize the nation. There was precedent in the lore for the Prometheanism that characterized the new Ch'ü Yüan. But when the modern intellectuals sought transformative and populist values there, they had to bring the lore well beyond its classical or post-classical traditions. Ch'ü Yüan was now seen as the radical reformer who used his revolutionary art forms to express the needs and desires of the masses; he was the "genius," "superman," and messiah who alone in his day perceived what his society must do and where it must go.

The doubts and insecurities of the modern intellectuals are conveyed in this new Ch'ü Yüan lore where, in spite of its clarion calls and powerful imagery, it falls back on the theme of self-sacrifice and the inability of the prophet himself to lead his people to the promised land. Before 1949, the Ch'ü Yüan lore dramatizes vividly the new intelligentsia's ambivalence about their relationship to the masses. They argued that though the Fifth of the Fifth festivals give evidence of Ch'ü Yüan's closeness to the masses, he was only capable of being a leader because he transcended them.

After 1949, especially during the 1950s, Ch'ü Yüan was celebrated with unprecedented fervor. But the commemorations and monument building on his behalf, and the flood of scholarship and polemic about him betrayed a disquietude.

Intellectual leaders of the new society apparently wanted to continue to use Ch'ü Yüan lore as a means of understanding the new roles of intellectuals; but there was profound concern over the romantic legacy it carried from the previous generation. Ch'ü Yüan and his poetry were fine as national treasures, well representing to the world the venerability and power of China's national culture. But how to square his "individualism" with collectivist values? It was appropriate that he should symbolize revolt against outdated and oppressive political and literary forms. But how to reconcile the notion of his willfulness and his transcendence with the dictates of historical materialism? The pivotal issue in the lore of Ch'ü Yüan since 1949 has been a pivotal issue in the entire intellectual history of the People's Republic: is the revolution to be voluntaristic—a function of individual will and spontaneity? Or is it predetermined and a function of history?

In the process of coming to terms with this dilemma, writers and critics, historians and policy makers have worked into the Ch'ü Yüan lore of recent decades a variety of cognate problems. They have raised such questions as the propriety of using ancient exemplars for leaders of the socialist revolution; and they have asked how to use new criteria, derived from Marxist traditions, for making judgments on figures from China's past. Along the way, the delicate question of Ch'ü Yüan's "class background" has been debated, as well as his relationship to the classical schools of political philosophy. Finally, there is the manner in which the lyrical idealism and romanticism of his art fit with modern "socialist realism."

Myth and History

The data for this study come from a wide variety of sources—poetry, painting, drama, biographical references in historical works, literary criticism, folktales, common customs and festivals, and in modern times especially, historiography and cultural policy statements. I have tried to let the subject define the data and the boundaries of my study by using the figure of Ch'ü Yüan as the force that holds it all together. Thus, while there are a number of substantial problems raised in this study (such as the nature of loyalty, or the relationship of art and politics), I pursue them only as far as they are developed in the lore on Ch'ü Yüan; I recognize fully that this never exhausts everything that the Chinese have said on the subject, and that it does not always represent the predominant point of view. In this fashion, a coherent though changing body of ideas, images, and sentiments has emerged. These make up a long, resilient, and important tradition, which, up to now, has at best been partially understood and appreciated. It can provide insights not always available in more systematized and formal expressions of Chinese culture.

Specific scholarship has suggested the usefulness of this approach. From modern Chinese historical scholarship dating from the 1920s, I was alerted to the potential in using new kinds of data and investigating traditions parallel to or overlapping with those elements of the so-called great tradition which have been the subject of conventional cultural history (the standard philosophical schools and the development of mainstream orthodoxies). Chinese historians contributing to the New History, for example, argued that by expanding the range of subjects and data, historians would have a more intelligent grasp of conventional subjects, but they might very well also create new contexts in which to reevaluate China's past altogether.[2]

I have heeded the advice of the New Historians to temper our conventional views of China—from the cosmopolitan center—with an understanding of the role of folk culture and the place of ethnic, local, and regional culture. I have followed their suggestions to take seriously the rich bodies of myth, legend, and folklore and to see them as Chinese formulations of Chinese problems. Experimental scholarship of the New Historians demonstrated to me that the networks of myth, symbol, and ritual spanning Chinese history should be considered media which conveyed continuing and changing answers to perennial cultural questions.

Leslie Fiedler's "literary anthropology" has also encouraged the present study.[3] His *Return of the Vanishing American* was directed at defining "the myths which gave a special character to art and life in America," a goal he accomplished through an imaginative use of American legend, folklore, fiction, and "pop culture." The book focuses on the tensions born of the formative confrontations between "civilization" and "wilderness," "European" and "Indian" which have continually replayed themselves in American self-perceptions to the present day. Fiedler uses an adaptation of Lévi-Strauss' structural analysis; however, his study embodies a strong sense of history and contexts. He introduces what are in effect legendary archetypes that represent the problems at hand, and he shows how their transformations occur to make it possible for regional cultures and successive generations to deal with unresolved problems in ways intelligible to themselves. His study is an example of how we can profitably characterize a culture by its chief dilemmas. It demonstrates that we can explain the origins of these dilemmas without committing ourselves to a genetic or a "cultural essence" argument that denies historical understanding.

A goal for both Fiedler and the Chinese New Historians is to discover the uniqueness of cultures by discovering their basic problems as defined by their participants. They both acknowledge that this may often be achieved only by looking at ideas that suffuse the entire culture and may not be found in formalized, systematic statements. "Myth" is central to this process of investigation, not as the antithesis of "truth" or historical "fact," but rather as a medium through which a culture expresses, with a variety of symbols, its most pressing dilemmas, its perceptions of life's most vexing contradictions. Through myth, a culture mediates those tensions. "Lore," in the broad sense, is the stuff of which myths are constructed—the rituals, legends, and tales; the poetry, songs, and pictures—which, over time, dramatize and illustrate a culture's feelings about itself.

Unifying Themes

There are three broad and overlapping themes which cut across the stages of Ch'ü Yüan's evolution. These themes structure the various lore of Ch'ü Yüan and give them coherence over time. Through the themes, the mythology of loyalty and dissent articulates itself and shows its continuities and transformations. The three are devoted respectively to problems of time, space (the South), and the question of madness.

Time. In classical lore, Ch'ü Yüan was known as "the entangled one." His tragedy, ending in his suicide, was seen as the result of the conflicting loyalties, the webs of court intrigue, and the bonds of time—all of which entangled him inextricably. Considerations of time are prominent from the earliest literature associated with Ch'ü Yüan. Two kinds are designated. First, there is time as fate or circumstance, which, out of the reach of human will, determines whether a talented and virtuous official has a wise sovereign and is permitted to exercise and implement his abilities. Second, there is time as a measure of human mortality, emphasizing the limitations of passing time as a source of anxiety and humility to idealistic and ambitious officials such as Ch'ü Yüan. From the classical period onward, the lore suggests that officials, like Ch'ü Yüan, may cut through their entanglements and through the bonds of time with their art and literature. Literature becomes politics by another means, and it becomes a way to achieve immortality and power for those whose efforts in the temporal political world are impotent and evanescent. In the folk rites and festivals for Ch'ü Yüan, these notions of time are complemented. Cosmic time and the cycle of the seasons are background to the ritual of recalling the soul of Ch'ü Yüan in his rice-god mask and praying and sacrificing to share in nature's renewed power and fecundity.

The modern lore makes a significant departure on the subject of time. The degree to which Ch'ü Yüan's revolutionary character was entangled and limited by his times remains a key issue, but no longer is it a question of cosmic time. Neither unpredictable "fate" nor the cycle of nature are at the center of the modern lore. As we might expect, the time with which Ch'ü Yüan must contend is linear historical time. In place of natural cycles there are the progressive historical stages of modern historicism.

Space. The South—its rivers, its flora and fauna, its local cultures—has played both supporting and leading roles in the various stages of the Ch'ü Yüan lore. As the mythology of loyalty and dissent has evolved, the South has become a more complex and important symbol, particularly in the exile or banishment theme. In the basic story of Ch'ü Yüan, the southern countryside is cognate with his ordeal. It is both the setting and instrument of his punishment. Post-classical officials routinely memorialized Ch'ü Yüan when they themselves were either sent to serve in some remote southern post or when they were actually exiled to the South for political malfeasance. Being in the South meant being away from the metropolitan centers of power; the presence of the South's tribal peoples and its primitive ruggedness meant the absence of civilized high culture. Southern exile could mean the end of a career and a life. This aspect of the lore makes the South akin to that rocky peak where Prometheus endured his passion: "The remotest region of the earth, / The haunt of Scythians, a wilderness without a footprint."[4]

While this imagery evolved in Chinese literature, another image of the South began to develop and to infuse the lore. With each new wave of northern nomadic invasions, from the third century A.D. onward, the South was increasingly seen as a potential refuge for "exiled" Chinese ethnos and for China's high culture. The Yangtze Valley was here perceived not as the edge of civilization, but as a moat protecting the exiled culture from further encroachments from the barbarians. Implicit throughout the Ch'ü Yüan lore is a sweeping analogy between the exiled official and the exiled high culture itself.

The lore of Ch'ü Yüan is but one instance of the association the Chinese make between the South and a cultural style. Derived in part from the imagery I have just cited, the South comes to be associated with deviance and dissent, with eccentricity and defection. The Ch'ü Yüan lore begins by showing that the South is a place to which deviants and dissenters are transported. Eventually, it says that the South is the place from which they come. The Yangtze River becomes a mythological frontier of experience as well as a geographical frontier.

In modern times, a significant transformation occurs when historians begin to treat the South as an independent variable in the evolution of Chinese civilization. Southern culture in modern times is considered to have an innovative, nonconforming, and revolutionary spirit. A basic feature of modern Ch'ü Yüan lore is its embodiment of a cultural history that divides Chinese civilization into a northern and southern branch. The dialectical play of the two produces the special qualities of Chinese national culture. In this scheme, the persona of Ch'ü Yüan becomes secondary to the character of southern culture. Through him, southern culture is said to have first fully interacted with the northern culture; and first through him the South gave full expression to its visionary, artistic spirit, and its unbridled, passionate individualism.

Madness.   The last theme is madness. The notion, as associated with the Ch'ü Yüan lore, is used in two connected and complementary ways: tactical madness, and "mad ardour." The first is familiar in the Western tradition as Hamlet's method to gain time in his dangerous political game. In Chinese literature, this is the madness feigned by sages and talented officials "in order to escape the hate and envy of their contemporaries, the despotism of princes, and the follies committed by those in power."[5] It is the delicate weapon of those worthies who have not met their "proper time." In our study, we shall see counterculture "madmen" (hermits, fishermen, rustics) urging politicians to avoid disaster by emulating their style—to retreat from politics into the safety and anonymity of the countryside.

Madness, in the second sense, characterizes public figures like Ch'ü Yüan who refuse to withdraw voluntarily from public action or temper their passionate zeal. This is a mad ardour to realize ideals and implement absolute values. It differs basically from the first kind of madness, which is a pose of eccentricity and a convention of passive protest. Ch'ü Yüan's madness is the madness of a Joan of Arc. It shows itself as a pursuit of the True Way which invites the characterization of heresy because of its "excess." It is fanatical, tempestuous, and visionary. In the twentieth century, Ch'ü Yüan was initially attractive to the moderns because of these qualities. By mid-century, this "romantic" legacy was a source of ambivalence toward him and the model he offered to the new intelligentsia.

From classical to modern times, transformations of the Ch'ü Yüan lore have followed a course that can be summarized by indicating the chain of symbols associated with the idea of the countryside. A reversal of values is reflected in a reversal of associations: The premodern lore linked the countryside (or the South) with the abandonment of public service, with private life; it associated an immersion in the countryside and in the culture of the folk with madness, and in turn, with impotence and death. Implicitly, this chain of associations was counterposed to one that linked the cosmopolitan culture of the capital, successful public service, and reason. In the twentieth century, it is the metropolis and traditional cosmopolitan high culture that are linked with impotence and death. Only in the countryside and among the folk is public service thought to be fulfilled. Only there is political reason, power, and success to be found.

1

Encountering Sorrow:
Classical Foundations of the Myth

Chieh Yü, a madman from Ch'u, came past Confucius
singing as he went:
> *Oh phoenix, phoenix*
> *how dwindled is your power!*
> *As to the past, reproof is idle,*
> *But the future may yet be remedied.*
> *Desist, desist!*
> *Great in these days is the peril of those*
> *who fill office.*

Confucius got down [from his carriage], desiring to speak
with him; but the madman hastened his step and got away,
so that Confucius did not succeed in speaking to him.

　　The Analects of Confucius

In the mythology of loyalty and dissent, there are really two
madmen of Ch'u. They are, in a sense, doubles, personifying
personal alternatives in a political crisis. One is Chieh Yü,
the recluse who feigns madness and mockingly advises Confucius. The other is Ch'ü Yüan, the stalwart official whose
mad ardour was his undoing. The recluse is a gray eminence

17

who materializes only long enough to deliver his famous message to Confucius and disappears before the Master can interrogate him. His advice seems clear enough: when the sage-like minister has been drained of his political influence, rather than explain away or carp about his failures, he should think about future prospects; he should withdraw a safe distance from politics. This anecdote is a dramatic fragment of the tradition which emphasizes Confucius' status as an uncrowned king, his lack of political fulfillment, his fruitless search for a wise king-patron who could implement his sage advice. Over the centuries, madmen like Chieh Yü reappear, sometimes in the guise of a scruffy fisherman, a wild-eyed hermit priest, or an eccentric scholar-official retired in the woods.[1] Whatever the mask he wears, the messages are fairly constant: political loyalty often goes unrewarded; talent and wisdom often go unused. When there are no worthy princes, even the best officials may meet a bad end. When there is a disjunction between moral insight and power, it is often best to retire in anonymity to the countryside. When the time is not right for wisdom and goodness to show themselves, perhaps the best course is to hide one's talent by feigning madness. Let the world think you stupid and survive. This is the only way out if the state is not well governed and you have missed your time.

Ch'ü Yüan, like Confucius, missed his time. Many have viewed his refusal to follow the advice that Chieh Yü gave to Confucius as the mark of a special kind of political madness. Some have faulted Ch'ü Yüan for his lack of discretion; others have questioned the soundness of his wisdom and loyalty. But most who have written about him have expressed the deepest reverence and sympathy for this official who refused to compromise his values, to hide his wisdom, to feign stupidity, to save his skin.

Biography and Polemics

In the second century B.C., the great historian Ssu-ma Ch'ien wrote a biography of Ch'ü Yüan as part of his monumental *Historical Records (Shih chi)*. This is the locus classicus for all the considerable future lore that deals with Ch'ü

Yüan. Outside of the *Ch'u Tz'u* itself, there is no earlier independent text which supplies information about him. The biography is no mere chronicle. It is a passionate and compassionate portrait with which Ssu-ma Ch'ien himself identified; and it was one of many such biographies through which Ssu-ma Ch'ien evaluated his personal political dilemma as well as the general condition of contemporary Han politics.[2]

Ssu-ma Ch'ien's biography of Ch'ü Yüan tells us that Ch'ü Yüan was the scion of a great family of the state of Ch'u, a vast southern territory located in and below the central Yangtze Valley. He was one of the highest state ministers serving King Huai (r. 328–299 B.C.). The biography focuses on events during the time when Ch'ü Yüan had two pressing tasks: to devise new laws for the state and to carry out a foreign policy. There are no details whatsoever about the former, but the fundamentals of the latter are quite clear. The problem created by the expanding hegemony of the state of Ch'in forced a choice between two diplomatic alternatives: a "horizontal" (east-west) alliance with the expanding Ch'in imperium or a "vertical" (north-south) alliance with those states resisting the Ch'in juggernaut and trying to preserve their independence. Ch'ü Yüan favored the vertical alliance against Ch'in, a fact that provides the central substantive issue in the biography. The biography goes on to tell us of court rivals envious of Ch'ü Yüan's influence with the king and in league with a traitorous spy from Ch'in. The traitors, of course, favor the alliance with Ch'in and slander Ch'ü Yüan to shake him and his policy from the king's confidence. They tell the king that Ch'ü Yüan, through his work on the legal reforms, is presuming upon the king's power. The king, taken in by the ruse, promptly sends Ch'ü Yüan on a distant diplomatic mission to the "vertical" allies. When Ch'ü Yüan returns, to find the king being drawn into a transparently dangerous deal with the Ch'in, his protests are quickly met with a second, and final, expulsion from the court. This time it is terminal banishment to the south, in the tropical countryside of Ch'u. King Huai, to whom Ch'ü Yüan remains loyal, is duped into a tentative alliance with Ch'in, and he

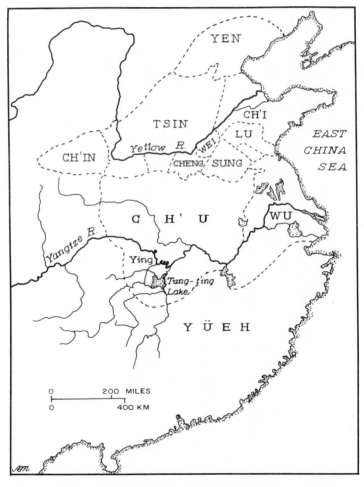

MAP 1. China, Fifth Century B.C. The Kingdom of Ch'u at Its
Zenith.

soon loses his life at the hands of the duplicitous allies. Ch'in then invades Ch'u, and Ch'ü Yüan, after hearing of the destruction of the capital, commits suicide by drowning himself in the Milo River, just northwest of present-day Changsha, in Hunan province. According to Ssu-ma Ch'ien, Ch'ü Yüan wrote his most famous poem, the Li Sao, to lament his loss of King Huai's confidence. The biography makes the poem into a kind of suicide note, expressing the poet-minister's despair at the blindness of the king and the resultant destruction of the country.

Ssu-ma Ch'ien himself was a victim of slander and suffered castration as punishment for his alleged malfeasance, his continued loyalty to his king notwithstanding. In the context of this personal identification, what were the historian's evaluations of Ch'ü Yüan's problems and their consequences? Ssu-ma Ch'ien wrote that King Huai was misled by the culprits because he "could not distinguish the truly loyal;" when he lost his state and died ignominiously in Ch'in, he suffered the "fate of those who do not know how to judge men!" Of Ch'ü Yüan's reaction, Ssu-ma Ch'ien observes: "In fine phrases he censured the actions of the king, and with examples and analogies argued for the right. Such is the nature of Ch'ü Yüan's poem [the Li Sao]." It was his fate "to be faithful and yet doubted, to be loyal and yet suffer slander—can one bear this without anger?" As for Ch'ü Yüan's suicide, the biography does not directly evaluate it, but instead incorporates the Ch'u Tz'u poem "Fisherman" (attributed to Ch'ü Yüan), which sounds the "madman of Ch'u" theme: a rustic asks the exiled Ch'ü Yüan why he persists in his useless and dangerous struggle; why not safely retire? Of what use would his death be? The biography itself says only that Ch'ü Yüan "chose to die rather than seek a place in the world. . . Like a cicada slipping from its shell, he shook off the filth that surrounded him and soared far beyond its defilement."[3]

In his epilogue to the joint Ch'ü Yüan/Chia I biography, Ssu-ma Ch'ien had second thoughts:

> At first when I read Ch'ü Yüan's [works], . . . I was moved
> to pity by his determination, and at times when I visited

Ch'ang-sha [while in exile] and viewed the deep waters where
he had drowned himself, I could never keep from shedding
tears and trying to imagine what sort of person he was. Later,
when I read the lament which Chia I wrote for him, I began
to wonder why a man with the ability of Ch'ü Yüan, who, if
he had chosen to serve some other lord, would have been
welcomed anywhere, should have brought such an end upon
himself![4]

As Ssu-ma Ch'ien's own biographer suggests, the issue of
suicide was a sensitive one with him, for he chose to live in
disgrace in order to write his monumental history for the
purpose of "arguing for the right." He attributed such a goal
to Ch'ü Yüan as well.[5]

To Ssu-ma Ch'ien, Ch'ü Yüan was one of many who
exemplified the inescapable bonds between politics and misfortune, misfortune and literary creativity, and therefore, politics and literary creativity. Ssu-ma Ch'ien's exquisite "Letter
in Reply to Jen Shao-ch'ing," written after his punishment,
expresses this linkage and clearly attempts to explain and valorize his own situation.

> Confucius was in distress and he made the *Spring and Au-
> tumn* [Annals]; Ch'ü Yüan was banished and he composed
> his poem "Encountering Sorrow"; after Tso Ch'iu lost his
> sight, he composed the *Narratives from the States*; when Sun
> Tzu had his feet amputated, he set forth the *Art of War*; . . .
> most of the three hundred poems of the *Book of Odes* were
> written when the sages poured forth their anger and dissatis-
> faction. All these men had a rankling in their hearts, for they
> were not able to accomplish what they wished. Therefore
> they wrote about past affairs in order to pass on their thoughts
> to future generations.[6]

The *Historical Records* biography of Ch'ü Yüan is enriched
by the biography of Chia I (201–169 B.C.). By placing these
two biographies in tandem — in violation of the usual
chronological ordering — Ssu-ma Ch'ien achieves a triangula-
tion of sentiment and values. Chia I also expresses deep feelings about Ch'ü Yüan in his poem "Lament for Ch'ü Yüan,"
which occupies a prominent place within the biography. It is
the first of a very long line of poetic celebrations of Ch'ü

Yüan and it is particularly significant for containing the earliest suggestion that Ch'ü Yüan committed suicide.

Chia I's career parallels that of Ch'ü Yüan and their mutual biographer. As a promising court official he was slandered because of jealousy and competition for power at the court. His king, once appreciative of his talents, quickly cooled toward him and soon packed him off—in effect exiled him—to be tutor at the distant court of the king of Changsha, in the sweltering tropical locale where both Ch'ü Yüan and Ssu-ma Ch'ien were likewise banished. "He heard that the region of Changsha was low-lying and damp," says the biography, "and he feared that in such a climate he would not live long. . . . He understood that his banishment from the court was meant to be a reprimand, so he was sad."[7] His trip to his place of banishment was the occasion for the "Lament for Ch'ü Yüan," the model for a persistent convention: to write laments for Ch'ü Yüan in time of personal political misfortune, often en route to or while in southern exile; and to throw the written lament or some other poetic offering into the Hsiang or Milo River. The *Shih chi* biography only says that Chia I composed the lament when he crossed the Hsiang, but a later account establishes the entire convention:

> Chia I and Teng T'ung shared the same position as Palace Attendants. Chia I disliked [Teng] T'ung's conduct and repeatedly criticized him at court. For this reason [Chia I] was banished from court and demoted to the position of Grand Tutor of Ch'ang-sha. When he was going to his office he felt deeply frustrated. As he crossed the Hsiang River he threw in a lament which said, "The unworthy are honored and illustrious / Flatterers attain their ambitions" as an expression of sorrow for Ch'ü Yüan, who encountered the calamity of slander and evil. He also used it as a self-commiseration, since he too had been accused by Teng T'ung and his group.[8]

The central problem of the lament is Ch'ü Yüan's suicide. While Chia I is most sympathetic and even empathetic, he suggests a possible alternative to suicide (from which Ssu-ma Ch'ien no doubt took support for his own difficulty) viz., withdrawal from the world until the time is right.

You met such an unlucky time!
. . . .
Oh, how you suffered!
All alone you met this disaster.
. . . .
I follow the divine dragon of the nine-layered pool;
He hides deep and unseen to conserve his worth.
. . . .
I shall remain aloof from the filthy world
and keep myself intact.
. . . .
It was through hesitating and confusion that you
met this trouble.
It was your own fault![9]

Chia I seems to have been the first to apply this kind of critique to Ch'ü Yüan; however, the tactic of withdrawal and self preservation was formulated earlier. Chia I argues that since the time was unpropitious for Ch'ü Yüan to realize his political ideals in his native state, if he cared not to bide his time there in safety, he should have done as Confucius (or by implication, any of the other great classical itinerant political advisors), that is, find another state where one's talents would be welcomed and appreciated. ("You could have gone through the nine provinces and assisted a ruler.")

By the time of the preeminent philosopher Tung Chung-shu (179–104 B.C.) but well before the compilation of the *Ch'u Tz'u*, these motifs had jelled into a convention, and Ch'ü Yüan became a familiar name in the "frustration, born-out-of-time" literature that was a hallmark of Han politics. In the following example, Tung's poem "Neglected Men of Worth," the main themes are developed by building up a series of allusions to familiar exemplars which are used in a flat, stylized fashion. The figure of Ch'ü Yüan has begun to move ever closer to an interdependent identity:

Upright I have awaited my chance until now I am
approaching the grave.
Time goes on, I cannot expect to be understood,
My heart is depressed, I cannot hope for a position.
. . . .

When I hide my talents they scoff at my intransigence.
. . . .
When I consider conditions in ancient times,
Then too men of integrity were isolated and had no one to
  turn to.
. . . .
Pien Sui and Wukuang drowned in the deeps
Po-i and Shu-ch'i climbed the hill to pick herbs.
If even saints like those were distraught
What is to be expected when the whole world has gone astray?
Men like Wu [Tzu-hsü] and Ch'ü Yüan
Were really without anyone they might look to.
Though I am not up to [the conduct] of those men
I shall go on a distant voyage, always admiring them.[10]

By the first century A.D. the genre of poetry derived from
the *Li Sao* had undergone a resurgence, and respect for Ch'ü
Yüan had grown to cult proportions as evidenced in the
poetry anthologized in the *Ch'u Tz'u*. In this setting, Yang
Hsiung (53 B.C.–A.D. 18) wrote his controversial "Contre
Sao" *(Fan sao)*, a critique of Ch'ü Yüan's behavior that has
raised the hackles of Ch'ü Yüan worshippers into the twentieth century. Though Yang starts his critique sympathetically
enough with the issues that had concerned Ssu-ma Ch'ien
and Chia I, especially the suicide, he introduces new political
considerations, such as public commitment and political
loyalty.

The *Han History (Han shu)* biography of Yang Hsiung in-
cludes a description of how the "Contre Sao" was written:

[Yang] wondered why Ch'ü Yüan, whose writings were
superior to those of [recent poets], when he found himself
refused, wrote the *Li Sao*, threw himself into the river and
drowned. Yang was so saddened by this piece that whenever
he read it he would cry. He considered that if a gentleman
meets his proper time he enlarges [his sphere of] action. If he
does not meet his proper time he [withdraws like a] dragon or
snake. Whether he meets his proper time or not is due to
fate. Why need one drown himself? [Yang wrote his piece
and] from the Min mountains he threw it into the current of
the River as a lament for Ch'ü Yüan.[11]

The "Contre Sao" itself makes these points which are accurately reflected in the biography: the proper and wise strategy for an official like Ch'ü Yüan should be to withdraw from court and preserve himself until a sage-ruler appears:

> It is best for a divine dragon to
> hide deep in a pool
> and await an auspicious cloud which
> will take him up.

The necessity and moral validity of this strategy is not negated by the fact that the whole is brought about through the uncontrollable and (somewhat mechanistic) actions of cosmic flux: "That the sage and wise do not meet their proper time / Is certainly due to time's fate" (*shih ming*). And finally, the weighty example of Confucius is adduced to legitimize leaving one's state, finding (or trying to find) other places to practice one's principles, and returning to one's state when it is propitious to do so:

> Formerly, when Confucius left Lu
> Reluctantly and tardily he began an extensive journey.
> In the end he returned to his home capital:
> What need did he have of the Hsiang [River] depths
> and its billowy rapids?

If Yang Hsiung was being unfashionable in his chastisement of Ch'ü Yüan, he was not, apparently, meaning to be an iconoclast. To the contrary, by citing the example of Confucius he is forcefully arguing with his contemporaries that their paragon Ch'ü Yüan is flawed and unorthodox.[12]

The momentum of Yang Hsiung's "Contre Sao" was maintained by the historian Pan Ku (A.D. 39–92). In his great *Han History (Han shu)*, Pan Ku tried to undermine respect for Ch'ü Yüan by forcefully dismissing his behavior as singularly unworthy of emulation. He claimed that Ch'ü Yüan's actions were all selfish and not deserving of the loyal or pure characterization that was part of the dominant image. Ch'ü Yüan was merely parading his talents and making an exhibition of himself in the *Li Sao*; he drowned himself out of resentment and bitterness—hardly worthy and constructive motives. Though Pan Ku found fault with the content of some of Ch'ü Yüan's poetry, he haltingly acknowledged that while they were not of scriptural or canonical status (as the *Odes* or *Shih ching*), "nevertheless their language is beautiful and elegant, setting a standard for some major genres of poetry; and even if Ch'ü Yüan was not a man of comprehensive wisdom, he possessed talent of exquisite quality."[13] That said, Pan Ku still had no use for Ch'ü Yüan the public figure who wrangled in the midst of bad company, was critical of his superiors, and only sought to advance himself. In the end, Pan Ku's Ch'ü Yüan violates whatever purity he might have possessed by killing himself.[14] Citing the scriptural *Odes* for his conclusion, Pan Ku suggests that Ch'ü Yüan would have done better to emulate those paragons who served their lords "by protecting their own person."[15]

In the long run, the most important response both to Yang Hsiung and Pan Ku was made by Wang I (fl. A.D. 110–120), himself a native of Ch'u. Wang's commentary and gloss of the poetry attributed to Ch'ü Yüan is the earliest we have and it has been the point of departure for all future readings of the *Ch'u Tz'u* (to which Wang himself contributed). Wang I's introduction to the *Li Sao* is an empassioned defense of Ch'ü Yüan which uncompromisingly dismisses the accumulating criticism as well as the political strategies (one hesitates to call it philosophy) which inform them. In his stylized biographical sketch of Ch'ü Yüan we see the model for the collection of tags and labels which become typical: he is emphatically "loyal and true" *(chung, chen)*; the mere mention of "slander" is all that is required to evoke visions of the inherent danger of court politics and politics in general.[16]

Wang's introduction to the *Li Sao* begins with an implicit linkage of Ch'ü Yüan with Confucius and an orthodox lineage which Pan Ku wished to deny him. Wang is cautious here. Sometime during the first century A.D. the important honorific *ching*—scripture—had been applied to the *Li Sao*. Wang I carefully notes that it is incorrect to use the term here. Nevertheless, he, not unlike Ssu-ma Ch'ien, artfully inserts Ch'ü Yüan and the *Li Sao* into a distinguished and very catholic tradition which began when Confucius compiled the *Odes* and the *Spring and Autumn Annals* during a time of adversity.[17]

Wang I then aggressively puts his own interpretation on Ch'ü Yüan's political conduct in answer to the Han detractors. The ideal minister, like Ch'ü Yüan:

> takes loyalty as the highest [value], and values the maintenance of integrity. [Ch'ü Yüan] therefore used bold words to preserve his state; he killed himself to achieve Righteousness (*jen*). He was like Wu Tzu-hsü who was not adverse to having his body floated on the river; like Pi-kan who did not regret having his heart cut out. Then, loyalty was established and proper conduct was achieved. Glory shone forth and their names were praised.

Wang is intolerant of those whose politics are not aggressively direct, who do not plunge into the fray. He has no use for those who flatter a superior or remain passive when they ought to admonish him. It is "shameful, worthless, and mean" to shrink back in order to avoid a feared calamity. Nor has he stomach for the classical ruses: it makes no difference if you cherish ultimate values (*tao*), but confuse the workings of your country. Feigning stupidity or madness and not speaking out get us nowhere. Ah, but Ch'ü Yüan, "advancing he did not hide his advice; retreating, he had no regard for his life." He was loyal and pure; his honesty was "smooth as a whetstone, straight as a dart."[18]

Thus, Wang explicitly rejects Pan Ku's criticism and is particularly sensitive to the argument that Ch'ü Yüan was not loyal because he criticized his superior and because he was basically self-aggrandizing. Outraged and aghast, Wang's muscular prose declares "Could it be said that Po I and Shu Ch'i [those paragons who sacrificed their lives rather than violate the rules of kingly succession] grieved against their superior in order to advance themselves!" Did not the people of the *Odes* grieve against their lord and remonstrate with their superior when they said:

> Alas, my son, That you should still confuse right and wrong!
> When I have not led you by the hand, I have pointed
> at a thing.
> When I have not face to face declared to you,
> I have held you by the ear.

Wang I concludes that the Li Sao does indeed "base itself on" the Five Classics, Pan Ku's criticism notwithstanding. Indeed, Wang's citation from the Odes suggests that Ch'ü Yüan would have done better not to be so compliant to his lord, to whom he related in the passive role of the wife. Instead, he should have been more aggressive, assuming a father's or teacher's role: "Would it not have been better for him to treat his lord as one confusing right and wrong and held him by the ear?"[19]

With the incorporation of the Li Sao and other poetry attributed to Ch'ü Yüan in the Ch'u Tz'u anthology, and then with Wang I's commentaries, the lore of Ch'ü Yüan is engulfed by imperial Han Confucianism. This was facilitated by the fact that the Li Sao does employ references to the Golden Age, to sage-kings and to government by talent; though neither it nor any other poetry attributed to Ch'ü Yüan contains a reference to Confucius or his model politician, the Duke of Chou. As the modern critics in China have been arguing for a generation, Ch'ü Yüan and his poetry were largely co-opted by the Han Confucianists in a fashion similar to the co-optation of the Odes.[20] Wang I was central in this process, which he accomplished through his polemics with Yang Hsiung and Pan Ku, and through his application in his commentaries of the principles used for interpreting the Odes. Wang's interpretations are strongly symbolic and allegorical. Everywhere he sees political allegory, parable, and metaphor. Although this is appropriate to reading the Li Sao, it is quite forced and without foundation for a work like the Nine Songs, one of the most controversial of the Ch'u Tz'u poems attributed to Ch'ü Yüan.

An issue that branches off of Wang I's claims about the status and significance of Ch'ü Yüan's poetry is the relation of the poetry to the *Odes*. It is an issue inseparable from the question of the transmission of orthodoxy (*cheng t'ung, tao t'ung*). In the modern era, it has been claimed that Ch'ü Yüan's poetry constituted a revolutionary break away from the conservative, aristocratic strictures of the *Odes*. From the time of Wang I, however, the relationship of the two primordial bodies of poetry was assessed along these lines: from the point of view of the origins of literary genres, it was asked whether or not all genres derive from the classics (*ching*). If so, then the *sao*, the poetic genre of the *Ch'u Tz'u*, is derivative of the *Odes*, or specific sections of it. But this raised the next question: if the *sao* comes from the *Odes*, does it preserve and perpetuate the ultimate values of the *tao*, as the *Odes* do?

Another line of criticism entertained the idea that the two bodies of poetry were completely independent traditions.[21] When the question of the function of the *sao* is raised in this context, some argue that it was the first revival of the spirit of the *Odes* after it had fallen into decline; therefore, righteousness and morality (the *i* and *li*) could be learned from it.[22] Opposing this evaluation of the *sao* poetry were those who said that the poetry of Ch'ü Yüan blurred the moral principles of the classics and contributed to the gradual decline of the spirit of literature.[23] One major source for these opposing views was the early comparison of the *Odes'* style and the *sao* style: the former functioned as a medium for making moral judgments and the latter as a (mere) instrument for political remonstrance.

Clearly, Wang I's position—with prior support from the significant, if un-Confucianized, opinion of Ssu-ma Ch'ien—was to see the *sao* tradition as consonant and continuous with that of the *Odes*; hence, his application of the same principles of interpretation. Wang could not have been unaware that this placed him in a most prestigious position, for he now stood in relationship to the *sao* poetry as Confucius had stood to the *Odes* (which he reputedly compiled). Just as Confucius was a transmitter of the values of the Golden Age and of the *tao* via the *Odes*, so Wang I would do the same via the *Li Sao*. This guaranteed the renown of Ch'ü Yüan along with Wang I.

The compilation of the *Ch'u Tz'u* anthology during the first century A.D. was both symptom and source of Ch'ü Yüan's prominence. In addition to the poems attributed to him, it contained *sao* style poetry which not merely imitates the scornful and self-righteous tone of the *Li Sao*, but openly sympathizes with Ch'ü Yüan. In the anthology, poems like Liu Hsiang's (77–6 B.C.) "Nine Laments" (Chiu t'an) go as far as to use Ch'ü Yüan as a protagonist, through whom the poet speaks and makes his criticism of contemporary Han society.[24]

From this body of poetry as well as the biographical and polemical literature, the dominant structures of the Ch'ü Yüan lore are derived. They give us an official's-eye view of government. The authority and legitimacy of the king are made to seem a function of his relations with his officials, whose loyalty and talent nevertheless lead them inevitably to disaster. In order to see these themes more vividly, I first want to bring to the foreground the *Li Sao* poem itself, and then a series of archaic paragons who repeatedly appear in connection with Ch'ü Yüan. The poem, the figures, and their political implications can better be dealt with now that we have a sense of the mainstream of Han thought which absorbed them and gave them renewed life.

The Li Sao Poem

Of the poems attributed to Ch'ü Yüan, the *Li Sao* provides the most biographical insight, but that in itself is very little. Though it dramatically evokes the estrangement of a minister and his king and the minister's subsequent political despair, it has little to do specifically with the Ch'ü Yüan who emerged in Han biographical literature. It did, however, serve as a source for the basic themes and moods of that literature, and did so in a fashion that set the tone and style for the Han lore of Ch'ü Yüan. The poem warrants examination both for the political messages it seems to convey, and to provide a larger context for evaluating the myth of Ch'ü Yüan during the

Han and in subsequent times. We must look at the love
metaphor which structures the poem along with the symbolism of the shaman's magic journey. These are used to portray the frustrated poet-minister's anxious sense of time and
pessimistic sense of politics.

The poem presents Ch'ü Yüan and his dilemma through a
lavish use of flower symbols. He is associated with orchids
and irises, or sometimes simply with fragrant grasses; his
enemies are weeds or foul smelling flora. Later literature
often refers to him with the orchid symbol. Here, the flower
imagery is meant to suggest his purity of spirit and the beauty
of his inner talent and virtue. The lush countryside of Ch'u is
no doubt an inspiration for this imagery, but it may equally
indicate the poet's reliance on archaic Ch'u shaman lore.
The *Li Sao*'s preoccupation with flower metaphors and props
for Ch'ü Yüan (garlands, food, etc.) seem to echo the use of
flower-bedecked boats and flowered costumes in shaman
rituals.[25]

These flower symbols festoon the basic story of the virtuous
minister who loses favor with his king. In contrast to the
harsh and violent imagery of Han loyal-minister lore, a love
metaphor is used to convey this story. The official and king
are depicted as estranged male and female lovers. The poet
actually depicts himself in the first part of the poem as a
woman and later as a man. In the female role, he competes
with jealous, slandering courtesans for the king-lover's attention. As a man, throughout most of the poem, he actively,
though vainly, quests after his beloved. The Han critic, Wang
I, was overly fond of finding political allegory in every poem
attributed to Ch'ü Yüan, especially those which feature
amorous themes. Even the *Nine Songs*, which seem to be
merely transcriptions of sometimes erotic shaman liturgies,
were given political glosses. Although it was fashionable in
Wang's day to force such interpretations on the archaic love
poetry anthologized in the *Odes*, few subsequent commentators have questioned that the intent of the *Li Sao* love
theme was political. In recent times, for example, the great
translator, Arthur Waley, sardonically called it a "politico-

erotic ode," and suggested that the strange way that sex is mixed with politics in the poem indicated that the poet was a bit demented.[26] I am inclined to think that the poet was very lucid and successful in his use of the love metaphor to portray the passion of his dedication. Equally clear are the portrayals of the minister's attempts to resolve disharmony and recapture the intimacy of what should have been the interdependent relationship of virtue and power. In other literature, both contemporary with the *Li Sao* and from later times, one frequently sees the equation made between minister and wife, king and husband. In some instances, these clichés were given greater significance by placing them into cosmologic contexts where the minister-wife and king-husband were to be understood as human expressions of the complementary primal forces (*yin/yang, k'un/ch'ien*).[27]

To activate the estranged lover's theme, the *Li Sao* poet uses the imagery of the shaman's magic journey to the outer realms. First it is used in the sense of a quest to find the beloved and reunite with her (to regain the favor of the king and renewed political power). Second, when the poet-minister fails to find his woman, the quest journey becomes an escape — an attempt to forget about his woman and seek another altogether (to leave his king and homeland where his talents are unappreciated and go elsewhere for royal recognition and patronage). Altogether, the distant journey to the ends of the earth, the fairy realms, and the corners of the cosmos provides the self-esteeming poet an opportunity to act out his feelings of superiority and to transcend the filth and corruption of the secular world. There he had become as pearls to the swine. But his intent is not to make the distant journey an end in itself as it became in later poetry. The burden of the poem, like the whole of the Ch'ü Yüan lore from Han times onward, is that the poet cannot escape, nor does he wish to. He feels compelled to carry out the quest. In the poem, when the quest fails, he consults a shaman, but cannot follow his advice. The shaman assures him that there are other fish in the sea, and encourages him to quit wasting his time and "go farther afield," where such a comely fellow as he is guaranteed success. Though he starts his escape journey, it is abruptly halted when, from stellar heights, he catches sight of his old home and apparently is drawn back to it. The poem ends cryptically with his return to earth, then a final expression of discontent with his treatment by his country, and finally his disappearance to the abode of someone called P'eng Hsien. The latter is properly understood to be something like a master of the occult, and not an exemplary suicide. Though the poem certainly does not have an upbeat denouement, there is no hint of the suicide which became the critical fact of Ch'ü Yüan's biography from the time of Ssu-ma Ch'ien.[28]

If we look at the journey itself, as distinct from the quest, we see another dramatic way the poet has successfully conveyed his central message of political frustration and inhibition of rightful power. David Hawkes, the modern translator of the *Ch'u Tz'u*, has demonstrated that the magic journey is common in the literature of the Ch'in-Han era (255 B.C.–A.D. 220). Its purpose is to acquire and/or affirm power, and it is accomplished in the same manner as Ch'ü Yüan's trip to the various parts of the cosmos. Kings, magicians, mystics, and poets are all depicted in Han literature as successful cosmic tourists who obtain or legitimize their political, spiritual, or artistic powers from this ritual journey. Ch'ü Yüan attempts to visit with cosmic gods and goddesses in the hope that they will give him their support. But in the *Li Sao*, where Ch'ü Yüan is a combination of politician, shaman, and poet, the journey is nevertheless a failure. What begins as a liberating, dream-like flight from mundane corruption, ends as a harried, nightmarish confrontation with the recalcitrant residents of the Four Quarters. Driven by a sense that his time is running out, the poet compulsively seeks his woman in her various incarnations, only to experience his initial rejection over and over again. For all his persistence and ritual propriety, the journey does not work for him any more than his efforts in the chaotic real world bring the results he expects. Just as the magic has gone out of his love, the power has gone out of his magic.[29]

Plate 1. "Lord of the Clouds," fourteenth-century illustration of the *Nine Songs*

In the *Li Sao*, questions of time weave in and out of the themes of frustration and ill-used talent, and through the quest and journey motifs. There are two kinds of time at issue. First, there is the time or timing spoken of in the Han polemics on Ch'ü Yüan. Linked to "fate" (*ming*), it determines whether or not virtuous officials like Confucius or Ch'ü Yüan will have their wisdom recognized and used by a good king. This sense of time is at the heart of that literature, inspired by the *Li Sao*, which became known as the "poetry in which the scholar-official fails to meet his time" (*shih pu yü fu*).[30] In the *Li Sao* the poet is explicit about his ill-timed career. He lives in a topsy-turvy time of chaos. Evil and ugliness are taken for good and beauty, and rewarded accordingly. True goodness and beauty are ignored or defiled. Power and recognition are prizes of the greedy, the envious, the flatterers, while the talented are victims of slander and the whims of fickle kings. Though the *Li Sao* poet recognizes all this, he persists in his "passion for purity." He refuses to heed the criticism of his aloofness and his campaign to convince the world of his righteousness.

The second notion of time expresses itself as the poet's overwhelming sense of aging, encroaching death, and the limits which mortality places on human ambition. The flower, in addition to symbolizing the purity of the poet, also signifies this sense of evanescence, temporality, and human vulnerability.[31] Repeatedly, throughout the poem this is expressed in other ways as well. On the first leg of his quest-journey, for example, the poet vainly implores the Charioteer of the Sun to keep the day from ending. Later he says: "Swiftly I sped, as in fearful pursuit, / Afraid Time would race on and leave me behind."[32] And again: "For old age comes creeping and soon will be upon me, / And I fear I shall not leave behind me an enduring name."[33] For Ch'ü Yüan, time in its dual meaning is doubly the enemy: it has married him to an inept king, and it cuts away at his ability to remedy this misfortune.

The poet-officials who imitated the *Li Sao* and celebrated Ch'ü Yüan in the *Ch'u Tz'u* anthology were likewise snared by time. On one side was their awareness of mortality, and on the other, that sense of time which demanded that they retire and wait for a new chance to achieve fulfillment. But with a compelling sense that time is running out, how can one accede to advice like that of Chieh Yü the madman—passivity and strategic patience? If the time were ever to come, we might ourselves no longer be fit: "I should like to wait a little until the proper time comes," writes Liu Hsin in his "Nine Laments," "But the day is getting dark and draws towards evening / Time steals on, remorseless, with ever advancing step."[34]

A Gallery of Exemplars

From the days of Ssu-ma Ch'ien, the lore of the ill-fated minister developed through a juxtaposing of Ch'ü Yüan with a variety of cognate paragons and exemplars, and by drawing upon a host of analogies, anecdotes, and parables. Through the matrices of the major figures with whom Ch'ü Yüan was paired or compared, his persona was given extended range and meaning. The literary device in question here is typical of the Han period, and much Chinese literature beyond that time.

The Three Virtuous Ones (San jen), referred to by a Western scholar as "the three sages of perfect goodness," usually appear individually in the relevant literature.[35] Because Wang I brings them into his defense of Ch'ü Yüan, they reappear in the later stages of the lore. Together they represent a continuum of the possibilities that confront the worthy minister who remonstrates with his unappreciative and potentially dangerous king. All three of the Virtuous Ones served King Chou (r. twelfth century B.C.), the notorious last king of the Shang dynasty; and like Ch'ü Yüan, they were also the king's kin.

The first, Wei-tzu, criticized the king's excesses, and ultimately, after the king failed to respond positively, quit the court and left the country. Chi-tzu, the second of the trio, protested the king's excesses and as a result was thrown into prison. When released under the amnesty of the succeeding dynasty's first king, he too left the country on the grounds that he could not serve a "usurper" sovereign—one who has violated the laws of hereditary succession. This is a major issue in Chinese political mythology and one which I will differentiate from the main themes of the Ch'ü Yüan lore. Pi Kan is the last of the three and the most popular in political literature. His criticism of the king was rewarded by disembowelment at the hands of the king, who then had his remains minced and pickled (and, in some stories, distributed for consumption throughout the kingdom). The themes here are developed in a moral guide to politics called *Han Ying's Illustrations (Han shih wai chuan)*. It raises questions resonant with Wang I's defense of Ch'ü Yüan and reintroduces the motif of tactical madness:

> When Pi-kan was put to death for remonstrating [with the Tyrant Chou], Chi-tzu said, "To speak, knowing [one's words] will not be put to use, is stupid. By sacrificing oneself to make the wickedness of one's prince apparent is not loyal. These are two things that should not be done. If, however, they are done, there is no greater misfortune." Whereupon he let his hair down his back and, feigning madness, left. . . . The Ode says:
>
>> People have the saying,
>> "There is no wise man who is not [also] stupid."[36]

Han Ying's Illustrations cites various examples of this perverse notion that a minister's suicide is disloyal because it reflects badly on the sovereign and gives him the reputation of a destroyer of sages.[37]

Wu Tzu-hsü (sixth century B.C.) is the exemplary suicide most closely associated with Ch'ü Yüan in the literature we are examining. The two are frequently referred to in tandem; and they share common political themes. Wu Tzu-hsü's biography in the *Historical Records* is informed by issues similar to those of Ch'ü Yüan's. Wu, a native of the state of Ch'u, becomes embroiled in politics when his father, a state official, criticizes the king and is killed. Rather than remain in Ch'u to avenge his father's death and surely be killed him-

Plate 2. A Good Official Is Pickled by an Evil King

self, he flees to the Kingdom of Wu (the lower Yangtze Valley) in the hope of future justice. When he does return to Ch'u, now under a new king, Wu Tzu-hsü, like Ch'ü Yüan, is caught up and destroyed by his involvement in foreign policy. He is slandered by traitors to the state, banished, and (in the *Historical Records'* version) made to commit suicide, after which he is sewn in a leathern sack and set adrift on the Yangtze River. His loyalty, integrity and persistence are highlights of the biography, and they are the points of departure for the morbid observations which are typically made on his political career.[38]

Already in the third century B.C. Taoist classic *Chuang-tzu* we read that "men of ardor are regarded by the world as good, but their goodness does not succeed in keeping them alive. . . . if your loyal advice is not heeded, give way and do not wrangle. [Wu] Tzu-hsü wrangled and lost his body."[39] And in the *Lun Heng* (Critical essays), the philosopher Wang Ch'ung (A.D. 27–c.100) warns that talented energies, like those of Wu Tzu-hsü and Ch'ü Yüan, might not only go unused but might even be destroyed.[40] In *Han Ying's Illustrations*, Wu Tzu-hsü is used, along with many others, to state and re-state a political philosophy biased toward officials: "When a feudal lord has five admonishing ministers, though he be without principle, he will not lose his state."[41]

The *Ch'u Tz'u* anthology uses Wu Tzu-hsü in a stylized, allusive pairing with Ch'ü Yüan and other figures who by late Han times seem to be called up reflexively one by the other in the poets' imaginations. Here is an example from "Ai shih ming" (Alas that my lot was not cast) by Yen Chi (fl. 155 B.C.):

> [Wu] Tzu-hsü died to fulfil the right;
> Ch'ü Yüan drowned himself in the Milo.
> They would not change though faced with bodily destruction;
> For loyalty and faith admit no alteration.[42]

And from Wang Pao's (c. 58 B.C.) "Chiu huai" (Nine regrets):

> I grieve for the orchid and the iris [Ch'ü Yüan's
> symbols in the *Li Sao*]

> That lie about, stalk across stalk, in dead heaps.
> . . . .
> When I think of the olden times,
> I see that many met with an evil end.
> Wu [Tzu-hsü] floated down the Great River.
> Ch'ü Yüan drowned himself in the Hsiang.[43]

And again in the "Chiu chang" (Nine declarations) attributed to Ch'ü Yüan himself:

> So a loyal man is not certain to be used,
> Nor a wise man certain to be employed.
> Wu Tzu-hsü met a bad end;
> Pi Kan was cut up and made into pickles.[44]

Shen-t'u Ti is another major figure linked with Ch'ü Yüan both by the suicide-drowning theme as well as recurrent political themes. In the *Chuang-tzu* he is first introduced in a typical barrage of names:

> Those like Hu Pu-hsieh, Wu Kuang, Po Yi, Shu Ch'i, Chi Tzu, Hsü Yü, Chi T'o and Shen-t'u Ti—all of them slaved in the service of other men, took joy in bringing other men joy, but could not find joy in any joy of their own.[45]

Later, the same text tells us that "Shen-t'u Ti offered a remonstrance that was unheeded; he loaded a stone onto his back and threw himself into a river, where the fish and turtles feasted on him."[46] *Han Ying's Illustrations* uses Shen-t'u Ti to draw together most of the political themes we have thus far been pursuing:

> Shen-t'u Ti thought he was born out of his time [*fei ch'i shih*], and was about to cast himself into the river. Ts'ui Chia learning of this stopped him saying, "I have heard that [the function] of the saintly man and the humane gentleman between Heaven and Earth is to be father and mother to the people. Now is it right not to come to the rescue of a drowning man by reason of [fearing] wet feet?"
> Shen-t'u said, "Not so. [Of old], King Chieh by putting Kuan Lung-feng to death, and King Chou by killing Wu Tzu-hsü, and Ch'en by killing Hsieh Yeh, had their states

destroyed. Therefore the loss of a state or the destruction of a
family is not [caused] by the lack of saints and sages, but is
the result of not using them. Whereupon embracing a stone,
he sank into the river."[47]

Finally, we come to the brothers Po Yi and Shu Ch'i, the
most frequently cited of all the exemplars dealt with here.
From the Confucian *Analects* through the *Li Sao* itself, and
into late Han literature, they are stock-in-trade for political
discourse. They chose to starve to death in the mountain wilderness where they took refuge because they were unable to
flee their native state. The motive for their drastic action was
their refusal to serve the new king who, though pious, had
breached hereditary right—he had failed to nourish his
father properly and committed regicide. Moreover "he did
not mourn his father properly and killed his hereditary
lord."[48] In all this, the brothers are illustrating principles
quite apart from those associated with the Ch'ü Yüan lore,
which focuses on the question of government by virtue and
talent (indeed, virtuous and talented officials, not kings). As
such, the Ch'ü Yüan lore and the matrix of exemplars we
have examined is antithetic to aristocratic values, or at least,
is unconcerned with the question of kingly succession.
Rather, it is preoccupied with the issue of what makes for a
good king at any time. In spite of their fundamental connection to the problem of hereditary succession, Po Yi and Shu
Ch'i are, more often than not, reduced to an abstraction of
purity and persistent devotion to principle, as in this next
example from *Han Ying's Illustrations*. It brings most of our
themes and exemplars together, and returns us to the opening
questions raised by the madman Chieh Yü. Confucius is
doing the talking here, responding to a challenging question
about his living in obscurity. Is there some defect in his personality, he is asked; after all, why does he not implement his
"accumulated virtue," his "piled up righteousness" *(jen)*?
Confucius is made to justify his obscurity with the standard
litany of political disaster and mayhem:

Do you think that the wise are never punished? Then how was it the Prince Pi-kan had his heart cut out and died? Do you think the just are [always] harkened to? Then how was it Wu Tzu-hsü had his eyes torn out and hung from the eastern gate of [the capital] of Wu? Do you think the scrupulous are [always] employed? Then how was it Po-i and Shu Ch'i starved on Mt. Shou-yang? Do you think the sincere are [always] employed? Then how was it that . . . [Chieh] Tzu-t'ui climbed a hill and was burned to death. Many superior men of wide learning and subtle plans have not met with the right time; I am certainly not the only exception. A man's ability depends on natural endowment; his success or failure is a matter of opportunity [*shih*].[49]

Summary: Ministers, Kings, and Power

The Ch'ü Yüan lore which proliferated during the Han is a rich example of what H. G. Creel has called "the propaganda of the official class."[50] It is a luxuriant body of literature which carries certain political themes to their extremity. These are themes which Marcel Granet demonstrated were central to the new politics emerging in the Warring States period: that "the king has prestige when he has good counselors" and that "the minister nearly always occupies greater status than the king in their common history." And further, "the personality of the minister supplants that of the king," whose chief merit is to promote the best vassals. "His merit is greater if he can attach to his court new faithfuls who are worth more than [those in other courts]."[51] These are basic motifs in the mythology of the founding king and kingly succession: to begin a successful dynasty, the king requires a charismatic minister, while the king's role is nearly reduced to recruiting such a minister.[52]

In the literature we have considered, the relationship of minister and king is developed in a more general context that does not concern itself with succession: Ch'ü Yüan's dilemma had nothing to do with establishing a kingship or the legitimacy of his king. But it is related to the problem of where the founding king gets his virtuous minister. In the literature from the Warring States and Han periods, he is almost always raised from obscurity. Thus, in the *Li Sao*, Ch'ü Yüan nostalgically rehearses examples of laborers, butchers, and the like, whose talents were brought to the court of the wise king who recognized them.[53] Wang I's poetry in the *Ch'u Tz'u* likewise recalls the ages past when obscured political talent was "recognized and raised up."[54] But the king's wisdom must not quite end there. He must also be able to recognize the difference between truth and the slanderous falsehood that the lore depicts as the inevitable outcome of rivalry and jealousy at court. These problems are in turn the result of promoting the virtuous and favoring them.

In mutual dependence, the king requires the virtue of the official, and the official requires the recognition of the king. However, this will not be possible if the virtuous one is "born out of time." The meeting of the two is a function of "meeting with the right time." Hence, that handbook on political survival, *Han Ying's Illustrations*, warns that even Shun, one of the great Golden Age sage-kings, "would have been well off to escape punishment of execution" if he had lived in the times of the evil kings Chou or Chieh.[55] The *sine qua non* of political wisdom in this lore is the recognition of and compliance with the restrictions of cosmic time. Whether or not Ch'ü Yüan exercised this wisdom is the question at the heart of the "Contre Sao" tradition.

Ch'ü Yüan became the major exemplar of a tradition complementary to that of "obscure virtue raised up." Though the same mechanisms of timing are at work, he is the virtuous, high-and-mighty minister who falls into obscurity. It is this aspect of the lore that becomes popular in the literature of the T'ang and Sung eras (seventh to thirteenth centuries). Usually shorn of its cosmological implications, it becomes a convention for lamenting the precariousness of official life.

From the Ch'ü Yüan lore emerges the idea that the ill-fated official can use his literary talents as a political force. The linkage of politics and literature persists in the lore; however, literature is not depicted as an expression of power. Rather, it is seen as the product of frustrated political power.

It becomes sublimated politics, a way of exercising power by another means. The poet-officials learn to deal similarly with the unyielding encroachments made by kings and by time upon their mortality: consistent with their ideas about the link between literature and politics, they sought the power of an immortality lodged in their literary creations. Through these, the officials thought themselves in control of all moral space. And the immortality which literature gave them guaranteed at least a share of the political space in which mortal kings were only temporary residents.

It was the political wisdom of Frazer's *Golden Bough* that "The king must be guarded, and he must also be guarded against." Our Chinese officials seem to epitomize this political ambivalence. And for letting down their guard, they regularly suffered. It is their mode of suffering that we should note next—the evocations of ritual sacrifice, which continue in all aspects of Ch'ü Yüan lore into modern times. Marcel Granet strongly grasped this in his classic study of the relation between the Chinese king and his officials:

> Putting [the minister] to death (voluntary suicide, forced suicide, execution) whether it takes the form of immolation and of an attempt to cannibalize the victim, or whether it takes the form of an expulsion and a complete repudiation, or whether it has the character of a communal rite or of a rite of aversion, whether it appears more as a religious act or more as a penal sanction—it always has something of a sacrifice and an ordeal about it.[56]

Granet also noted that no matter who appeared triumphant in the struggle between king and minister, there was no simple victory. In this lore, "to destroy, to kill, is to contract a debt which the future will determine who is to pay. Only the king who is supported by Heaven, only a Sage whom Heaven inspires can consume the vanquished or hurl his repudiated flesh to the Powers of Evil."

Thus, the Ch'ü Yüan lore, and the "propaganda of the official class" of which it is a part, consistently blur or negate any paradigms of complementarity and harmony in a series of

ways which ultimately require the mediating idea of loyalty to
restore the minister to his proper role. The problem results
from consistently depicting all but the sagest of kings as fools,
dupes, or murderous butchers; depicting monarchy basically
as a personnel bureau for recruiting virtuous talent; depicting
officials as the only source of political and ethical knowledge
and as the regular sacrificial victims of the kings. The odd
picture that emerges from this literature is that ever since the
Golden Age, politics do not work correctly. Indeed, there is
consistent skepticism, even pessimism, about the possibility
of it ever working. Hence, the background of nostalgia for the
good old days when politics apparently did work. I am not
disagreeing with the modern historians who say that the idea
of Golden Age politics was a means of formulating and
legitimizing the new politics beginning around the third century B.C. I am saying it was also a way of arguing that since
there once had been a politics that worked, there could be
one again—a hedge against the despair on the brink of
which this literature often seems to rest.

   In Ch'ü Yüan lore, the instrument for keeping king and
official together, in their appropriate relationship, and making government work, is the idea of loyalty. On the face of it,
this suggests the official's concession to a passive role. But
there is no easy and no one answer given as to just what
comprises loyalty; nor how to construct the hierarchy of loyalties demanded by life's complexities. The object of loyalty is
an unresolved issue. Is it the king? This is emphasized by
Ssu-ma Ch'ien's rendition of the Ch'ü Yüan story, until his
concluding remarks where he suggests leaving the king rather
than committing suicide. Is it principles? The repeated allu-
sion to Confucius and other itinerant sages suggests approval
of serving anyone who will implement their values. Some
(especially, modern) critics perceive in this literature a tension
between loyalty to "the self" and to the state. I do not think it
too much to conclude that all of these loyalties simultaneously exerting their demands are the "entanglements," as
Yang Hsiung put it, which led to Ch'ü Yüan's tragedy in the

classical formulation of his story. In the *Li Sao*, Ch'ü Yüan himself remarks in a characteristically portentious tone: "How well I know that loyalty brings disaster." And so, since we are not any closer to understanding why a politics premised upon loyalty should work, we shall follow the advice of the madman Chieh Yü and desist, on this issue, until we have the aid of the Sung scholastics in the next chapter.

2

A Minority of One:
Traditions of Loyalty and Dissent

People will not follow your example:
You turned your back upon the State,
Disdained the customs,
And were contemptuous of death itself. . . .
Alone you struggled with those troubles.
        "The Ch'ü Yüan Temple"
        Su Shih, A.D. 1066

"To obey, but to resist. There is the whole secret!" So goes a late-nineteenth-century French formulation of the problem of being a political person.[1] The Chinese who commemorated Ch'ü Yüan between the end of the Han epoch and modern times seemed to believe that he had resolved the dilemma implicit in such a formula. This balance of obedience and resistance presents a problem and paradox similar to the British notion of a "loyal opposition." In China, however, in both political theory and practice, "faction" and "party" were continually decried. There was no theoretical accommodation made for a loyal opposition. Thus, one (individual or

48

group) could be considered subversive, or perhaps treasonous, even if "obedient" in the French sense (accepting the necessity of authority), and "loyal" in the British sense (accepting authority in the present institutional forms).[2]

In the many centuries surveyed in this chapter, the Chinese bureaucracy grew enormously in size and complexity. So did the power of the monarchy. The literature on Ch'ü Yüan reflects periodic state efforts to exert persistent social and political pressures on the bureaucrats to conform and compromise "scruples and high ideals in the service of a questionable master."[3] Looking at the politics of the Ming period (1368–1644), modern scholarship suggests that for an official:

> To refuse [to compromise and comply] was to find himself in an embattled minority. What was worse, it was a minority without status and with almost no cohesion as a group. In a sense it lacked even a raison d'être. Within Confucianism the concept of a 'minority' had no place. The scholar stood alone, with comfort and support coming only from personal friends and distant admirers. He could only retire to his home ground, strive for economic self-sufficiency on the land . . . or devote himself to teaching.[4]

Independence and/or resistance on the part of scholar-officials have tended to be expressed in individualistic and not collective ways: "individual heroism and individuality of thought—rather than . . . the conscious assertion of their interests as an opposition group."[5] This is not to say that Chinese political history is not often riddled with factional struggles, or that it is uncommon to see interest groups within officialdom trying to affect policy. Indeed, many of the examples of exiled officials cited in this chapter are instances of individual members of a faction suffering a collective sanction. However real or prevalent, factions or collective action by officials were at best suspect by the monarchy, and apparently never capable of legitimation on constitutional grounds. On moral grounds, protest groups were periodically established and active with great prominence. Still, informing even this collective activity are some persistent beliefs, which the Ch'ü Yüan lore served to illustrate and preserve: that "ordering the realm" was an individual responsibility; and that each official individually bore the burden of implementing ultimate values.

As scholar-officials in succeeding epochs confronted these problems, Ch'ü Yüan's political experience continued to have relevance, but not merely as the expression of an unambiguously loyal official, as some modern critics have asserted.[6] Ch'ü Yüan did certainly continue in much literature to be known simply as the epitome of "loyal and true" service. But his lore, at least from the eighth century onward, was deeply enriched by efforts to understand and appreciate Ch'ü Yüan as a nonconforming, uncompromising, obstinately individualistic person of integrity. His experiences, culminating in his suicide, became a model for a political and moral style that has been translated as "mad ardour": "the daring of the magnanimous man, driven by a restless energy, to fulfill limitless ambitions, not for worldly success but for the attainment of absolute values."[7] For Ch'ü Yüan as for those who identified with him, this mad ardour is not the same as the eccentric behavior by which the hermits and recluses expressed their renunciation and withdrawal from a contemptible world.

The political style of Ch'ü Yüan, like that of some Neo-Confucians, for example, signified:

> Neither world renunciation nor idiosyncrasy, and far from either the self-indulgence of many Wei-Chin (third and fourth centuries A.D.) hedonists or the weird habits of Taoist 'immortals.' . . . [Theirs] was the independence and uncompromising spirit of men totally dedicated to the service of mankind, and mad . . . only because the depth of their human concern set them at odds with a complacent society. It was a sign of their true humanity, their genuineness as individuals, their authenticity as Confucians.[8]

These are the most important themes of the Ch'ü Yüan lore as it developed over almost two millennia following the compilation of the Ch'u Tz'u.

The continuity of the Ch'ü Yüan lore and the continued popularity of the figure of Ch'ü Yüan was carried out through the media of the popular festivals and customs and through new literature as well as the ever-present literature of the Han. The newer literature always assumed a familiarity with the classic materials; the *Historical Records* biography remained the sole source of biographical information, and its approach to Ch'ü Yüan's life and death informed all future discussions. It was rare to find anyone even writing a summary biography of Ch'ü Yüan, and instead it was common practice to append, without comment, the *Historical Records* biography to one's new edition of the *Ch'u Tz'u*. Likewise, Wang I's commentary on the *Ch'u Tz'u* persisted as the point of departure for all future readings; and so his vigorous and sympathetic portrait of Ch'ü Yüan was as well known as Ssu-ma Ch'ien's biography.

We should not confuse the popularity of the *Ch'u Tz'u* poetry and the derivative genre with the popularity of the figure of Ch'ü Yüan or the growth of his lore. Over the centuries, revived interest in the poetry has not always been accompanied by a particular interest in Ch'ü Yüan. Modern scholars have demonstrated in detail how the literature of the *Ch'u Tz'u*, especially the poetry attributed to Ch'ü Yüan, waxed and waned in popularity, while its style, mood, and imagery persistently enhanced all areas of literary and artistic culture. They argue that there has been a tendency for writers and artists to turn to and revive interest in this literature in "times of trouble" (for example, eighth-century T'ang; the Southern Sung; the seventeenth century). No one, however, goes beyond this broad generality to analyze the motivations for interest in the *Ch'u Tz'u* by a particular person at a specific time. Their notion of "influence" sometimes becomes a quantitative catch-all category, filled with any and all allusions to and imitations of *Ch'u Tz'u* poetry no matter how brief or detailed, profound or superficial.[9] By examining the lore of Ch'ü Yüan, which they do not do, there is opportunity to come to some understanding of why—apart from questions of the aesthetic attractiveness of *sao* poetry—the

Ch'u Tz'u was appealing to successive generations, and what messages it conveyed to officials who explicitly remarked on the political experience of Ch'ü Yüan. The themes I have selected to describe and analyze suggest that, to whatever degree the *Ch'u Tz'u* literature or the figure of Ch'ü Yüan have had prominence, their understanding has not been simply a revival or repetition of the Han understanding. Over the centuries, a dialogue has continued with the Han lore, but new contexts make for new significance. For example, the figure of Ch'ü Yüan must be understood against the emergence of the poet as a social type, and the proliferation of types of poets. Ch'ü Yüan's experience with the encroachment of the Ch'in state upon his native Ch'u must be seen against the pattern of northern nomadic incursions upon the Chinese cultural epicenter and the eventual shift of that center in a southeasterly direction. Finally, the issue of Ch'ü Yüan's loyalty must be understood in new ways, partly as a result of the dynastic complications caused by these same incursions, partly as a result of the development of monarchy and bureaucracy and new relations between them.

I have isolated some motifs and themes which reflect both continuity and breaks with the Han foundations of the Ch'ü Yüan lore, and I will illustrate them through the variety of media that have made the lore so rich. As the modern scholars have suggested, there do seem to be nodes of time wherein interest in Ch'ü Yüan and/or the *Ch'u Tz'u* have been rather intense and coherent. These have guided my selection of a few illustrative materials from a vast literature created over a great span of time.

Orchids and Chrysanthemums

On a small and very delicate scale the main political themes of the Ch'ü Yüan lore can be seen in the flower symbology associated with it. The *Li Sao* itself abounds with flower symbols. The *sao* poet continuously compares himself to the orchid, for example, in order to convey both his purity, moral integrity, and his concern for his mortality. In the Han lore related to Ch'ü Yüan, this subtle imagery contrasted sharply with indelicate images of political blood and gore depicted in texts such as *Han Ying's Illustrations* and the *Lun Heng*. After the Han, the flowers prevailed and became a very common shorthand for alluding to the travails of Ch'ü Yüan; indeed, the implications of the flower symbol became more complex.

Independence, aloofness, and aloneness are qualities that became signified by the chrysanthemum, which is associated with Ch'ü Yüan because in the *Li Sao* the poet is depicted as feeding on them while wandering in banishment. Using this motif, here is a poem by Wang An-shih (c. 1045):

> The sun is lusterless above the city;
> As autumn comes, its brilliance fades.
> A mass of cold air floods even the sky;
> What then of the humble grass and trees?
> Yellow chrysanthemums, perfect in nature,
> Lone flowers defying the press of the mob,
> Among the dew and frost, I pick you.
> You will serve to still my morning hunger.[10]

Critics seem to agree that the poet here is identifying with Ch'ü Yüan—the pure, dedicated official, ready and willing to serve, but only as an individual.

Added to the stock political implications, the use of the flower symbols in poetry and painting came to convey a strong sense of bucolic isolation from metropolitan political involvement. Ch'ü Yüan (Ling-chün) was thus often evoked in a natural setting, like this one in a gently ironic colophon to a fourteenth-century "Ink Orchid" painting by Cheng Ssu-hsiao (1241–1318):

> Once by the river Li, I passed through the region
> of the Hsiang.
> The [orchid] flowers I saw grew only in small clusters.
> It seems lately Ling-chün
> has changed his mind.
> So blooming from thousands of acres, they now flirt
> with the spring wind.[11]

A modern historian tells us that by the time this poetry-painting combination was composed, due to the Mongol conquest of north China: "poetry and painting had become part of an underground culture in the south, lamenting a lost time and turning into a sort of resistance art, and flower paintings tended to be looked upon increasingly for their allegorical significance."[12] The poet in the next example was known as a Sung loyalist. Both his political sentiments and those of the painter whose work inspired him were akin to the famous I-min recluses who dramatized their anti-Mongol sentiments by retreating to the countryside and refusing to hold any official posts. Thus Ch'ü Yüan, quite inappropriately from the perspective of the Han tradition, became associated with the tradition of political resistance—with loyalism, the political recluse, and the hermit. This next poem is by Ch'iu Yüan (b. 1247), and it was composed for and on the painting "Narcissi" by Chao Meng-chien (1199–1276):

> The ice is thin, the sand banks are dark,
>   and the short grasses are dying;
> She who picks fragrant flowers is far away,
>   on the other side of Lake Hsiang.
> But who has left these immortal's jade pendants
>   in a moonlit night?
> They surpass even the "nine fields of orchids"
>   [planted by Ch'ü Yüan] in an autumn breeze.
> The shiny bronze dish is upset,
>   and the immortal's dew spilled;
> The bright jade [vase] is smashed,
>   like broken corals.
> I pity the narcissus,
>   for not being the orchid,
> Who had at least known
>   the sober minister from Ch'u.[13]

Poets: Public and Private

The paintings of the I-min recluses featured not only the orchid but the chrysanthemum as well. In these flowers they saw the embodiment of Ch'ü Yüan and the renowned poet T'ao Ch'ien (T'ao Yuan-ming, A.D. 365–427) respectively.[14]

Their treatment of the subject seems to imply not a contrast but an identity of the two figures' significance. Such a pairing was inapposite in the context of the bulk of Ch'ü Yüan lore, but it was not uncommon: T'ao Ch'ien is said to have cultivated the flowers while in self-exile. He is well known also for cultivating a peculiar life style and attitude toward public service which has relevance to understanding the development of the Ch'ü Yüan lore.

Successive epochs in Chinese history understood Ch'ü Yüan in the context of new sets of exemplars. Old ones did persist, but in increasingly stylized and mechanical usages. As it became arcane to speak of Ch'ü Yüan in terms of Wu Tzu-hsü or Pi Kan, it became common to understand him in terms of T'ao Ch'ien and others—poets or poet-officials who have enjoyed great popularity within the officials' culture. These exemplary poets are notable for being social and political dropouts who advocated retreating or in fact retreated themselves to bucolic isolation and wrote poetry as a pastime. In addition to T'ao Ch'ien, we must look at the highly popular Li Po (A.D. 705–762). Together, their lore throws into strong relief the contrasting elements of Ch'ü Yüan's lore: the persistence of his sense of social and political obligation, the conception of his poetry as a means of political remonstrance and protest, and his unwilling exile to the countryside.

The lore of T'ao Ch'ien depicts him as a virtuous and successful official who exiled himself into bucolic retirement out of a sense of loyalty to a fallen dynasty. (Sung dynasty loyalists who refused to serve the Mongol Yüan dynasty in the thirteenth century considered T'ao's action to be exemplary of their own protest eremitism.)[15] In his retreat, he regularly drank wine to excess and wrote poetry. Two illustrations are relevant here. In his poem "Lament for Gentlemen Born out of Their Time," we see a latter day expression of themes formulated earlier in the lore of Ch'ü Yüan. T'ao Ch'ien summarized it this way in his preface to the poem:

> Worthy men who cling to the right and set their minds on the true way hid their talents in their times; those who kept themselves clean and conducted themselves decently exerted themselves to no purpose to the end of their lives. So, Po-i and the

Plate 3. Fourteenth-century portrait of Ch'ü Yüan

Four White Heads [who refused to serve under the Ch'in and Han] complained that there was no one to whom they could turn. Ch'ü Yüan gave vent to his cry 'It is all over.'

In the poem itself, T'ao Ch'ien addresses Ch'ü Yüan directly: "You may cling to your orchids / In vain your fragrances and purity—who believes in them?"[16]

In another poem, T'ao Ch'ien suggested an alternative to the public dedication and the undying desire to serve, which he skeptically observed in the experience of exemplars like Ch'ü Yüan. T'ao's poetry celebrated the bucolic life, but not as a complement to public service, nor as a means of temporary strategic withdrawal from political danger. Indeed, he is perhaps best known for his vision of an arcadian utopia in which the question of political service is only a bad memory. Thus, T'ao Ch'ien began as a "refuser" (like Po Yi and Shu Ch'i). He could have continued to serve public office, but left in protest over an issue quite outside the Ch'ü Yüan lore—the impropriety of an official serving a new king whose succession is of dubious legitimacy. T'ao ended as a pastoral recluse who impugned the very notion of public service. This contrast was certainly recognized by some of the many poets who addressed the problem of the individual and society through the tandem figures of Ch'ü Yüan and T'ao Ch'ien. Hsin Ch'i-chi (1140–1207), for example, seems to have found T'ao's answers the more compelling: "Remember that, drinking and sleeping, Magistrate T'ao / Eventually achieves supreme happiness; / While being sober all alone, Master Ch'ü / Cannot escape calamity."[17]

The third figure in this little typology of poet-officials, Li Po, represents the polar opposite of Ch'ü Yüan on the continuum of public service. As Arthur Waley summed it up, Li Po was:

A man who in the eyes of a society largely dominated by bureaucratic values had completely failed in his career or rather had failed to have a career at all. There were poets who had lost their jobs and poets who had returned voluntarily to private life. But that a great poet should never have had a job at all was almost unprecedented.[18]

He was an anomaly—"an educated man, of good birth with nothing to write after his name, not even the *cheng-chün* (summoned gentlemen) that marked the bearer as having performed the heroic feat of refusing a post when one was offered to him."[19]

The lore of Li Po's drunken bohemianism contrasts sharply with Ch'ü Yüan's regularly cited sobriety. Other elements of their respective lore contrast still further. Tradition has it, for example, that Li Po also was a drowning victim; however, he, in a drunken stupor, is said to have fallen out of a boat while trying to embrace the reflection of the moon in the water. Plenty of *yin* here, but no hint of that tension with the *yang* elements of the cosmos, nature, or culture that inform the Ch'ü Yüan lore. This is a parody of Ch'ü Yüan's sacrificial death just as Li Po's life seems to be a parody of Ch'ü Yüan's life ordeal.

When Li Po did, however obliquely, address himself to the conventional problem of public service, symbolized in the madman of Ch'u motif, he tellingly identified with the madman Chieh Yü, not with the official (Confucius, Ch'ü Yüan, etc.) who was the object of the madman's warnings. "*I am a madman of Ch'u,*" said Li.[20] He relished the role of the outsider, the eccentric whose position on the fringes of society he perhaps perceived as giving him the same power of perspective as the *sao* poet's magic flight. Indeed, Li Po was not satisfied with the madman role alone. He also claimed for himself the identity of an immortal banished to earth from the celestial realm, envoy on earth of the Thirty-six Heavenly Rulers. Waley concluded that "having failed to secure any footing in the hierarchy of earthly officialdom, Li Po could, as compensation, still fall back upon his status as Minister on Distant Service of celestial principalities. . . . A transcendental official in a service recruited not by the Board of Rites."[21]

The typology of poets—Ch'ü, T'ao, Li—is a continuum of attitudes toward public service in which the post-Han lore of Ch'ü Yüan may be measured. Ch'ü Yüan is forced out of service and never relents in his belief that service is both noble and his calling. T'ao Ch'ien leaves office of his own will, but still honors a set of values in which service is taken for granted. However, he does not accept the role of "high and virtuous official degraded," but instead comes to reject altogether the system in which that category is meaningful. Li Po, in effect, is never even a part of that system.

Concomitant with this public-service continuum are notions of individualism. Ch'ü Yüan's is a function of his self-righteous purity and persistent refusal to compromise what he knows to be the Right. His "chrysanthemum-like" aloneness is paralleled (and indeed, results in) his physical isolation, forced upon him by his banishment to the countryside. But as we move from Ch'ü Yüan to T'ao and Li, we approach a hedonistic individualism, increasingly anarchistic and escapist. For Ch'ü Yüan, the countryside is punishment and ordeal; the other two seek and recommend bucolic isolation as an end in itself or as a means of reaching spiritual sublimity.

Tristes Tropiques

Ch'ü Yüan's exile in the countryside of Ch'u became the central motif in the poetry of officials who identified with him in their own times of trouble and discontent. These officials, especially from T'ang times, created a literary convention in response to actual political exile or to the figurative exile imposed upon them by the need to serve in distant bureaucratic posts. Let us begin our look at exile poetry with Arthur Waley's sensitive observations on the role of this figurative exile in the life cycle of the poet-official.

Drawing on experiences of eighth- and ninth-century poets, Waley notes that "[literary] culture was essentially a metropolitan product" and so poets, such as those we shall consider here, "were as much dépaysé at a provincial town as Charles Lamb would have been at Botany Bay. But the system of Chinese bureaucracy tended constantly to break up the literary coteries which formed at the capitals, and to drive the members out of the little corner of Shensi and Honan which to them was 'home.'"[22] Schematically, the lives of these literary officials passed through three stages. First, at the capital drinking, writing, engaged in discussion, and "burdened by [one's] office probably about as much as Pepys was burdened by his duties at the Admiralty." Then, having failed to curry favor with the Court, the official "is exiled to some provincial post, perhaps a thousand miles from anyone he cares to talk to." Finally, having "scraped up enough money to buy husbands for his daughters, [he] retires to a small estate, collecting round him remnants of friends of the old days."[23]

Because, in fact, officials were exiled in the regions south of the Yangtze River, the South in literary convention became associated with perennial problems of official life, and so with Ch'ü Yüan. However, the South was an ambivalent symbol: in contrast to the notion of the South as a forbidding place of exile, from as early as the fourth century A.D. it also gradually came to be thought of as a protective bastion of Chinese civilization when it was under the threat of destruction from nomad barbarians advancing from the north. A recurrent image in poetry is the Yangtze River as a moat, sealing off and guarding ethnic Chinese (Han) culture in retreat from its northern nomad assailants.[24] We are primarily concerned with a contrasting imagery: the South as alien and hostile to Han Chinese culture; barbarian, threatening, and even lethal to exiled poet-officials, themselves embodiments of Han culture.

Geographically speaking, the location of 'the South' was a function of the ever-expanding Chinese state. Until the T'ang period, the Wu, Yüeh, and Ch'u regions (the Yangtze Valley and below) bore the mostly negative burden of southern imagery. Thus Ch'u and Ch'ü Yüan were conventionally thought of as barbarian. In characterizing Ch'ü Yüan, even an accomplished Western historian like Henri Maspero could succumb to long-lasting Chinese regional chauvinism. Closely following the oldest conventions, Maspero referred to him as "a poet of barbarian origins . . . who renewed Chinese poetry." And he described him as "a man of Ch'u, Ch'ü Yüan was a barbarian; Chinese was not his mother tongue; from that perhaps came a certain clumsiness of expression which the Chinese have remarked ever since; and from that also perhaps came his pedantry, his desire to show off his knowledge of antiquity, . . . [all reflecting] the slightly puerile vanity of a good student satisfied with his laboriously acquired erudition."[25] During the T'ang, the South came to be identified geographically with subtropical Nam-Viet and Hainan island, places which then began to play the previous roles of mystery and uncivilized foreboding earlier performed by Ch'ü Yüan's homeland.[26] Nevertheless, Ch'ü Yüan and the Hsiang River Valley remained the focal points of the exile convention and what I call the Southern mode in poetry.

We have seen the beginnings of the exile theme in the literary treatment of Ch'ü Yüan by Ssu-ma Ch'ien, Chia I, and other Han writers. The basic elements were: recalling and mourning Ch'ü Yüan when in the Yangtze Valley near the Hsiang River; remarking on the frightful climate or terrain; writing a poem dedicated to Ch'ü Yüan and perhaps sinking it into the water as an offering; and conveying a melancholy sympathy for the troubles of an official's life which could end in exile so far from civilization.

Here is a sample of a T'ang variation on this theme with some of the main elements present. The great poet Tu Fu (712–770), always lamenting the demands of an official career, especially the constant displacement and travel it required, wrote the following to Li Po around A.D. 759 while Li was in the neighborhood of Lake Tung-t'ing and the Milo River:

> The cold wind rises above this remote district.
> Have you no advice for me, my friend? When will
> the flying wild geese bring me a letter from the
> river-and-lake region where the autumn waters are
> high? Literature seldom leads to a life of
> worldly success; Daemons are usually pleased to
> meet their victims. You had better talk with the
> ghost of the unjustly used Ch'ü Yüan; Drop a
> poem into the waters of the Milo for him.[27]

In contrast to the private sentiments and experiences expressed in Tu Fu's poem, on rare occasions there were in-

stances of exile poetry in which the poet's banishment was
linked to much broader and calamitous historical events.
Here, the exile was considered to be a result of an egregious
imperial policy which led to the destruction of the state by
northern barbarians. In this vein, the poet might suggest that,
like Ch'ü Yüan, his good advice on foreign policy was not
only rejected by the king, but resulted as well in his expulsion
from the court. Typically, the poet expresses his remorse in
verses which are inspired by his encounter with the ruins of
the ancient capital of Ch'u, the city of Ying. Using this symbol, he writes a lament for the fall of his own state in north
China. This scheme is dramatically played out, for example,
in Yü Hsin's (513–581) monumental "Lament for the
South," written on the occasion of the fall of the Liang state.
In Lu Yu's (1125–1210) "Lament for Ying," the occasion is
the Southern Sung appeasement of the Golden Tartars (Chin)
who then controlled north China.[28]

With a scope that tended to be much more limited and
personal than these laments, the "Southern" became a fixed
mode in the repertoire of poet-officials great and small. To
achieve its mood of melancholy isolation and loneliness, it
relied heavily on an evocation of primitive wilderness and
physical separation from the familiar civilized world.

The Ch'ü Yüan lore first became interwoven with the exile
theme in poetry during the generation of Liu Tsung-yuan
(773–819), who was one of China's greatest literary stylists.
Liu himself had his turn at exile in 805 when he and other
members of the Wang Shu-wen clique were expelled from
the capital. Liu was then given a post in Yung-chou, a
thousand miles away in southern Hunan province; he never
again regained a position in the capital, and when he was
reassigned a post one last time, in 815, he was sent still
further south to Kwangsi, where he died four years later. In
the poetry and essays of his Yung-chou period, Ch'ü Yüan
lore and the full panoply of exile literary conventions come
together most dramatically. Liu's sympathy for and identification with Ch'ü Yüan were considerable, and so the future
preeminence of Liu's writings became an important medium
for perpetuating the myth of Ch'ü Yüan.[29]

Liu's attraction to Ch'ü Yüan can be seen in his use of the *sao* style in a number of poems, and in his unique parody of Ch'ü Yüan's *Heavenly Questions*.[30] Dramatically illustrating this empathy are poems he composed on the occasion of his first banishment, and on the eve of his second. For the former occasion he wrote "Encountering the Wind at the Milo River," a piece in which he was still capable of expressing some optimism about his future in politics. He felt certain that his political difficulties were temporary and not likely to result in terminal banishment:

> On my way south, I did not grieve like that Ch'u official,
> For I have expectations of reentering the Capital's gates.
> The spring winds return to the Milo; but
> I do not take troubled waters to mean that
> times of peace are impossible.[31]

In 815 he was less sanguine when he wrote his famous "Lament for Ch'ü Yüan," again on his way south to another new post.[32] Along the Hsiang River route he made a pilgrimage to the Milo River where he summoned up the memory of Ch'ü Yüan:

> After you by a millennium, once again I am in
> exile and passing by the Hsiang River.
> I seek you out at the Milo, holding the fragrant
> Heng and Jo grasses,
> And in a hurried moment I wish to devote some words
> to you and thereby to achieve some enlightenment.
> You did not follow along with the world
> and only pursued the Tao.
> World affairs were confused, and society diseased.
> Noble men were ignored and petty men served the court.
> And while the hens cackled meaninglessly, the cock's
> beak remained closed.

For the most part, Liu's long poem is a personal restatement of the main themes of the *Li Sao*: the topsy-turvy image of a political world in which the worthless are followed, the worthy ignored; the calamity that follows when good political advice is ignored. Liu lavishes praise on Ch'ü Yüan for his loyalty, talent and his brave encounter with the consequences of his steadfast values. He strikes the appropriate maudlin pose, weeping at the thought of Ch'ü Yüan's experiences, and he underscores the pedagogic role that Ch'ü Yüan played by recording his experiences: "If you had said nothing, what hope would there be for future generations?" Momentarily, Liu takes heart from this positive result of Ch'ü Yüan's (and perhaps his own) political tragedy, and he further boosts his spirits with a reflection on the experience of Confucius. Liu recalls that Confucius was in effect exiled from his native state of Lu, yet this did not diminish his sageness or fame. By the same token, he recalls that a contemporary of Confucius, also from the state of Lu, Liu Hsia-huei, managed to stay on in Lu and achieve a successful, worthy, official career. But this did Liu Hsia-huei little good in the long run, for who ever heard of him; and what are his achievements next to those of the "exiled" Confucius?

If Liu Tsung-yuan gained satisfaction from his thoughts on the fame of Confucius and Ch'ü Yüan despite their exile, it was only momentary. His poem ends on a realistic and somber note when he acknowledges that he must retreat and remain silent. His words are no longer effectual. Unlike the Han poets, he does not attribute the official's frustration to "time's fate." He concludes: "since there is no way to end these bad days for our society, at least they can be forgotten (for the moment) while reminiscing about Ch'ü Yüan."

Though the lore of Ch'ü Yüan's banishment was endemic to T'ang officialdom during Liu's era, not all who reflexively compared their plight to Ch'ü Yüan's were as worshipful as Liu Tsung-yuan. Han Yü (768–824), who like Liu also rose to future literary fame, suffered through his exile in Ch'u from 804 to 806. While he explicitly identified with Ch'ü Yüan, neither he nor his poet friend, Meng Chiao (751–814), with whom he assessed the problem, had any sympathy for Ch'ü Yüan's suicide and the "stinking reputation" he had got from that act.[33] Despite such demurrers, the experience of Ch'ü Yüan remained appealing not only because it had come to represent the pain of exile but also because it dramatically marked the intersection of politics and art—the public and the private.

Recent biographers of Liu Tsung-yuan, for example, agree that in his case and generally throughout the T'ang literati, the art of literature was an epiphenomenon of politics. One modern biographer writes:

> Only the agony and distress of a ruined or frustrated official career, as in the case of Liu Tsung-yuan, could drive the T'ang intelligentsia into serious literary pursuits. These men remained at heart servants of the state. They simply transferred their endeavors from a political to a literary plane. Thus social and political themes predominated the formal literature of the T'ang.[34]

And another writes that "Liu was not a literatus who served in office, but a politician who wrote as an avocation: and because of the frustration of his political hopes."[35] If these observations are correct (even in the sense of accurately reflecting the T'ang literati's self-evaluation), then we can understand the particular appeal of Ch'ü Yüan, as Ssu-ma Ch'ien's biography depicted him. To sum up this fundamental relationship of politics and art, I turn to the beautiful formulation of J. D. Frodsham: "Chinese poets were almost invariably members of the bureaucracy, cultivated officials who yet secreted poetry as naturally as oysters produce pearls."[36]

I am apt to mislead the reader about exile poetry's attitudes toward public service if the genre is misconstrued as a kind of nature poetry and its protagonists as varieties of recluses or hermits. Liu Tsung-yuan (as Ch'ü Yüan) "never considered himself a hermit," one biographer writes, "his exile was involuntary and, as he always hoped, temporary."[37] While Chinese nature poets typically professed:

> A genuine longing for the hill and stream environment . . . Liu considered such a place less than desirable. An unwilling denizen of the back country, he drew upon its images to express his feelings, but where the nature poet found relief from the trials and tensions of official life, Liu found a painful reminder of his estrangement.[38]

If Liu differed from the nature school in his poetic attitude toward his natural environment, he also differed from his exemplar Ch'ü Yüan. The latter was, after all, a southerner, and the place of his banishment was nonetheless his beloved homeland, which, convention has it, he resolutely refused to leave. This aspect of the Ch'ü Yüan lore seems a bit at odds with itself in the southern motif which expresses contempt for and fear of Ch'ü Yüan's South.

Some officials stationed in Ch'ü Yüan's homeland did not assume the role of the exile and cultivate the self-pitying attitude of Liu Tsung-yuan. By the time of the poet Po Chu-i's (772–846) generation there was in evidence a growing literature written by northerners stationed in the Yangtze Valley which celebrated the beauties and joys of the South. A legacy of standard tunes and clichés was already available for this purpose when, for example, Liu Yü-hsi (772–842) was stationed in the heartland of Ch'u (Hunan province) and apparently decided to make the most of it.[39] Liu's accounts were among the earliest records of Ch'ü Yüan's links with the Dragon Boat Festival. Liu also wrote poetry which he claimed was inspired by local language and folksong. In doing so, he identified with Ch'ü Yüan in a manner quite different from Liu Tsung-yuan and the exile tradition:

> Of old, when Ch'ü Yüan was living in the region of the Yüan and Hsiang [rivers], the people of those parts summoned the spirits in crude and rustic language; he then wrote the *Nine Songs,* and even today they sing and dance them in Ch'u. So I also wrote nine "Bamboo Branch" *tz'u* [poems] and had trained singers to perform them.[40]

Here, Liu is following Wang I's tradition for explaining the origins of the *Nine Songs* and Ch'ü Yüan's "civilizing" effect on the primitive culture of provincial Ch'u.

Even Liu Yü-hsi, with all his fascination for the culture of the South, betrays a northern bias in spite of himself. In a reminiscence on Chang Chiu-ling (A.D. 673–740), who was himself banished to a southern post fifty years earlier, Liu does acknowledge that Chang was exiled in Ch'ü Yüan's

homeland, but the ethnic and even status implications of that
fact are Liu's point: Chang, he says, was concerned about
becoming a prisoner in his southern post:

> So he committed his [poetry's] symbolism to animals
> and birds and transferred his phrasing to herbs
> and trees, in a mood of dark depression, in the
> same spirit as that of the Sao-man (Ch'ü Yüan).
> So, alas! when [Ch'ü Yüan]
> himself was sent to a far-off retreat, once his
> expectations [of return] were lost, he could not
> bear it. How much less a Hua-man
> [a Han Chinese] of gentry stock
> required to go off to that ill-favored land![41]

While it is true then that the exile theme and the Southern
mode depicted Ch'ü Yüan's South as barbarous, Ch'ü Yüan
was treated, after the fashion of Wang I, as an avatar of
civilized political values and as a civilizing force within Ch'u
culture. Wang I's secular and allegorical approach to Ch'ü
Yüan's poetry prevailed, and it resulted in blurring the peculiar regional forms and values embodied in the poetry. Thus,
where the ecstatic visions of the Southern shaman were in
evidence in the Li Sao or Nine Songs, they were interpreted
as metaphors for the common experiences of officialdom; erotic and Dionysian elements became symbols for an Apollo-
nian bureaucratic culture.

Another feature of the Southern mode is suggested by the
poetry of Li Ho (771–817), in which we have an exception to
this treatment of Ch'ü Yüan which proves the rule. At the
same time that poet-officials like Liu Tsung-yuan were expressing a hostile attitude toward the South, Li's art uniquely
and momentarily revived the traditions of the divine river
goddesses and the wild exotic qualities of the Ch'u shaman
songs. He shared his T'ang contemporaries' explicit empathy
with Ch'ü Yüan, but unlike the conventional poet-official,
he was perhaps (in Frodsham's description) "by temperament
something of a shaman manqué" and about as close to the
poete maudit as one finds in Chinese letters. Li Ho's appreciation of the wildness of Ch'ü Yüan's literary vision contrasts

sharply with that of the exile poets who shuddered at the threatening tropics of Ch'u. Thus, even at a time when Ch'ü Yüan was much adored, it was apparently not for the Dionysian elements of his art and the culture they represented, for Li Ho, who best revived these elements, enjoyed no popularity until modern times.[42]

For a final illustration of the Southern mode, let us look ahead some time at a full-blown, ornate example of the genre — a long poem by Wang Yang-ming (1472–1529), one of China's greatest philosophers. The poem is entitled "Mourning Ch'ü Yüan," and was composed in 1507. Coming fully eight centuries after the T'ang poets developed the exile convention, Wang's poem is evidence for both its longevity and its importance as a medium for the Ch'ü Yüan lore.

This poem was written after what a modern biographer describes as "the most traumatic experience" of the philosopher's life. In the year before composing it, he had been imprisoned for about two months and flogged forty strokes in the audience chamber of the emperor, "probably in the presence of high-ranking officials." Then he was banished to the remote southwest province of Kweichow "to be an insignificant officer in the neighborhood of Miao tribespeople." What was his offence? He had sent a memorial to the throne criticizing the imprisonment of two officials who had offended the emperor by asking him to dismiss a powerful eunuch.[43]

The poem was composed by Wang Yang-ming as he made his way south to Kweichow, and en route, encountered the Hsiang River. It is structured by a series of alternating references to the wild and forbidding natural scenery and to Ch'ü Yüan's political plight. In his poem, Wang is anchoring his craft somewhere in the deep Yangtze gorges at nightfall during a freezing winter rain storm. The clouded sky, soughing wind, the sleet and ice and choppy waters introduce and set the desolate mood. Wang wonders where among these rugged, towering peaks could "the entangled one's" abode be found. He expresses disappointment and grief for not being able to see the ruins of Ch'ü Yüan's home. Then the poem conjures visions of the inhospitable terrain (immeasurable peaks, unfathomable chasms) and its terrifying inhabitants: dragons swim in the caves and grottos; apes scream mournfully from the sides of the gorge; bears roar and tigers stalk their prey in the dark woods; evil hill spirits and forest demons leap and whistle in the gloom. "I recall your destitution," writes Wang to Ch'ü Yüan, "and I wonder where in all this you can have found a place for yourself. . . . In or out of court, you were entangled by the greedy," Wang recalls, and then concludes that "envy entangles the upright and straight, and slandering them brings calamity." Wang Yang-ming's use of the southern mystique was aimed at creating a sympathetic remembrance of Ch'ü Yüan's life and, more generally, a warning about the evils endemic in court politics. Wang uses the natural setting, in what was by his day the conventional manner, to suggest the tragic isolation and misery of Ch'ü Yüan in exile. Wang adds to this an occasional analogy between the denizens of the forests and the courtiers responsible for driving Ch'ü Yüan from office. He concludes his poem with a reverential summary of Ch'ü Yüan's loyalty, his exile and suicide; and, as was the custom, Wang takes a Parthian shot at Yang Hsiung who dared to censure Ch'ü Yüan and suggest that he was less than a paragon.[44]

Contre Contre Sao

With all the attention given to Ch'ü Yüan by the T'ang poets, it was not until the Sung, in the eleventh and twelfth centuries, that some of the lore of Ch'ü Yüan and the basic literature associated with it were fairly systematically organized and reassessed. Arbiters of taste and scholarship, like Su Shih (Su Tung-p'o, 1036–1101) and Chu Hsi (1130–1200), added a rich new stratum to the Ch'ü Yüan, Ch'u Tz'u tradition, and through their efforts guaranteed not only the preservation of earlier strata but the vigorous continuity of the entire tradition down to the seventeenth and eighteenth centuries, when it received an intellectual charge that brought it down to modern times.

Underlying Sung contributions to the lore of Ch'ü Yüan

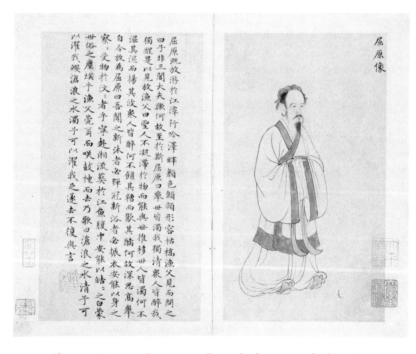

屈原像

屈原既放游於江潭行吟澤畔顏色顦顇形容枯槁漁父見而問之曰子非三閭大夫與何故至於斯屈原曰舉世皆濁我獨清眾人皆醉我獨醒是以見放漁父曰聖人不凝滯於物而能與世推移世人皆濁何不淈其泥而揚其波眾人皆醉何不餔其糟而歠其醨何故深思高舉自令放為屈原曰吾聞之新沐者必彈冠新浴者必振衣安能以身之察察受物之汶汶者乎寧赴湘流葬於江魚之腹中安能以皓皓之白而蒙世俗之塵埃乎漁父莞爾而笑鼓枻而去乃歌曰滄浪之水清兮可以濯我纓滄浪之水濁兮可以濯我足遂去不復與言

Plate 4. Fourteenth-century album leaf portrait of Ch'ü Yüan

are some technical works. For the first time since the Han, concerted efforts were made to produce an authentic edition of the *Ch'u Tz'u* and a complete new commentary. The result was Chu Hsi's *Ch'u Tz'u chi chu*, a work which stands between Wang I's recension and commentary and all later ones. Chu Hsi's work was based on the efforts of Su Shih, and more importantly, Hung Hsing-tsu's (1090–1155) *Ch'u Tz'u pu chu*.[45] Altogether, the interpretations continued and often enhanced the T'ang adulation of Ch'ü Yüan. Since the word of Su Shih, and especially Chu Hsi, had the weight of orthodoxy in future generations, their evaluation was of particular significance. Moreover, they cast evaluations in the framework of a polemic with the critics of the Han. Just as the Hung-Chu recension and commentary was conceived as the successor of Wang I's work, so their picture of Ch'ü Yüan was explicitly meant to correct and supplant the "Contre Sao" tradition of Yang Hsiung, et al. Hence, it is known as the "Contre Contre Sao" (Fan fan sao) tradition.

Chu Hsi further contributed to the lore of Ch'ü Yüan in a special appendix to his edition of the *Ch'u Tz'u*, the *Ch'u Tz'u hou yü*, in which he anthologized two dozen or so poems that illustrated the extended development of the *Ch'u Tz'u* poetic tradition. The contents range from the Han (Yang Hsiung's "Fan Li Sao" for example), through the T'ang (including Liu Tsung-yuan's "Mourning Ch'ü Yüan"), and down through Sung poetry. The issue is not that these poems by prominent poets would have perished without the efforts of Chu Hsi. Rather, as any good literary anthology is apt to do, this one made it possible for readers to recognize that individual works belong to a genre, and even to a complex tradition that comprises literary forms as well as particular sentiments, moods, and political values. By placing this anthology between the same covers as the *Ch'u Tz'u* and his own extensive commentary, Chu Hsi obviously becomes as much a creator of the tradition as a transmitter.

A generation before Chu Hsi, we can detect in Su Shih's poetry an effort to comprehend, sum up, and place the Ch'ü Yüan lore. His grand poem "The Ch'ü Yüan Temple" is the best example of that effort, and I agree with the critic who evaluated the poem as a summation of all previous attitudes toward Ch'ü Yüan.[46] Though the poem employs most of the motifs we have met in the exile genre, and the poet approaches Ch'ü Yüan in the familiar ritual fashion, the product is a uniquely gentle and reverent evocation of Ch'ü Yüan's memory for the purpose of making a philosophic point of universal significance. The setting in the Yangtze gorge is a familiar one also, but few of the qualities of the southern motif appear—the landscape is not obtrusive and hostile and the mood is contemplative rather than desolate and despairing. Su Shih composed the poem in 1066 when he was sailing up the Yangtze, not into exile (that came earlier and later), but homeward to Szechwan where his father had just died. "While sailing a frail craft to Ch'u," he wrote in the preface to the poem, "I chanced to pass the temple built in memory of Ch'ü Yüan. High mountains towered above the river, and, while I gazed, I cried aloud my thoughts. . . ."

Like his later and more famous poem "Red Cliff" (Ch'ih pi fu), in which allusions to Ch'ü Yüan also play a role, the main themes of "The Ch'ü Yüan Temple" are the frailty of the lone individual in the face of social pressures and human mortality. The first half of the poem summarizes Ch'ü Yüan's plight and centers on the question of whether he could achieve through his death what he could not achieve in life. The second half is informed with the question of whether and what the world has learned from Ch'ü Yüan's example.

In these lines from the poem Su Shih summarizes the tragedy and points to its implications:

> Banished across the waters a thousand *li*
> Towards the south.
> So that in life, you had no home,
> And in death, no grave.
> Alas! Man is but mortal,
> And it is hard to meet with death.
> Alone and powerless you wavered
> On that river-bank.[47]

Su Shih's object was not merely to tell us again that an official's life is not a happy one. He wanted to know what had become of Ch'ü Yüan's example, in this time when Ch'ü Yüan's home was a ruin mourned by passing travelers, and his children scattered and forgotten. Su Shih was unsatisfied with Liu Tsung-yuan's "What hope would there be now if you had said nothing"—and wanted to know if indeed anyone had changed their behavior as a result of Ch'ü Yüan's words. Certainly not any of his own contemporaries, Su Shih observed. Today, people have not the courage of their convictions and are too closely tied to the chaotic world; and so they accuse Ch'ü Yüan of folly for his stubbornness and his suicide. Since, in Su Shih's view, there was no hope of attaining human perfection, why not be satisfied with maintaining one's own purity and avoiding evil? But he saw little chance of even this for a people who would not follow the example of Ch'ü Yüan turning his back upon the state, disdaining customs, and showing contempt for death itself. If some critics saw Ch'ü Yüan as intemperate in his lone struggle, Su Shih nevertheless considered that intemperateness itself a virtue. And, all things considered, he saw no need to mourn Ch'ü Yüan, since he had found solace in the grave.

In other writings, Su Shih alluded to Ch'ü Yüan in discussions of the perennial quest for solace or the Buddhistic search for the tranquillity of nonbeing. These writings, in their celebration of wine, inebriety, and Taoistic self-cultivation often suggest the images of T'ao Ch'ien and Li Po more than Ch'ü Yüan. But even in these contexts Su Shih explicitly does bring forward Ch'ü Yüan: "He who alone had awakened to the truth, and found Tao in the raging torrents of the Milo."[48]

In none of these evocations of Ch'ü Yüan did Su Shih mention the question of loyalty. This was a mundane issue, after all, which would have been very much out of place in a poem like the "Red Cliff", a dreamy speculation on the relativity of "permanence" and "impermanence," and the evanescence of human life. Flooded with allusions to the venerable river goddesses and with symbolic moons, rivers, and oceans, this very famous poem summons up images from the *Li Sao* and the *Nine Songs* to evoke those notions of temporality and mortality which were as apposite to the Ch'ü Yüan lore as the issue of political loyalty.

I will not speculate how Su Shih could so exquisitely exercise such a Buddhistic sense of time, futility, and absurdity and still be concerned with the loyalty issue. But he was, and he could even be hard-nosed about it. Su Shih's poem "The Enlightened Ruler Listens to Loyal Counsel" speaks generally of the mutual responsibility of the minister and king to give and receive good advice. He argued that the successful king knows that "the Way of Government does not rest in mere docility of council. He fully understands that loyalty of intention may underlie the thwarting of his will; that the man who does not pander to the emotions probably has the welfare of country at heart."[49] As for the minister, he should play out his role, giving advice at the cost of his own interests and at the risk of his life. These are the tests of his loyalty.

In this argument, Su Shih emphasized the responsibility of the king to accept advice, and the dangers to the minister if the king does not. In his "Discussion of the Minister Chia I" (a figure closely related to the Ch'ü Yüan lore), the emphasis was on the responsibility of the loyal minister to be patient and eschew the role of a prima donna when the king falls short of sagehood. Su Shih was unsympathetic with Chia I's criticism of his king (Han Wen Ti) and saw no excuse for not serving him. That king, said Su, was good enough, and if Chia I could not serve him, it was his own fault. Who was Chia I waiting for—a sage like Yao or Shun? One's way must be *won* at court; one must *work* into the good graces of the courtiers, patiently. In brief, Su Shih claimed that Chia I had great ambition but little tolerance; great talent but not enough knowledge of the realities of politics.[50]

From these statements, as well as from poems like the "Ch'ü Yüan Temple," it may be fairly deduced that Ch'ü Yüan fulfilled Su Shih's criteria for a loyal minister and that Su Shih did not find his suicide inconsistent with them. This said, however, we would be missing the point if we did not emphasize that, for Su Shih, loyalty was obviously not the issue that made Ch'ü Yüan lore attractive (any more than it was to the T'ang poets). Su Shih correctly perceived in the *Ch'u Tz'u* material for a more profound and transcendent set of questions. For Su Shih, Ch'ü Yüan's suicide was not a sign that the poet had passed the test of loyalty, but that he had passed a test of spiritual authenticity and independence. Ch'ü Yüan's accomplishment lay in his resistance, not his obedience.

Hung Hsing-tsu's and Chu Hsi's contributions to the "Contre Contre Sao" tradition do pivot on the question of loyalty.[51] Unlike Su Shih, they directly and explicitly structured their appraisals of Ch'ü Yüan in light of the Han literature on the subject. Hung Hsing-tsu's argument was a response to all of those in the Han and the Northern-and-Southern dynastic periods who successively had formulated the standard criticism of Ch'ü Yüan's behavior. Hung relied on exemplars whom we met in the Han lore, such as the Three Virtuous Ones. He used them as the means of measuring the trueness of Ch'ü Yüan's loyalty and the validity of his suicide. Hung could see no less loyalty or wisdom in Ch'ü Yüan's suicide than in the acts of remonstrance by which Pi Kan risked death. And what of leaving the state and preserving oneself as an act of loyalty? Hung suggested that Ch'ü Yüan, like the Three Virtuous Ones, was the kin of his overlord (thereby uniting the obligations of loyalty and filial piety). This was a bond that obviated the possibility of fleeing. Ch'ü Yüan's unblemished virtue and loyalty could be better appreciated, according to Hung, if it were understood that he was in effect a combination of two of the Three Virtuous Ones: like Wei-tzu, he was forced to retire from the court; and like Pi Kan, he chose not to run away from his problem but to confront death with a reputation unblemished.

Hung Hsing-tsu's argument concluded with a panegyric reminiscent of Wang I's rhetoric a thousand years earlier: "Though banished and out of office, he only knew love and unalterable affection for his lord; . . . he completely fulfilled the duties of a [loyal] minister." At the end, Ch'ü Yüan's dilemma was that "to die was difficult, and not to die was difficult." Though in the short run Ch'ü Yüan failed, Hung said, one hundred generations were to hear his songs thereafter: "Ch'ü Yüan died, but he did not die," for later generations read his poetry, wrote about him, and took him for a standard of loyalty.

Where the Ch'ü Yüan lore is concerned, these are echoes of distant themes first sounded by Ssu-ma Ch'ien: that the power and effectiveness of the official must be postponed; it must be sublimated in the literary arts, which in turn are his source of immortality. Though Hung did not mention the problem of "mistiming" so prominent in the Han literature, I think his panegyric was his response to that issue as well.

When Chu Hsi made his contributions to the debate, he took a more reserved and ambivalent tack. He pedantically questioned Hung's use of the Three Virtuous Ones as a standard of judgment; given the broad differences in historical context, were they really comparable to Ch'ü Yüan? Was not Ch'ü Yüan, after all, superior for having chosen death where the others had had death thrust upon them? Turning to the earliest critics of Ch'ü Yüan, Chu Hsi dismissed them for dwelling merely on trifling faults of conduct. After all, he said, there can be no complete purity or rectitude; no one can be without transgressions. Where is perfection to be found? Even the *chün-tzu* (the ideal Confucian person) has faults. Ultimately what matters, according to Chu Hsi, are the motives behind the actions; the purity and cleanliness of the mind. These should be judged, not the actions as such.

When Chu Hsi came again to the question of Ch'ü Yüan's suicide, however, he made a demurrer that raised the ire of future generations of Ch'ü Yüan worshippers who caused Chu Hsi and Yang Hsiung to be tarred with the same brush. Chu Hsi argued that Ch'ü Yüan's fault was that his behavior strayed too far beyond the golden mean. Chu Hsi apparently could not tolerate the emotional excesses which led to the suicide. He claimed that this was loyalty to a fault. It would have been better, he seemed to be saying, if Ch'ü Yüan had spent his energies defensively guarding against the dangers of flattery and slander which ruined him at court.[52]

Thus, there were evolving in Chu Hsi's time strong new notions of loyalty and new models for them. It should not be assumed that Chu Hsi's judgment on Ch'ü Yüan reflected any equivocation about giving up one's life as an act of political loyalty. He had said that "to die after having done everything according to the right way is the proper [political] fate." And he shared a common Southern Sung reverence for that age's leading hero, Yüeh Fei (1103–1141), the general who was executed by the Southern Sung court. Although Yüeh had been a staunch defender of the South against the northern nomads, he had questioned the court's foreign policy and as a result was silenced with a false charge of insubordination and suspected treason. Chu Hsi respected him not simply because Yüeh had died for the state, but rather because the general was willing to oppose a policy he felt was not in the state's interests, and then to accept the consequences of that opposition.[53] Modern scholarship says that at this time, Neo-Confucian ethics were beginning to claim that no matter how wrong the policies of the Sung court might be, the proper fate for Yüeh Fei was to remonstrate but to accept the consequence of death:

> [These ethics] supported absolutism to the extent of making loyalty a personal commitment unto death in absolute obedience to the emperor. . . . The classical praise of Yüeh Fei was the epitome "chin chung pao kuo" or "utmost loyalty to requite the state." Its word order implied the Neo-Confucian priority: personal loyalty [that is, to the person of the emperor], comes before loyal service to the state. Absolute obedience to the ruler is a prerequisite without which loyalty in whatever form was simply inconceivable.[54]

Here then was an attempt to give firm resolve to a perennial tension in the notion of political loyalty—the conflict between the personal loyalty to the king and loyalty to the best interests of the state—which we have seen dramatized in the Han lore of Ch'ü Yüan.

If Yüeh Fei was the new exemplar of loyalty for Sung, Feng Tao (A.D. 882–954) was the chief counterexample. He was remembered as the minister who had served in the courts of successive dynasties, and he was the target of the admonition from Sung's influential politician and historian Ssu-ma Kuang: "A loyal minister does not have two sovereigns, a loyal wife does not have two husbands."[55] On the issue of an official preserving himself, Ssu-ma Kuang wrote: "If it is clear that a minister can do nothing about correcting the faults or errors of his sovereign, it is proper for him to take action assuring his own survival."[56] Unfortunately, Ch'ü Yüan is not mentioned in Ssu-ma Kuang's general history, the monumental *Comprehensive Mirror (Tzu-chih t'ung-chien)*, therefore, his application of these principles to the case of Ch'ü Yüan is a moot question. In regard to Feng Tao, however, Ssu-ma Kuang did not dismiss Ch'ü Yüan's final solution: "The great man should achieve righteousness through sacrifice and not prolong his life if that meant the destruction of righteousness."[57]

During the Southern Sung, a significant body of literature and special terminology to deal with the issues of loyalty began to emerge.[58] This was a sometimes obsessive concern which continued at least to the end of the seventeenth century. It was probably provoked by problems of national security. The problem of loyalty was enlarged beyond king/official relations to include such questions as whether to trust and embrace groups that had rebelled against the nomads in the north. Questions also arose in response to the problem of "loyalism," that is, the special kind of loyalty problems brought about by dynastic changes. An expression of this was the eremitism to which we have alluded when discussing Ch'ü Yüan and T'ao Ch'ien. The inherited lore of Ch'ü Yüan was of limited use here since its political focus was not dynastic change and the two-masters dilemma it posed. In spite of the omnipresent association of loyalty with Ch'ü Yüan, from T'ang times onward the Ch'ü Yüan lore was not generally used as a medium for formulating the relationship of officials and kings, and certainly not as a medium for expressing the views of those—like the Sung theorists—who increasingly sought to subordinate the official to a monarchy of absolutist pretensions. Officials continued to identify with

Ch'ü Yüan not for his exemplary subordination, but for his willfulness, his estrangement, and—Chu Hsi notwithstanding—his "excessive" behavior.

Li Sao Continued

In the seventeenth and early eighteenth centuries, the dilemmas of political protest were pandemic in scholar officialdom. Protest groups that sprang from the disintegration of the Ming polity were followed by similar organizations, after the Manchu conquest in 1644, whose concerns encompassed anti-Manchu loyalism as well as critiques of monarchy and bureaucracy. From such troubled times we draw some of our last illustrations of the Ch'ü Yüan lore before the twentieth century. While the great bulk of literature related to Ch'ü Yüan in these centuries continued to be in the form of commentaries on the *Ch'u Tz'u*, significant new treatments of him are found elsewhere, particularly in a genre of drama called *tsa-chü*.

Overall, these dramas treated Ch'ü Yüan in the partisan fashion that has prevailed in all forms of literature since the Sung. He was defended against the "Contre Sao" tradition and even against Chu Hsi's evaluation. The Ch'ü Yüan that was most appreciated was not the loyal one, but the estranged, isolated, and obstinate one. Seventeenth- and eighteenth-century writers argued in effect that the popularity of Ch'ü Yüan and his poetry was a function of a paradoxical quality of his life and art, that is, his ultimate achievement of orthodox values through a proximate violation of them. They insisted that a Confucian-Mencian orthodoxy was maintained in the values conveyed by his poetry. And they assessed his suicide as the result of his conscious search for a meaningful death. It was not that he took life lightly, but that he used his own death as an instrument to arouse his lord to the political truth (*i szu wu chün*).[59]

In the context of this kind of appreciation of Ch'ü Yüan, a number of *tsa-chü* were composed in the seventeenth century. Yu T'ung's (1618–1704) "Reading the Li Sao" (Tu Li Sao) appears to be the earliest extant example of this genre of

Ch'ü Yüan lore.[60] It lends itself well to the evocation of the *Li Sao*'s flamboyant, histrionic protagonist. This is a three-part piece that deals with that phase of Ch'ü Yüan's life most favored by dramatists—the final days of his banishment. He is depicted as orphaned and wandering like a wild man in the Ch'u back country. Thematically, the dialogues and soliloquies do not go beyond a rehearsal of the old problems of good officials who are ignored or abused by their kings, and the issue of fleeing a country in hard political times. The author is explicitly sympathetic with Ch'ü Yüan's political choices and with his suicide. Correspondingly, he is contemptuous of the criticisms made by Chia I and Yang Hsiung. Most striking about this drama is its enlargement of the wild, heterodox, and frenzied aspects of the story. Part one depicts Ch'ü Yüan at the temple wall, composing his poem, *Heavenly Questions*, and then consulting with an oracle. Part two features a female shaman. And in the last part Ch'ü Yüan meets with the scruffy fisherman (not in the original *Li Sao*) who cannot discourage him from suicide.

The peculiar emphases of this play present an occasion to note a convention that had been emerging in connection with the Ch'ü Yüan lore since at least T'ang times. It depicts exiled Ch'ü Yüan undergoing a transformation of mien and behavior into that of a wild or mad person—one with long dishevelled hair and strange dress, who fed on nuts and berries as he wandered alone through the countryside and then (in Li Ho's phrase) "raved wildly by the wall, as he wrote his Heavenly Questions."[61] This motif, which associates wildness or a kind of madness with primitive nature, would seem to have had its ancient beginnings in the philosophic Taoism of Chuang-tzu and to be carried through Chinese literature in various forms, such as our "tactical" madman, the fisherman, the mad monks of the southern Zen Buddhist school, and the "Mad Zen" (K'uang Ch'an) schools of philosophy.[62] I suspect that the Ch'ü Yüan lore was enriched by these, mostly Taoist and Buddhist derived motifs: wildness, madness (and often, southernness) suggest not merely eccentricity, but also individualism and estrangement, autonomous artistic vision, and social-political protest; perhaps even defection. All these themes appealed especially to some of the modern worshippers of Ch'ü Yüan.

The next play for consideration, Cheng Yü's "The Milo River" (Milo Chiang), is much informed by this "wild" motif too.[63] Its mood and setting are similar to those of Yu T'ung's play and its cast has but two players, Ch'ü Yüan and the fisherman. The play was preserved thanks to the efforts of Wu Wei-yeh (1609–1672), a member of the Ming loyalist group, the Revival Society (Fu she). Wu included this play in a 1661 anthology of plays. The format is quite simple and structured to permit chanting of the Li Sao. In between each verse a vernacular summary is chanted according to what I assume were popular tunes. The action consists merely of Ch'ü Yüan, again in his last days, confronting the fisherman who offers him wine and food and induces him to sing the Li Sao. Ch'ü Yüan speaks at length about himself, and with the immodesty of the Li Sao itself he flaunts his perspicacity and brilliance. He further takes issue with his critics, Chu Hsi for example, who say he has been loyal to a fault, and with those who say that the poetry of the Ch'u Tz'u is inferior to the poetry of the Odes. With defiance he tells his critics that despite their deprecations, he is celebrated by the folk in the Dragon Boat Festival.

"Li Sao Continued" (Hsü Li Sao) is a phrase or title used repeatedly throughout Chinese literature, poetry in particular, to suggest an affinity of mood or situation with Ch'ü Yüan. Chi Yung-jen's (1637–1676) quartet of tsa-chü bears that title though Ch'ü Yüan himself is a principal in none of them.[64] He is alluded to occasionally in the plays, but the author was more intent on writing, as he tells us, in the tradition of the Li Sao rather than about Ch'ü Yüan, to whom he pays explicit homage in the foreword. Chi Yung-jen is said to have written the quartet while in jail. He had been caught up in the intrigues of the separatist San Fan rebellion and, in the end, he was murdered by a participant in the rebellion whom

A. 13th century

B. Dated 1498

C. Dated 1593

D. Circa 1600

Plate 5. Portraits of Ch'ü Yüan

he refused to support. While there is no suggestion in his standard biography that he was himself anti-Manchu, the text of his quartet leads to that conclusion.

The tone of Chi Yung-jen's plays is set by the first of the four, which amounts to a lecture on the absurdity of Chinese politics and history. It seems to be at the same time an oracular warning to the Manchu regime in particular. The body of the text recounts the endless succession of dynasties, emphasizing the inevitable demise of all regimes, those of the North being especially precarious and short-lived. The leitmotif is the fate of the South (Chiang-nan) with each new cycle of a northern regime. The heroic defense of the South against the North by Yüeh Fei and Wen T'ien-hsiang (1236–1283) are adduced, but the overall mood is one of Buddhist-like resignation in the face of irresistible flux and temporality.

These same themes reappear in our final example of the use of the Ch'ü Yüan lore as an expression of extreme estrangement and of that double-edged loyalty (loyalism) that is in effect subversive. In Wang Fu-chih's (1619–1692) commentary on the *Ch'u Tz'u* there is a straightforward appreciation of and identification with Ch'ü Yüan. Wang was a native of Heng-yang, Hunan—or as he put it, from Ch'ü Yüan's place of exile in the Hsiang River valley.[65] During the period of the Manchu conquest he personally participated in the Ming loyalist resistance. He was a member of the reformist and anti-Manchu Revival Society and a participant in the "Ch'u faction" which fought for "moral reform and preservation of national interests." When that faction lost to its competition, Wang was impeached by his rivals on "trumped-up charges," barely escaped with his life, and ended his political career forever at the age of thirty-one. For the rest of his life he refused any compromise with the Manchus, and his subversive writings about them occasionally required him to hide out and even take refuge with the primitive tribespeople of the region.[66]

Wang's impoverished life in the countryside was not fully that of a recluse, for he attempted to keep in touch with cosmopolitan developments. His mastery of the Taoism of Chuang-tzu did not inhibit his writings from developing an undying spirit of resistance to the Manchus and deep involvement in sophisticated political theory. His political life and times were sufficiently like those of Ch'ü Yüan, Wang himself said, to warrant full empathy and unqualified appreciation. He could not agree with Chu Hsi that Ch'ü Yüan's loyalty was in any way faulty, saying that his spirit of loyalty and devotion was firmly and deeply rooted, and that it transcended life and death. Wang wove his sympathies into an imitation *sao* style poem, the "Ninefold Brightness" (Chiu chao), and used his commentaries on poems like the *Heavenly Questions* to outline his theory that an alien regime in China, like one without the *tao*, could neither rule legitimately nor long.

Summary

Some features of the lore discussed in this section both contrast with the Han lore and point the way toward its modern transformations. The most notable feature is the virtual disappearance of the imagery of a Promethean contest between minister and king for power. Absent are the explicit pretensions of the official to a political role, in effect, superior to the king's. By the same token, the context of references to political power is not cosmic, nor the official's role perceived as informed by one of the two elementary cosmic forces. This must in part reflect the greatly increased size of the bureaucracy, from the T'ang onward, and the gradual enlargement of the monarchy's control over it. The heroic proportions of the ancient ministers and their political expectations were difficult to maintain when an official could not escape the fact that he was but one of a large and growing group, more and more structured by examinations and routines, and increasingly managed by a court of increasingly despotic practices.

There was an epic quality to the earlier lore: the materials here surveyed display a shift to the lyrical side of the *Ch'u Tz'u* tradition. Beginning with the T'ang, contributors to the lore were not primarily interested in Ch'ü Yüan's embattled relations with his king nor with his court rivals, but rather with his passion—the ordeal of his isolated exile and banishment. The focus was shifted from the outer and public expressions of politics to the inner and personal. Admiration for Ch'ü Yüan became a function of the consistency, perseverance, and the completeness of his commitment. His success or failure was not measured by formal accomplishments, but rather by his ability to demonstrate that in a crisis he remained steadfast to his values. With perhaps only the significant exception of Chu Hsi, the post-Han lore is content to accept Ch'ü Yüan's loyalty to his king as a commonplace, and to show more serious interest in his loyalty to a body of values, a loyalty which he demonstrated in personal expressions of feeling and in his own disposition of his life.

This lyrical tendency is highlighted by modern scholars when they point out that for the long period surveyed here, Ch'ü Yüan, his plight, and his poetry were expressly used by the literate elite as a means of emotional release—a conventional, even ritual, medium of catharsis for those many individuals perennially frustrated and hurt not merely by the king but by "the system" as well. One chanted the *Li Sao* and wept. One recalled Ch'ü Yüan's suffering, and through the tears recalled other political worthies' and one's own malaise as well. Ch'ü Yüan's feelings became as important as his actions; and his expression of those feelings in his poetry as important as these two together. The lyricism, the open concern with self and sentiment, was of the greatest appeal to the moderns. And related to this was their perception of Ch'ü Yüan specifically as a poet, a role which decidedly begins to emerge only in the late T'ang.

The moderns often choose to forget Ch'ü Yüan's role as an official or even as a poet-official. This should not lead us to miss the useful insights that the post-Han lore gives us into a special view of the relations of art and politics, private sentiment and public obligation. Before the twentieth century, those who most cherished the Ch'ü Yüan—*Ch'u Tz'u* tradition could think of no higher praise than claiming Ch'ü

Yüan's poetry to be at the same time an expression of personal sentiment, a medium of universal values, and a tool of political remonstrance. Just as feelings and the disposition of one's self were carried over into the public realm, so public values and obligations were internalized. Whether one had fulfilled one's public duties, whether one was truly loyal—these were things that could be measured (some said, *best* measured) by examining the true nature of one's feelings, the "state of one's mind." Thus, "personal space" is externalized, "political space" brought within. Is not all of this the burden of the formula *i szu wu chün*—"He used his death to bestir his lord"?

The prominent role which locale (Ch'u, Chiang-nan, the South) played in the post-Han lore was intimately related to the predominant lyrical mode and the emphasis on sentiment. The South and its flora and fauna were major factors in the melancholy exile theme. Rivers and gorges were indispensable settings and props for memorializing Ch'ü Yüan and expressing one's own personal feelings.

When we add the theme of "resistance" to the emphasis on self, sentiment, and locale we shall have a stock of seasoned timber out of which the moderns, especially the "romantic generation," began to fashion anew the lore of Ch'ü Yüan.

3

Man and Superman
in Republican China

Our great ancient poet, Ch'ü Yüan, looks like a romantic.
Kuo Mo-jo, "Romanticism and Realism," 1958

SIGNIFICANT transformations of the Ch'ü Yüan lore began
early in the twentieth century, during an epoch with an insa-
tiable appetite for heroes. Old paragons were rejected or skeptically set aside; new ones were sought in obscure corners of
history, within China's own countertraditions, and from other
peoples' culture. Through each new wave of iconoclasm and
with each new batch of imported exemplars, Ch'ü Yüan's
prominence increased, his suitability to twentieth-century problems was enhanced. It was common during the
anti-traditional New Culture movement (from about 1915
onward) for long-venerated figures (like the Golden Age sage-
kings, or Confucius and Lao-tzu) to be dismissed by so-called
antiquity doubters as mere legends, or scorned as mediums
for conveying corrupt or dead values. Ch'ü Yüan did not entirely escape this iconoclasm, but efforts to undermine, or

87

merely to "reevaluate," his historicity were met with extraordinary and almost universal resistance and contempt. In a generation rife with skepticism and determined to scrutinize the past with a fastidious new historiography, Ch'ü Yüan remained off-limits.[1] The new Chinese intelligentsia, struggling to shape their own identity, seemed compelled to seize upon every aspect of the inherited Ch'ü Yüan lore that could provide some guidance for what they might be, and that could valorize what they had already become.

By the time the monarchy was overthrown in 1911, the intellectuals who drew upon the lore were significantly different from all of those in the past whom it had inspired or provoked. The poet-officials we have looked at had been part of an ongoing, integrated system in which the politics of state and bureaucracy were supposed to have been affected by their lives. Many acted as though they believed that happened. They were, except in the worst of times, brokers between state and society, embodiments of prestigious cosmopolitan culture, teachers and preservers of universal values. The Ch'ü Yüan lore had served them generally as a means of expressing their frustrations or resentments at the failure of their ideal role to be realized fully. The new intellectuals we talk about in this section were not at all sure what their own roles were to be. The institutions which had been the reason-for-being of the poet-officials were now gone and in disrepute. This left the new intellectuals neither here nor there—severed from both the state and society. Like their predecessors in the old bureaucracy, the moderns decried the failure of the state to use them and to pay attention to their wisdom. But unlike the old bureaucrats, the new intellectuals lacked a coherent ethical sanction for their demands to be heard and followed, and their plaints were not made as participants from within a supportive system. They did not remonstrate with heads of state about the proper workings of inherited institutions. Instead they sanctimoniously shook their finger in the face of the whole culture and called for the reevaluation or abandonment of institutional legacies.

Fundamentally, the new intellectuals sought from the

Ch'ü Yüan lore a license for change and the legitimization of their own stewardship of the changes they sought for China. Because of this, they transformed Ch'ü Yüan's political resistance into revolutionary leadership; his concern with self and personal sentiment into expressions of liberation from malevolent tradition; and his South into the cultural hothouse of creative vision and radical innovation.

Along with this effort to find transformative value in the Ch'ü Yüan lore, Chinese intellectuals of the twentieth century looked for populist values. They gave virtually no attention to Ch'ü Yüan's relationship to his king: instead they made his relationship to the common people the locus of his problem of public duty and loyalty. They saw his martyrdom not as a product of king/minister relations, but rather of his cultural heritage, his skepticism, and the disjunction of his populist ideals and social realities.

During the first half of the twentieth century, Ch'ü Yüan's public role and suicide were primarily understood according to two contradictory notions of public duty—both exploited by China's so-called romantic generation of the 1920s and 1930s. The first notion was heavily populist and emphasized the democratic pathos of merging with the people and heroically sacrificing one's life on behalf of the collectivity. It argued that aloofness and separation from the masses was in itself a source of self-destruction for the society's intellectual leaders. The second notion was radically individualist. It relied on such European formulations as the German Romantics' "storm and stress" ethics which spoke of the moral individual against an immoral society. This was a literature which depicted the public hero as a sacrificial victim (often a poet), or as the superman whose genius bore sympathy for the masses, but nevertheless conflicted with and was ultimately crushed by them.

It was this latter notion of public duty which enjoyed the earliest and longest prominence in twentieth century China, and it has provided the most persistent medium for identifying with Ch'ü Yüan. Before we begin a detailed exploration of the search for transformative and populist values in the

Plate 6. "Kutsugen" [Ch'ü Yüan] by Taikan Yokoyama, 1898

lore, we must look more generally at its relationship to those ideas of public service and martyrdom which were the points of departure for the modern understanding of Ch'ü Yüan.

Patriotic Martyrdom

Public martyrdom for public causes was a constant factor of Chinese politics from the turn of the nineteenth century. Most of it was involuntary, but much of it was conscientious self-destruction, sanctioned by a long tradition of "hortatory suicide," of which Ch'ü Yüan was but one exemplar. Nineteenth-century reformers and turn-of-the-century revolutionaries shaped their own self-images, and justified their actions with a host of heroic models from China's past. These ranged from bandit chieftains drawn from popular fiction, to seventeenth-century anti-Manchu loyalists, to ethereal Buddhist saints. Ch'ü Yüan was by no means more prominent than other heroes at this time, but allusions to him markedly weave in and out of the prolific and colorful patriotic literature turned out by scores of embattled scholar-officials who had now become rootless intellectuals.[2]

Borrowings from the Li Sao and analogies with Ch'ü Yüan were used over and over to memorialize revolutionaries killed either in one or another anti-monarchical insurrection before 1911, or in post-revolutionary efforts to unseat Yuan Shih-k'ai, the Republic's first president. This was a standard convention at least from the time of the executions of the young leaders of the Hundred Days of Reform in 1898. For example, the great scholar and reform leader K'ang Yu-wei (1858–1927), whose poetry was generally inspired by the Ch'u Tz'u, paid tribute with standard images from the Li Sao to a friend executed by the court:

> Orchids from the Li river and angelicas from the Yuan:
> I think of my friend.
> Cinnamon wine and fragrant rushes: I sacrifice to those
> fallen for the fatherland.
> Without peer in the world, his valor is alive,
> his soul resolute.[3]

The 1898 martyrs were of course still loyal to their sovereign, the Kuang Hsü emperor. But Ch'ü Yüan lore proved nonetheless useful for those who revolted against the monarchy; and subsequently, for those of the New Culture era who turned the attack on the whole "Confucian" institutional and intellectual heritage.

Among the important early examples of this anti-traditional use of Ch'ü Yüan, none is more important than that of Lu Hsün (1881–1937). As essayist and short story writer, his innovative styles and devastating social criticism earned him a uniquely venerated place in modern Chinese letters, and eventually, canonization by the Chinese Communists. During the first decade of the twentieth century, Lu Hsün expressed a deep empathy for Ch'ü Yüan as well as an interest in elements of China's countertraditions and foreign culture. At this time, one biographer writes, he created poetry "with melancholy patriotism similar to the mood of Ch'ü Yüan's works . . . the personal vision of a lone martyr."[4] Heralding the literature of later decades, Lu Hsün spoke of Ch'ü Yüan in the context of China's need for poets of destruction and rebellion, for genius, for a superman upon whom the future peace of the world depended. In a very undemocratic phase of his development, Lu Hsün believed that social levelling and equality, however beautiful an ideal, "represented a lowering of standards, a sacrifice of brilliant individuals to the mediocrity of the masses."[5] Citing endless examples from Byron to Nietzsche to Ch'ü Yüan, what Lu Hsün "feared most was that these creative individuals, these supermen or geniuses, would be crushed under what he called 'the tyranny of millions of unreliable rascals.' Had not China's own Ch'ü Yüan been rejected? Where now were her warriors of the spirit? Where . . . 'are those who raise their voices for truth, who will lead us to goodness, beauty, strength, and health? Where are those who utter heart warming words, who will lead us out of the wilderness? Our homes are gone and the nation is destroyed, yet we have no Jeremiah crying out his last sad song to the world and to posterity.'"[6]

Other major proponents of the New Culture developed the

image of Ch'ü Yüan as a model of public service and loyalty to a national collectivity (not to a person of authority), even at the cost of self-sacrifice. Li Ta-chao (1889–1927), co-founder of the Chinese Communist Party, wrote of his early fascination with ancient heroes and his youthful experiments with essays written in the style of the *Li Sao*. Li's biographer notes: "The Confucian concepts of loyalty and public service, as symbolized in the heroic figure of Ch'ü Yüan, nurtured in Li a highly romantic temperament, a fierce Chinese patriotism, and a burning desire to serve his country and people."[7] Shortly after his announced conversion to communism in 1919, he once more defined the goals of political participation in tones that invoked the heroic image of Ch'ü Yüan:

> The aim of human life is to develop one's own life, but there are times when the development of life necessitates the sacrifice of life. . . . There are times when ardent sacrifices extend the beauty of life further than normal development. . . . Tragic melodies usually make the most exciting music. The life of superior attainment always lies in ardent sacrifice.[8]

In statements such as these, sacrifice did not necessarily mean death, and death did not necessarily imply suicide. But tradition had it that Ch'ü Yüan did commit suicide, and just as that act was the focal point of traditional criticism of Ch'ü Yüan, so it was again in the first decades of the twentieth century. Suicide, in periods of great national distress (1905–1911, 1919, 1925 for example) was a prominent mode of political protest, and often the melancholy figure of Ch'ü Yüan helped to justify if not inspire the act of self-destruction.[9] A sign of the prominence of protest suicide during these years is the literature criticizing this extreme expression of public concern. In 1915, for example, Ch'en Tu-hsiu (1878–1942), the other co-founder of the Communist Party, wrote in a prominent New Culture journal that "self-sacrifice was a function of nonconstructive emotion instead of reason;" and he cited Ch'ü Yüan as an example of suicide out of a misguided sense of loyalty.[10] But unlike the traditional

"Contre Sao" criticism of his suicide, the generation of the New Culture did not advocate "retiring like the dragon," but insisted that the struggle be continued in any way possible. This was Mao Tse-tung's position in his 1919 essay "Against Suicide," which argued that oppressive society could drive individuals unconsciously and unwillingly to suicide; and that although suicide "represents a surrender to the dominating will of society, the individuals who understand that life is greater than society can act as their own redeemers."[11]

In the wake of the May Thirtieth Incident of 1925, critical observers wrote of another epidemic of patriotic suicides which they rejected as counterproductive. Some writers explicitly urged that Ch'ü Yüan not be emulated: young people should stay alive and continue to serve the country.[12] A similar sentiment was expressed by the intellectual community two years later over the drowning suicide of the eminent scholar, Wang Kuo-wei (1877–1927). His tragedy, moreover, was taken as the symptom of the Chinese intelligentsia's fundamental problem. On one hand, society still had not recognized the value of its intellectuals and had driven Wang to despair by failing to provide him a proper place. And on the other, Wang typically had courted his own destruction by separating himself from the masses, by becoming an aloof superman.[13]

Where Ch'ü Yüan was concerned, twentieth century literature required that this question of the relationships of public service and sacrifice, intellectuals and masses, all be understood within broad cultural contexts. Through this medium, key elements within the lore were reorganized and fused with current concerns of the new intellectuals. The traditional concern of the lore with the South was brought to the center of the stage and expanded greatly. A complex idea of Southern culture became not only an important means of understanding Ch'ü Yüan, but for understanding all of Chinese history.

North and South

From its inception in the Han dynasty, the lore of Ch'ü Yüan reflected a rather consistent set of attitudes toward the

South of China. Some writers contemptuously considered it "barbarian"; others thought of it as quaintly primitive. But without exception when Ch'ü Yüan's experience was the context, the South represented political exile. The South was where the court sent men who were low on the bureaucratic totem-pole, as well as dissidents and rival factions once they were defeated. The South thus became associated with those who dissent, those who protest. These associations were reinforced by other cultural forms that addressed themselves to social criticism (the philosophic Taoists or the "Mad Zen" philosophers) and with aesthetics (the "Southern School" of painting). In the twentieth century there has been a strong tendency to carry these associations one step further. The South has come to be thought of not merely as the place where dissidents and eccentrics locate themselves, but a place whose nature it is to produce dissent and eccentricity. This is true where Ch'ü Yüan's thought and art are in question, and in much broader considerations of Chinese culture as well. Accompanying a sense of the South as a unique culture has been a strong belief that at the heart of that culture is an innovative and revolutionary spirit.

In 1904, Liu Shih-p'ei (1884–1919), a prominent classical scholar and political activist, published a seminal essay on the dual origins of primordial schools of Chinese literature and scholarship. Arguing from a geographical determinism, the essay posited a contrasting set of northern and southern cultural characteristics which were a direct function of terrain, climate and ecology, and from which all future art and literature evolved. The northern culture of China typically "revered reality" and its literary tradition emphasized the recording of events or elucidating real life situations. The South prized imagination, illusion, and the visionary. Liu's essay cited the *Ch'u Tz'u* as one example in a train of literary developments determined by the physical world which begins in the Yangtze Valley. The most typical and general expression of southern culture to which the *Ch'u Tz'u* was heir was the tradition of the Taoist masters Lao-tzu and Chuang-tzu.[14]

Liu Shih-p'ei was a native of Kiangsu province and the scion of a great family of scholars. At the time he wrote the

essay he was deeply involved with a group of young intellectuals based in Nanking. Their anti-Manchu politics brought
them to an interest in protecting China's "national soul," or
"national essence," which they felt was embodied in certain
literary traditions. They emphasized those traditions, such as
the writings of the seventeenth century Ming loyalists, with a
definite southern locale: Just as "the South" had been a bastion of resistance to the Manchus in the seventeenth century,
in the twentieth it would be the source of Manchu destruction and the perpetuation of fundamental cultural traditions.
The Southern Society (Nan she), a poetry club affiliated with
national essence scholarship, was a strong purveyor of this
notion of the political and cultural mission of the South. Out
of this initially political intent for the north/south bifurcation,
there developed, as in Liu's essay, a radically new emphasis in
Chinese historical thought on the multi-ethnic, regional factor
in the origins and growth of Chinese civilization. This was in
sharp contrast to the prevailing myth of a unified, homogene-
ous China dating back to the Golden Age—or even to the
Yellow Emperor, mythical progenitor of the Han race.[15]

Another source for the north/south approach to Chinese
history was the interest of traditional literary criticism in the
relationship of the *Odes* and the *Ch'u Tz'u*. This was initially
brought about by a concern for the scriptural value of the
latter, and more generally, for the origin of literary genres. In
the decades following Liu Shih-p'ei's essay, many others
wrote about the North and South to determine their respective contributions to Chinese cultural styles, moods, and
forms. Whatever one determined to be the initial reasons for
the regional contrasts, it was generally agreed that their earliest coherent expression was to be found in the *Odes* and
Ch'u Tz'u respectively.[16]

One of the most important formulations of this approach
to northern and southern culture was made by Wang Kuo-
wei during the early New Culture period. His pronounce-
ments on Chinese culture were always of moment, and his
sharp, cogent analyses of antiquity were highly respected by
his peers. This would be sufficient reason for us to review his
opinion on the role of the *Ch'u Tz'u* and Ch'ü Yüan in the

formation of southern culture, but there is also another and more dramatic reason. Wang's mature life as a scholar and poet has about it much of the quality and mood of Ch'ü Yüan's political despair. He remained stubbornly loyal to the Manchu house after 1911, serving as tutor to the young scion; and then there was his suicide by drowning in 1927. Wang's essay "The Spirit of Ch'ü Yüan's Literature" boldly argued that after the fifth century B.C. there had formed two broad approaches to ethics and politics, and to the expression of these in literature: in the North an "imperial" approach; in the South, an "anti-imperial" one.[17] The North was aristocratic, this-worldly, and emphasized the interests of the polity. It dealt with collective problems through warm, sympathetic feelings and everyday emotions, and tried to solve the problems by reforming the old society. Its reforms used as a historical reference point near antiquity and the sage-king lore. Confucius and Mencius were of course practitioners as well as exemplars of the "imperial" style. In contrast, the southern style both derived from and focused on the commoner (*p'ing min*). It emphasized the individual person, not the collectivity, and tended toward escapism. Imagination was its medium for dealing with social problems, the result often being a radical effort to create a new society. Historically, its reference point was far antiquity, and Taoist literature (the *Chuang Tzu, Lieh Tzu*) gave it its prototypical expression.

Following an oft-cited evaluation made by Ssu-ma Ch'ien in the *Historical Records*, Wang stereotyped the southern mentality as being long on imagination and analysis but short on implementation. Being impractical, southern thought has tended "to seek peace" in abstract principles, and ultimately "without regret, to remove itself from the concrete world." However, the North "with a bold air, took its enduring plans, grasped the principles of reform, and did battle with contemporary society." (There is more than a chance similarity between Wang's historical descriptions and his enduring support of the Manchu monarchy, as well as his contempt for the modern southern radicals who led the Republican revolutionary movement.)

Having set up this general background, Wang Kuo-wei's

essay introduced Ch'ü Yüan as "a Southerner who studied in the North." His poetry in the *Ch'u Tz'u*, and all the other contributions as well, exhibit a compound of northern and southern culture: in form, mostly southern; in content, more an even mix. To emphasize the special qualities of this art, Wang juxtaposed it to the *Odes* and its prototypical approach to formulating human problems and their solutions. The literary genre emanating from the *Ch'u Tz'u* is informed by a "humorous" [sic] outlook on life, that is, one which emphasizes an alternation of cruel and compassionate human experiences, a persistent struggle between basic life forces.[18] In response to this struggle, the *Odes* did not advocate quitting the world and transcending the mundane. On the other hand, the *Odes* did not display the power of imagination which was the hallmark of its southern counterpart. It was Wang's conclusion that this was the South's contribution to Chinese culture—its "childlike imagination." He suggested that this was typical of the first stages of all cultural development—for example, as it was displayed in the mythologies of Hindu or Greek society.

Wang's essay set the stage for much of the ensuing discussion in China on Ch'ü Yüan and the *Ch'u Tz'u*. However, where he dealt with North and South with equanimity, or tended to express a preference for the northern cultural style, his successors praised the southern tradition, and the *Ch'u Tz'u* in particular, at the expense of the North and the *Odes*. The prime example of this is Hsieh Wu-liang's book, *A New Evaluation of the Ch'u Tz'u*, which greatly expanded on Wang's categories and arguments for the explicit purpose of glorifying the southern tradition and depreciating the northern.[19] It also argued in effect that the former was consonant with New Culture values while the latter embodied the values which were the target of New Culture iconoclasm. It significantly devoted its initial arguments to refuting the current doubts about Ch'ü Yüan's historicity and the traditional criticism of his life and art.

Though Hsieh's book rehearsed almost verbatim Wang Kuo-wei's north/south distinctions, it very quickly made a departure by arguing that Ch'ü Yüan's poetry is superior to the aristocratic *Odes* because his art relied upon the common people's ordinary forms of expression. This made the *Ch'u Tz'u* a product of the "ancient common people's literature." The populist motif, with its battle line drawn between "aristocratic culture" and the "common people's culture," was fast becoming a convention both in New Culture polemics and in the lore of Ch'ü Yüan as well.[20]

Hsieh Wu-liang's pioneering book is especially notable for its efforts to define the *persona* of Ch'ü Yüan within these broad cultural and literary contexts. He was depicted as creative, self-confident, and self-determining; fundamentally a patriotic person, and at the same time a socially transcendent individual, thanks to the influence of Taoism throughout southern culture. His patriotism was derived from his love of place and his social-political status (deeply rooted in the Ch'u ruling class), as well as his contact through his art with the folk of Ch'u. Hsieh was the first to make the much-debated suggestion that Ch'ü Yüan's patriotism, conveyed through his poetry, was the inspiration for the Ch'u rebels who overthrew the Ch'in tyranny and established the Han dynasty. The typically "revolutionary spirit" of Ch'u literature, Hsieh said, was revered and imitated by Han dynasty poets, and southern culture was much prized by the early Han ruling class. But within a few generations tastes changed, and even Ssu-ma Ch'ien, despite his reverence for Ch'ü Yüan, chauvinistically jibed that "things may get their start in the southeast, but things get done in the northwest." By the first century A.D., the South was in disfavor and the *Li Sao* and other prototypical southern literature began to be "northernized" through the use of commentaries and interpretative devices derived from the critical tradition of the *Odes*.[21]

The nature of the north/south contrast, as well as the character of the Southerner Ch'ü Yüan, were best summarized in Hsieh's schema of the embattled *Odes* and *Ch'u Tz'u*. First, the former is sentimental and other-directed; the latter is rigid, stubborn, and inner-directed. Second, the *Odes* are devoted to old customs, and to customary morality and

social-centeredness; the *Ch'u Tz'u* points toward the creation
of a new country, expresses the thought of the "superman,"
and supports ostentatious self-centeredness (which the ancients had criticized, but Hsieh approved). Third, the *Odes*
express faith in and servitude under Shang Ti (the preeminent god-force worshipped by the ancient Chou peoples),
while the *Ch'u Tz'u* (in the *Heavenly Questions* section) skeptically puts Heaven to the question. And finally, the former
is aristocratic but the latter is popular.[22]

In Hsieh Wu-liang's book Ch'ü Yüan thus becomes the
revolutionary, and his poetry the manifestoes, challenging
the tradition-bound culture of the North with weapons which
look very much like those wielded by the revolutionary
romantics of the 1920s. The *Ch'u Tz'u* was urged into the
two-culture (popular/aristocratic) mold which was being used
to shape the new image of Chinese civilization. Though formulations of the New Culture were still inchoate when
Hsieh's book first appeared, still his bias in favor of the *Ch'u
Tz'u* as the source of the Chinese populist literary heritage
immediately ran afoul of similar claims that the *Odes* itself
was derived from and/or still preserved pure folk elements.
The objects in both arguments were in any case the same: to
rescue the earliest monuments of Chinese literature from the
now discredited "Confucian" (or "Northern," or "Aristocratic") traditions of the anti-people. It was said that these had
co-opted what rightly had belonged to the popular tradition—Chinese culture's true and essential identity—and
made it serve, through corrupt interpretations, a purpose for
which it was not at all intended. In the 1920s, such argument
was used to demonstrate that the movement to promote vernacular literature was consonant with the true spirit of
Chinese culture.[23]

At the same time that Hsieh Wu-liang's book appeared,
Liang Ch'i-ch'ao (1873–1929), one of the deans of modern
Chinese letters, offered his ideas on Ch'ü Yüan in a lecture
at Southeastern University in Nanking.[24] Though Liang's
own scholarship had contributed mightily to the New Culture movement, this important lecture shows none of the ex-

travagances of either the Ch'ü Yüan doubters or glorifiers, and there is no design to enhance the image of Ch'ü Yüan and the Ch'u Tz'u by using New Culture criteria. For example, Liang makes him an aristocrat, with no further comments on the implications of this class affiliation. While Liang did not suggest that Ch'ü Yüan was a representative of aristocratic culture, neither did he claim that he spoke for the common people. Liang was primarily interested in exploring the nature of Southern (Ch'u) culture, its general contributions to Chinese civilization, and how the tensions between northern and southern characteristics informed Ch'ü Yüan's character and contributed to his suicide.

Liang's lecture was intent on establishing the importance of the mutual accommodation of Ch'u and the Middle Regions (Chung yuan—the northwest cradle of Chinese civilization) to the formation of the Chinese ethnos (Chung-hua min-tsu). Before the time of Confucius, Liang said, Ch'u had been considered "barbarian" by the Northerners; but soon after his time Ch'u culture slowly began to evolve toward the latter. Thus, by the time of Ch'ü Yüan, Ch'u had already become a part of the Chinese ethnos. Unlike other contemporary writers on this subject, Liang emphasized the positive contributions made by Ch'u to this heterogeneous and evolving cultural unit. "It was like new youth coming to a society that had already matured."[25]

Here is the imagery of Wang Kuo-wei again, but this time with positive implications for renewed, fresh cultural growth. (It should be noted that Liang himself was from Kwangtung province and, at one time anyway, was one of those "radicals" despised by Wang Kuo-wei. Further, in this discussion Liang was addressing a self-consciously southern audience at a school which more than any other at the time maintained the view that Chinese "essence" was best preserved in their cultural milieu.) Even when Ch'u culture amalgamated with the North, in Liang's telling, it retained some of its superstitious and irrational qualities (its shamanism, for example), those features which made it "like the song of a small child." When these combined with the rationality of the North, it

produced something new which was first expressed in literature, specifically the poetry of the *Ch'u Tz'u.*

In the person of Ch'ü Yüan the north/south amalgamation
displayed itself most vividly, and destructively. Liang specu-
lated that his suicide was a result of inner conflicts between
his two heritages. He was torn apart by a series of "contradictions" (in the psychological, not the Marxist sense): "aloof,
cold rationality" (northern) against torrid emotion (southern).
Ch'ü Yüan was very unlike what is usually considered
"Chinese," said Liang, especially where he displayed his "all
or nothing" [sic] attitude: witness Ch'ü Yüan's uncompromising obsession with purity. Liang means for us to juxtapose
this attitude to those of harmony or compromise. In fact,
what Liang is observing here is that "excessiveness" criticized
by earlier scholars. However, Liang is saying that the suicide
was a symptom of the excess and not the excess itself. He
thought that the immediate cause of Ch'ü Yüan's suicide was
his "love-hate" relationship with his own society in Ch'u,
symbolized as Ch'ü Yüan's beloved in the *Li Sao:* "For his
beloved he had both love and hate; the more he loved her the
more he hated her; two kinds of contradictory emotions
which daily engaged in battle."

Liang Ch'i-ch'ao seems to have been the first to discuss the
suicide in terms of more than the simple patriotic self-
sacrifice formula. His approach suggests that he was not
merely interested in Ch'ü Yüan's personality, but more am-
bitiously in a psycho-cultural approach to Chinese identity,
stressing a basic tension or contradiction in the vein of
Nietzsche's Apollonian/Dionysian polarity. His analysis also
was an expression of current interest in the "irrational,"
"primitive" side of the Chinese cultural personality. Much of
this kind of interest was promoted by the folklore enthusiasts
of the 1920s, many of whom were in turn guided by Sir
James G. Frazer's mythography. Liang chose to use Ch'ü
Yüan's suicide as a means of understanding these factors.
Having done so, what then did he think of the suicide itself?
He had to know that there was a weighty tradition of disap-
proval, but he chose in any case to use this point for his

appraisal of Ch'ü Yüan. Western values, Liang concluded, say that all suicide is cowardly, but "from my point of view, suicide [to escape the consequences of a social offence] is cowardly; but suicide for reasons of duty is glorious."[26]

None rhapsodized (or exploited) the glory of Ch'ü Yüan more than Kuo Mo-jo (1892–1978), the flamboyant poet and historian who surely saw himself as the *sao* poet incarnate. Kuo's prolific writings on the subject have been chiefly responsible for the modern course and tone of the Ch'ü Yüan lore, and especially for the integration of the lore into a Marxist framework—a task he began in the 1930s. The first results of his efforts were anthologized in his elliptical, poorly organized but nevertheless compelling *Ch'ü Yüan Studies*, a collection of his essays which became the point of departure for post-1949 studies of Ch'ü Yüan.[27] Its effort to place and analyze Ch'ü Yüan and "his age" is a dramatic illustration of a major concern of the historical materialist "social history controversy" during the 1930s—periodization of Chinese history according to Marxist categories. Be that as it may, it is still fundamentally concerned with two sets of problems which also attracted non-Marxists in the 1920s: the north/south cultural dichotomy, and the identification of Ch'ü Yüan's experience with those of the New Culture intellectuals.

Following the new archaeological scholarship, Kuo argued that the northern (Chou) and southern (Ch'u) branches of early Chinese culture were themselves products initially of the bifurcation of the Shang culture (1766–1122 B.C.). By emphasizing common origins for them, Kuo meant to undermine the notion of barbarian inferiority for Ch'u.[28] He argued that the "barbarian" designation for Ch'u was merely a propaganda device of the enemies of Ch'u in the North. The purpose of his study was to explain the nature and significance for Chinese history of the re-amalgamation of these two branches during the Warring States period (eighth to third centuries B.C.). From the all-important viewpoint of periodization, Ch'ü Yüan's epoch was one of transition from one major stage of history to another—from the bronze age to iron, from slave to feudal.[29] This revolutionary social change was reflected in a revolution in all aspects of philosophy and art, which in turn expressed themselves most fully in the life and art of Ch'ü Yüan.

Though Kuo's long argument was informed by materialist historiography, its narrative was basically structured by the north/south dichotomy which he explained by an analogy with classical Greece. The northern branch of Shang civilization, the Chou society, was culturally like Sparta—rational, realistic, and similar in social-economic arrangements, such as their slave systems. The southern branch, Ch'u, was Athenian—artistic and supernaturalistic, the heir to the artistic tradition of Shang.[30] Both branches went through a profound revolution, but it was in the North that the most progressive thought was initiated by the Confucian school. (This was a judgment not only in conflict with Kuo's contemporaries, but one that came back to haunt him during the anti-Confucian campaign of the 1970s.)

What were the elements of Confucian thought which Kuo felt were "in their time" revolutionary? Confucianism claimed (for example, in its idea of *jen*) that there was a universal "humanness" which contradicted the slave society notions of humans as chattel or beasts of burden; it insisted on government by qualified talent; it promoted political unification; and when considering the relationship of the realms of "heaven, earth, and humanity" it promoted a move from "spiritualism" to secularized, abstract principles.[31]

All of these elements can be found in Ch'ü Yüan's thought. So, Kuo argued, he was basically Confucian in ethics and morality and hence a revolutionary. The most important expression of this was Ch'ü Yüan's concern for the lives of the common people. In banishment he discovered the misery of the people, and this is what kept him from fleeing Ch'u, not his kinship to the king or his noble rank, as some had claimed. Though it was the fashion of Ch'ü Yüan's day to move on to safer or more profitable kingdoms, he stayed on to help the people, but also to encourage the unification of China under the leadership of Ch'u.[32]

To these Confucian revolutionary qualities, Ch'ü Yüan, through his art, added another stratum of revolution. This was the South's contribution to the great transformation of the time. In brief, Kuo argued that Ch'ü Yüan's genius created a new form of poetry, derived from the "natural forms of the folk songs," which resulted in the "overthrow of" and "liberation from" the strictures of the Odes. [33] The poetry of the Ch'u Tz'u, according to Kuo, is essentially vernacular (pai-hua). [34] Here was a "structuring of literature according to speech; a popularization (ta-chung-hua), a great literary revolution." [35]

At this point, Ch'ü Yüan and Kuo, himself a leading proponent of vernacular literature, began to merge. No wonder then, that Kuo should be defensive of his ancient counterpart when the latter was criticized. For example, other modern critics might be willing to grant Ch'ü Yüan his "advanced literary techniques," but his social thought they considered very backward. Many critics had difficulty accepting Confucianism as a "revolutionary" philosophy, and sometimes drove the point home by comparing Ch'ü Yüan to Tolstoy, Balzac, and Wang Kuo-wei. [36]

Kuo Mo-jo really had no answer to this kind of challenge beyond his original formulation. Instead, he quickly moved on to suggest that it was more important to consider the apparent contradiction between Ch'ü Yüan's northern rationalism and his southern artistic imagination. If one considered him a true artist, then the problem would be resolved, for it would be understood that he felt free to use any material at hand to convey his ideals. Ch'ü Yüan really did not believe in the supernaturalism, spirit worlds, heavens and hells that fill his poetry. These were just media for expressing his Confucian-derived social values. Basically, he was not a "believer" but a "doubter"—and this is evidenced in the Heavenly Questions. (Here, Kuo was typical of his contemporaries in his acceptance of the authenticity of the Heavenly Questions and in his interpretation which explained it as Ch'ü Yüan's challenge to all inherited ideas.) Kuo pleaded that the reader judge Ch'ü Yüan as an artist, not a philosopher; and that we understand his triumph to be the blending together of his northern-Confucian thought with his southern-romantic poetry. If Kuo Mo-jo's Ch'ü Yüan were "triumphant," how was his suicide to be explained? Kuo's answer, which became a standard one, was that there existed a severe disjunction between his ideals and the realities of Ch'u society at that time, so "he could not but be disillusioned."[37] Add to this his spirit of doubt and skepticism and there was plenty of motivation for self-destruction.[38]

Übermenschlichkeit

New Culture intellectuals were often ambivalent about public roles because of their ambivalent individualism. Holding institutional politics in contempt, their general notion of a public service role was that of educator or as elite ameliorator of common problems. Their individualism was an end as well as a means: both a product of liberation from the old society, and a force in liberating the masses and creating a new society. For a time, they seemed caught between the extremes of self-liberating sentiment and heroic action from within the masses. Like their Western models, Goethe's Young Werther or Lord Byron, they regularly betrayed a self-pitying, adversary relation with society. Just as often, any thought to merge was overwhelmed by feelings of contempt for and repulsion by the ignorant masses. This resulted in that Nietzscheian sense of self which we have seen in Lu Hsün and Wang Kuo-wei. Excluded from formal political action and leadership, the New Culture intellectuals saw themselves (not unlike Liu Shih-p'ei's generation) as *moral* leaders of the nation, poet-heroes, drawing their legitimacy from the example of the English Romantics, from Matthew Arnold's "poet critic," from Goethe, Nietzsche, and Wagner.[39]

In the late 1920s and on through the war against Japan, Ch'ü Yüan was a very prominent vehicle for dramatizing these new self-images of the intelligentsia. Persistently, the figure of Ch'ü Yüan was extracted from the indigenous myth complexes in which it had been understood, and placed in

Western mythological contexts which demanded that he be understood as a Socrates, Christ, or Dante. There was no longer a question of the "practicality" or rationality of his suicide. It was considered to be in the nature of things— merely the mode of his inevitable sacrifice for and by the masses, and an expression of the perennial struggle between genius and vulgarity, culture and society.

An extraordinary formulation of these ideas was expressed by the Edinburgh and Cambridge educated Lim Boon Keng (Lin Wen-ch'ing, 1869–1957) in his Tennyson-esque English translation of the *Li Sao*. His introduction admirably suits the mood of his translation and speaks, volubly, for itself:

> [The *Li Sao*] is the kind of poetry that will appeal to a Coriolanus or to a superman after Nietzsche's heart. Surely it is a perfect jeremiad to the noisy multitudes, who in their muggy ignorance and noisome fulminations against their superiors, betray the emptiness and the weakness of their character. It is a stately and proud vindication of the right of the strong man to be the shepherd of the people, to lead them to freedom and happiness. . . . Ch'ü Yüan says that it is during a wild revolution, when great changes occur, that strange readjustments are possible. Real progress, then, is a forward movement made by a people when they are duly organized and directed to apply the ideals of their sages to the routine of everyday life. The aim of the *Li Sao* is the foundation of the ideal state, in which government for the happiness of the proletariat is in the hands of the best, wisest, and strongest men of the state. Such a government is akin to that dreamed of in the *Republic* of Plato and in the classics so piously preserved by Confucius and his school.[40]

Lim described Ch'ü Yüan as a "fanatical idealist obsessed with the ideal of purity," an Olympian who "feels his love for his fellow men as a light which he would fain give to others." A superman like Ch'ü Yüan, Lim said, was needed in contemporary China—a leader "who would, out of his own abundance, propagate the gospel of true and pure living, to deliver the common herd of our fellow creatures from the quagmires and filth created by themselves, from their own

evil propensities and suicidal policies." China needed a patriot and man of principle like Ch'ü Yüan "to stop all lies and
shams, and to tell the crowd to do honest work and not to
think of clamoring for the moon, before they can stand up
and walk. Moral hygiene is even more necessary than antive-
nereal prophylactic."[41]

Completely missing in Lim's essay are the themes of Ch'ü
Yüan as the loyal minister whose unused talent leads to his
despair. He was now the leader and chief himself, and there
was no question of subordination. The relationship of consequence was between the leader and the masses. The
leader's only desire is "by his goodness, to benefit others"; the
masses only duty is to benefit themselves through obedience.

These themes were developed well beyond Lim's treatment
in a book which in bulk and passion has no equal in the
genre—Kuo Yin-t'ien's *The Thought and Art of Ch'ü Yüan*
published in Chungking in 1943.[42] It is most impressive not
for its technical scholarship, but for its groping construction
of a radically new reading of the poetry of Ch'ü Yüan and the
interpretation of his character after the fashion of a Western
epic hero. The book is outstanding for its recognition and
analysis of the basic structural elements of the *Li Sao*, that is,
its quest and journey themes, and its special notions of time.
The heart of the book, however, is devoted to illustrating
Ch'ü Yüan's qualities as a "hero" and "genius."

Kuo used the north/south cultural approach, but it was not
central to his argument and its implications were different for
him. Typically he saw the North as conservative, utilitarian,
rational, and realistic. The North's "predominantly quiescent
attitude toward contemporary problems completely advocated
inheritance, conservatism, and negativism . . . and therefore
it opposed Ch'ü Yüan's advocacy of the reform of the Ch'u
nation's ideals. The North said that the human world must
be harmonious with the cosmos; it will improve slowly and
does not need personal intervention."[43] And what of Ch'ü
Yüan's South? It of course had an innovative, liberated and
destructive spirit; its mode was illusionary and romantic.
Kuo's departure from the conventional analysis occurred

where he insisted that Ch'ü Yüan was not a Southerner
in extremis, like the Taoists were. He had rejected Taoist
philosophy because it was selfishly individualistic and advocated non-action (*wu-wei*). Ch'ü Yüan searched for the
realization of his ideals in the real world and rejected the
escapism of the Taoists, and Buddhists as well. His brooding
was not negative and his social philosophy was one of action,
not quietude.[44]

In Kuo Yin-t'ien's analysis, Ch'ü Yüan mediated between
North and South by rejecting the extremes of both. Just as he
rejected them in southern culture, so he rejected the northern tendency of "rationalism without humanism." He recognized the contradiction between "feeling and spirit" on one
hand, and "life action" on the other; and he resolved it with a
combination of "humanism with sentiment."[45] Kuo's favorite
literary device was antithesis and the book is riddled with it.
This seems to be his way of arguing against the criticism that
Ch'ü Yüan's behavior was excessive or wide of the moderate
middle way. Kuo seems to be saying that in pure form, as
Ch'ü Yüan might have found them, northern and southern
culture were excessive extremes, which he moderated
through synthesis.

There was an effort throughout Kuo's book to counteract
the stereotype of the South as innovative but undisciplined
and impractical. Ch'ü Yüan continued to play the role of
idealist, but his genius lay precisely where he sought to bring
ideal and real together, where he sought to implement his
visions within the mundane realm.[46] And though he failed to
carry out his plans, in Kuo's telling he was nevertheless optimistic "that good would win over evil," that "talent could
do great things," and that reality was "good and beautiful."

What was the source of Ch'ü Yüan's optimism? According
to this unique interpretation it was his belief in the "central
and basic authority of Shang Ti." This was the transcendent
being from whom good and evil derived, and who motivated
the former sage-kings and other historical exemplars of the *Li
Sao*.[47] Here Kuo was in conflict with a standard modern interpretation, like that of Hsieh Wu-liang, which held that a

belief in Shang Ti was the exclusive characteristic of the *Odes* and was challenged by Ch'ü Yüan in his *Heavenly Questions*. I think Kuo's argument required a transcendent god as a source of universal value to make it easier to convert Ch'ü Yüan into a Western style epic hero, an effort which we see in his comparison of Ch'ü Yüan with Dante and his explanation of their genius.

In Kuo Yin-t'ien's formulation, the drama and motive force of Ch'ü Yüan's experience derive from a contradiction between genius (*t'ien-ts'ai*) and its opposite, commonness or vulgarity (*su*). The latter must always cause the former suffering and inevitably destroy it; hence the fate of Ch'ü Yüan and his Western counterpart, Dante, who was introduced in the heart of Kuo's book as a device to drive its message home. Kuo asks us to understand Dante through Michelangelo's paean "Sonnet on Dante":

> To guide us he himself did not begrudge trampling
> In the abyss of evil, and afterwards, ascending to God;
> Heaven's gates opened wide to welcome his entrance,
> But his country's gates tightly closed and refused him.
> Ungrateful country! The outcome of your destruction
> And persecution of him could only be
> Calamity for yourself. You make humanity see that
> The finest of humankind must suffer the greatest miseries.[48]

Ch'ü Yüan, then, as Dante. The poet is author and subject in poetry structured by the quest motif. And narrative forces are derived from the quests for another's love, which in turn are allegories for the search for ideal good and beauty derived from God. How can the failure of their quests be explained? In Kuo's opinion the ancient Han formulation of "fate" and "time" was incorrect because "heroes and genius are not held back by the times."[49] Instead, the failures of the two poets in their earthly endeavors were really the reflection of the universal limitations of common humanity and the inevitable clash of genius with it. "That rational epoch," says Kuo of the Warring States era, "how could it know of the greatness of his passionate feelings? That impoverished

humanity—how could it understand his value as a provoca-
tive life force?"[50]

Genius such as that of Dante and Ch'ü Yüan, said Kuo
Yin-t'ien, "plants and cultivates a seed in the withered spirit
of humanity; and in order to bequeath to humanity wisdom
and soul, genius must ungrudgingly enter into the refuge of
evil, even to the extent of sacrificing its life."[51] Common
humanity does not understand genius, and so it actively
creates unnecessary conflict with it and persecutes it. Ch'ü
Yüan neither wished to drift along with his beloved common
folk nor to remain on the same plane as they, but rather to
transcend them, to dwell above in order to have a "bird's eye
view," the better to love and aid them. In his conclusion,
Kuo drew on the images of Socrates and Christ to strengthen
further his vision of Ch'ü Yüan as the savior-genius, sacrificed by his own society. Socrates drank his hemlock and
Christ was crucified for the same reasons that Ch'ü Yüan was
driven to his suicide. They all loved the common people, but
were not appreciated; they loved them but sought to transcend their commonness.[52]

Prometheus Bound: Kuo Mo-jo's Ch'ü Yüan

The writings of Lim Boon Keng and Kuo Yin-t'ien are
excellent examples of how the Ch'ü Yüan lore was reshaped
by New Culture values; however, they themselves were never
in a position to effect broadly the course of Ch'ü Yüan's
transformation. That responsibility lay in the contributions of
a number of literary critics and two poet-scholars, Kuo Mo-jo
and Wen I-to (1899–1946), whose devotion to Ch'ü Yüan is
at the heart of his modern cult. Both Kuo and Wen were
pioneering poets in the new vernacular genre, and both did
outstanding historical and anthropological research. Where
Kuo was interested in a historical materialist interpretation of
antiquity, Wen was interested in the ancient folklore of the
South and its generation of the Ch'ü Yüan myth. The prominence of both of these men in Chinese letters was a significant force for the persistent growth of the Ch'ü Yüan cult
before and after 1949.

Kuo Mo-jo openly admitted that in his poetry and drama he was writing about himself and his search, as an artist, for a proper place in the new China. At least as early as 1920 he was using the figure of Ch'ü Yüan as a vehicle for this purpose. As his own self-image changed over the years, so did his image of Ch'ü Yüan. The course of change followed his progress from the solipsism of a New Culture romantic, to populism and a Marxist-inspired revolutionary activism, and finally to melodramatic patriotism during the Anti-Japanese War. Yet in any one of his phases he (and hence, Ch'ü Yüan) never seemed to be far from the role of the poet-hero or genius-messiah celebrated in the writing of Lim Boom Keng and Kuo Yin-t'ien.

In antiquity, the term "entangled" (*lei*) had been used to characterize Ch'ü Yüan and his plight; Kuo Mo-jo used the same term in the title of his first work dealing with Ch'ü Yüan. "Hsiang lei" (The Entangled One of the Hsiang) is a one-act play completed in 1920 during a period when Kuo had formulated, with the help of Carlyle, the notion of the hero as poet. Kuo empathized with the formulation in *Heroes and Hero Worship* which equated the poet and prophet— "they have penetrated both of them into the sacred mystery of the Universe." He at this time claimed that under the additional influence of Goethe he was a "pantheist."[53] With this as background, I want to summarize the little drama, the better to catch the all-important mood and a sense of the typically broad-gestured, unrestrained style that went very far in breathing passionate new life into the figure of Ch'ü Yüan.[54]

The setting of "Hsiang lei" is a grotto at the edge of the sea where maidens perch on rocks above the water. Ch'ü Yüan is rowed up to them in a boat decorated with a dragon's head. It is early autumn and the appearance of Ch'ü Yüan and the boatman are ghostly, their white wispy hair like clouds, Ch'ü Yüan dressed in a billowy white robe. He is mad in appearance, and so disoriented that he fails to recognize his younger sister among the women on the rocks. He babbles about the Sage-King Shun and banishment, while his sister demands to know what is wrong with him. He rambles on about sages being mad, and he gains the sympathy of a waiting maid (nü hsu) who starts to recall that the father of Sage-King Yü was an emotionally unrestrained person, like Ch'ü Yüan, and that he ended by—. Ch'ü Yüan interrupts and blathers about being swindled, about sycophancy, and banishment. The waiting maid then makes her main statement: Calm yourself, she says, you are in a bad way; even mighty rivers must yield to things; bear suffering patiently; it takes time to carve out grottos. Even though you are like a volcano, still, volcanos do not erupt all the time!

Ch'ü Yüan finds her attempt to calm and inhibit him intolerable and he bursts into his main statement: Poetry is my life, he shouts, and then thunders on about his "free creation, freely expressing his self." And then a Whitmanesque conceit (which abounded in Kuo's poetry in the 1920s):

> I create dignified mountain peaks, vast oceans. I create the sun, moon, stars, constellations. I make the wind gallop with the lightning and the rain. Though limited to this single body I collect them and then disperse them till the universe overflows. Can it possibly be then that this body of mine is only some cosmetic material, meant to flatter [others]?

Still talking to the waiting maid, he cries: "Why do you belittle me? My blood must flow, my fire must erupt, and I must gallop no matter where I am! . . . You don't understand me. . . !"

After more dialogue of the same drift, Ch'ü Yüan concludes with a defense of sentiment. A truly good person, he says, is one who is able to cry freely; a poem which is able to cause others to cry freely is a good one; the real value of poetry is to make people feel deeply. That said, the old boatman hurries him off as it grows dark; and in a final gesture prefiguring his suicide, Ch'ü Yüan throws his garland of flowers onto the water. The sound of oars is heard disappearing into the distance. The waiting maid is left on her rock with the other ladies.

How different is this Ch'ü Yüan, preoccupied with self,

sentiment, and art, compared to the one in Kuo's *Ch'ü Yüan Studies*, where he emphasized devotion to the collectivity, action, and the "substructure" which is art's source. In the play, politics and banishment are reduced to incidental, vague, and confused memories, and, in contrast to the *Li Sao* which inspired it, the central issue is not Ch'ü Yüan's uncompromising adherence to principle. In the parallel scene in the *Li Sao*, the "maiden(s)" chorus "sobbing and sighing" expostulates with him: "Why be so lofty, with your passion for purity? Why must you alone have such delicate adornment?"⁵⁵ But in the play, he is not being asked to compromise his principles by the act of self-restraint. It is instead the purity of personal feelings, passion, and expression that are the targets. Here, the female chorus serves a role familiar from the Western tradition. They represent society, domesticity, the family; Kuo has them restraining, complaining, not understanding the creative spirit seeking liberation at whatever cost.

This same theme was elaborated by Kuo in a 1922 piece featuring, as he put it, one of Ch'ü Yüan's ancient heroes, Po Yi. Here we see Po Yi, alone in self-exile, wandering in unpeopled nature, and achieving there his liberation from "the obstructions imposed by civilization on his five senses." Kuo used the legendary figure as his version of "fallen humanity" attempting to regain its original purity. The state of Kuo's pristine humanity (*yuan-jen*) was one of spontaneity and freedom. Back then, Po Yi says, primordial humanity was sincere; they had no distinctions between things and the self; there were no nations, no nobility; and the so-called sages were really only shepherds, farmers, and artisans. It was the first of China's states that created organization, property, bureaucracy—all of these more evil than the deluge itself. He concludes by exhorting the enslaved, the penned-up, the sheeplike to liberate themselves; to remember that in civilization there are iron jails, bronze cages, and exploitative, avaricious sentiments. "*They* taught you to be yielding, to be faithful, to have respect, to sacrifice; they taught that these are the 'orthodox institutions,' 'civilization.' But I teach you to peel off the counterfeit person and return that natural core."[56]

By the time Kuo began his historical studies of Ch'ü Yüan in the late 1920s, he had considerably moderated these moods and sentiments, if not reversed them altogether. He had passed through a number of transforming experiences. One of the most important, he tells us, was his 1926 association, as propagandist, with the Northern Expedition. This expedition was the Kuomintang's military thrust northward from Kwangtung province to the Yangtze, in an effort to reconsolidate the Chinese state. Initially, Chinese intellectuals saw the effort in apocalyptic terms, but soon, many grew disillusioned with the tactics of the Kuomintang and with its limited effectiveness. In 1926, when Kuo reached the environs of Changsha in the wake of the troops, he performed the ritual remembrance of Ch'ü Yüan at the Milo River. He was still full of hope and exhaltation because of what seemed the army's success. And so, in his poem to Ch'ü Yüan, he expressed no empathy with the drowned poet's despair and suicide. However, as the messianic promise of the Northern Expedition faded, so did Kuo's faith that the Kuomintang and the Chinese intelligentsia would transcend history and lead the Chinese people into the promised land.[57] The anarchistic, antihistorical values of his youth gave way to a strong sense of the individual within the necessary constraints of institutions and history.

These new perspectives were expressed in Kuo's "The Age of Ch'ü Yüan." Here Ch'ü Yüan continued to be depicted as a revolutionary, but Kuo repeatedly emphasized that his feelings and art were a reflection of the major historical trend of his time, the liberation of China from slave society. Ch'ü Yüan's poetry was seen as a function of the times, but Kuo's interpretation tried to give his hero great scope to maneuver within that mechanistic formula. Thus, Ch'ü Yüan was able to draw on the music and song of the folk and to "elevate" these through his own poetic genius. Still, Kuo was troubled by Ch'ü Yüan's failure to be politically effectual (to make the diplomatic alliances, to reform Ch'u's laws), a fact which seemed to compromise his artistic genius; and Kuo was not satisfied with the explanation that "the limitations of Ch'ü Yüan's strength were a function of times and circumstances." After all, there were political and military figures in Ch'ü Yüan's time who did what he could not do—organize and lead the people forward in a progressive rebellion against the forces of the old slave society and against the tyranny of the Ch'in. Kuo Mo-jo, expressing his own frustrations (which he shared with his generation) came to admit that a poet, even a progressive one like Ch'ü Yüan, could sense and be moved by the people's strength; he could weep for them; but when it came to practical matters he had to stand at the sidelines of his age, a mere spectator. Thus, Kuo Mo-jo's later notion of Ch'ü Yüan's genius differed in two important ways from his earliest view and from those of Lim Boon Keng and Kuo Yin-t'ien. Commonality and the masses were not seen as its nemesis, and it could not transcend history.[58]

In the mid-1930s, Kuo's use of the mythology related to Ch'ü Yüan expressed a need for humility before the forces of history. It warned that the hubris of those who believed themselves autonomous individuals would lead to their destruction. This is the theme of "The Suicide of the Tyrant of Ch'u," a narrative about Hsiang Yü (third century B.C.), the Ch'u general who led those initial assaults against the Ch'in a few years before widespread revolt overthrew it altogether. Taking the bloody *Historical Records* biography as his point of departure, Kuo used him as an incarnation of ferocity and utter brutality, and argued that his anti-Ch'in militancy resulted in situations for the populace worse than Ch'in itself had perpetrated. Here was the military brute who, unlike the "impractical" poet Ch'ü Yüan (and Kuo Mo-jo), had the means to carry out the leadership of a people's revolt. But he failed because he thought himself independent of the "times and circumstances." In other words, he thought his initial successes against the Ch'in were solely due to his own prowess and self-enhancing heroics. In the end, the embattled Hsiang Yü committed suicide. But unlike Ch'ü Yüan, he got no sympathy or credit from Kuo, who evaluated this act, like

Hsiang Yü's life, as completely selfish and without any thought "for our China."[59]

It would not be too much to see in this study of Hsiang Yü a general indictment of the suffering brought upon China by its contemporary warlords. From what is known of Kuo's opposition to the Kuomintang Government under Chiang Kai-shek at this time, it seems quite reasonable to see Chiang himself as the particular target of the Hsiang Yü portrayal. In 1942, Kuo developed the themes of the Hsiang Yü story in his five-act drama "Ch'ü Yüan," the most famous use of the Ch'ü Yüan myth in modern times.

The drama was written and first performed in Chungking during the darkest days of the Japanese occupation.[60] The second United Front between the Chinese Communist Party and the Kuomintang showed severe strain. The Kuomintang was increasingly the target of criticism from all quarters for its mismanagement of the war effort, for corruption, censorship, and suppression of writers who were or appeared to be critical of it. Kuo's play is one of the most famous literary attacks on the Kuomintang. Because of its obvious criticism of Chiang and Madame Chiang, as well as its call for "unification and alliance" (that is, honoring the United Front), it became a wartime favorite for the Communists. For the anti-Communists it became "mere communist propaganda," a judgment which continues to be used as an excuse not to give any serious consideration at all to the play, even though it was a very popular example of a genre heavily indulged in during the war. Poets, historians, and dramatists of various ideological persuasions all produced a variety of material about melodramatic patriotism and national loyalty, regularly seasoned with attacks on the Kuomintang leadership. Nor is the play "Ch'ü Yüan" representative of a genre unique to China. It is comparable, for example, to Jean Anouilh's very popular drama "Antigone" written in Vichy France, and first performed in 1944 in Paris. Using classical themes and characters, both plays explored the conflicts of personal and public loyalties and duties during a time of crisis. Both attacked the deadly banality of the military mentality and the

murderous consequences of amoral politics. Antigone (a
latter-day Jeanne d'Arc for French audiences) and Ch'ü Yüan
were chosen to represent "the nation" and a stubborn adherence (in Anouilh's words) to "a passionate belief that moral
law exists, and a passionate regard for the sanctity of human
personality."[61] These were themes that were not merely incidental to the attacks on Vichy and the Kuomintang.

As political criticism, Kuo Mo-jo's play drew on the *Historical Records* biography of Ch'ü Yüan for its narrative line.
The king and queen (General and Madame Chiang, if you
will) are corrupt influences who bring about the fall of Ch'ü
Yüan and the nation. The king is made to be incidental to
the action: he is passively stupid—putty in the hands of the
queen and her courtier conspirators, the low and cunning
rivals of Ch'ü Yüan. Though her role in the *Historical Records* biography is minimal, and is rarely mentioned in Ch'ü
Yüan lore, the queen is depicted by Kuo as a ruthless, selfish,
and ambitious *femme fatale*, pivotal in the betrayal of both
the nation and Ch'ü Yüan. In Act Two she describes herself
to him:

> I like splendor, I like excitement; my will to conquer is too
> great, and I can be very jealous. When someone endangers
> my happiness and safety I must fight against him, until I
> sacrifice either my own life or his. . . . Actually your nature
> is in many ways like mine. You do not want to play second
> fiddle in any society. . . . perhaps you may be content with
> solitude, but I am not. I want to blossom, I want to flourish, I
> want a greater place in the sun, and if the small herbs and
> flowers die beneath my feet, I feel no pity for them. This may
> be the difference between our characters.

As in the *Historical Records* account, the queen's betrayal is
carried out as she conspires with foreign spies to negotiate the
alliance with the Ch'in State which Ch'ü Yüan opposes. To
discredit Ch'ü Yüan, the queen snares him in a "badger
game" (letting the king catch her in an apparent embrace
with Ch'ü Yüan, who she claims has surely lost his mind and

thrown himself upon her). Further to control Ch'ü Yüan and the like-minded, the traitor Chang I and the queen easily convince the king to control the "writers" of the kingdom:

> Chang I: I think a writer should confine himself to writing, without interfering with politics.
> Queen: Yes, quite right. When writers talk about politics they always talk nonsense.
> King: Yes, I shall make that my policy from now on, definitely forbidding writers to speak of politics; and if they insist on expressing their opinion, I shall certainly have them taken and shut in the temple. (Act Four)

The play deals with that phase of Ch'ü Yüan's life from the time of betrayal until his banishment. Kuo made him the embodiment of national unity and survival; and though we are never told how it was possible, the common people all know and love Ch'ü Yüan, recognize that he is the pillar of the nation, and that if he is harmed the nation will perish. In addition to the centrality of poets to national survival, another familiar theme in the play is the poet's ability to represent through art the dismal realities of the people's lives, their grievances and hopes. There is a specific effort to dramatize Ch'ü Yüan's radical literary populism, as in this speech from Act One:

> I . . . want to learn from you young people, with all my heart I want to learn from the sincere and common people. I want with all my heart to preserve the freshness, purity, and simplicity of my youth. . . . So when many people say my poetry is too vulgar and too free, having lost the authentic note of the traditional poetry, I am not in the least disturbed. I am doing my utmost to imitate the common people and to imitate children, so naturally it is vulgar. I am doing my utmost to break the rules of the traditional poetry. So naturally it is free.

But even Ch'ü Yüan, despite all his efforts, cannot completely shake off the old conventions, which are like "brands on the foreheads of slaves"—even if emancipated, the stigmata remain. Nor can he (or Kuo Mo-jo) completely abandon his aristocratic aloofness and contempt for the masses because of the limitations which they impose on his genius.

> Ch'ü Yüan (in Act Five): The common people are very exasperating too; they have no judgment of their own. Thus when [the traitor] Chang I said I was mad, everybody believed him at once. They consider the phoenix a chicken, the unicorn a lamb. How can I bear it? Thus, the more disgusted I feel. What do I want with their worthless sympathy?
> Diviner: That is true, most of the common people are too stupid to learn.
> Ch'ü Yüan: On the other hand my feelings are rather ambivalent; for although I hate their stupidity, in another way I love it.

Just as the play permits these sentiments to reveal themselves, if only momentarily, so does it show that Kuo had not completely abandoned for Ch'ü Yüan (or himself) other sentiments of the 1920s. In Act Five, Ch'ü Yüan, about to descend into banishment, stands captive in the imperial temple and apostrophizes nature and the thunderstorm that rages outside. Kuo identifies him with the cosmic element of fire, and has him cry out:

> I know that you are the life of the universe, my own life. You are myself! My blazing life, my smouldering wrath, will they not burst into a blaze? Burst, my body! Let the red flames leap forth like this wind, like the plunging sea, until all material things, all filth, are consumed in your flames, and let this darkness be consumed, the cloak of all evil.

Such volcanic outbursts notwithstanding, this Ch'ü Yüan remains essentially the one depicted by Kuo in his *Ch'ü Yüan Studies*—the Promethean chained to history; the intellectual suspended between polity and society; the patriotic poet, resolute, pure, and ineffectual to the death.[62]

The Unbound Prometheus: Wen I-to's Ch'ü Yüan

In 1947, when Kuo Mo-jo wrote an encomium for Wen I-to, recently assassinated by agents of the Kuomintang, he used Wen's tragedy as an example of the frustration and vulnerability that was characteristic of the artist's life in China. He paid Wen his highest tribute when he went on to compare him to Ch'ü Yüan, and to trace with approval the progress of Wen's thought from a position sympathetic with the "selfish individualism" of Chuang-tzu's Taoism to the populism of Ch'ü Yüan. Kuo concluded that Wen's death served the same popular and public ends as did the latter's sacrifice.[63]

"I am a worshipper of Ch'ü Yüan," Wen himself had written in 1944, during a period when he drew together and powerfully reformulated some of the major themes of the Ch'ü Yüan lore from the previous two decades.[64] Wen's preeminence as a poet and scholar coupled with his commanding prose have made his formulations a kind of grand summation of the lore on the eve of its proliferation in the People's Republic. In two separate essays he crystallized, as no one had before, the themes of Ch'ü Yüan the "people's poet" and the unbound Prometheus.

The first theme he galvanized in a sweeping, uncompromising little essay entitled "Ch'ü Yüan, People's Poet."[65] The main argument which the essay put forward with such confidence—that Ch'ü Yüan was not a member of the ruling class—has preoccupied Wen's successors ever since. He asserted that although Ch'ü Yüan was in name a member of the feudal aristocracy, in fact he was not so. Early in life he "suffered a fall" from the ruling class and consequently experienced the same kind of poverty and mistreatment as the masses. His great poetic works, the *Li Sao* and the *Nine Songs*, were created with the art forms of the people, the latter actually being "folk songs." Using these folk art forms, he wrote of the people's ills which were brought about by the crimes of the ruling class. For this reason, Wen concluded that the political achievements of his poetry were even greater than the artistic ones.

From the point of view of action, as opposed to art, Wen further argued that Ch'ü Yüan was even more "of the people," for he had encouraged the oppressed people of Ch'u to revolt and overthrow the old ruling class. It was not Ch'in that destroyed Ch'u, but a revolution of Ch'u's own peasants inspired by Ch'ü Yüan, who had made them see their own misery and recognize their class enemy. Over the ages, Wen concluded, the people have known that of the great poets only Ch'ü Yüan was one of them. They rejected T'ao Ch'ien even though he rhapsodized the peasants, and they also had no use for Li Po. Neither of them belonged to or really were on the side of the common people. And though the great T'ang poet Tu Fu did truly sympathize with the people, it was of no use, for they could not understand him. That the people commemorate the life of Ch'ü Yüan in their festivals is proof of his nearness to them.

Thus, in one short burst of exuberant prose, Wen I-to demonstrated that Ch'ü Yüan need not be considered an impractical intellectual standing on the sidelines of history, ineffectually weeping for the people. His Ch'ü Yüan was neither an "aloof and transcendent" genius, nor did he serve the people as an act of *noblesse oblige*. He had become one of them himself.

In his last essay on Ch'ü Yüan, Wen took this populist characterization to an extreme it never before or after reached. His "The Ch'ü Yüan Question," written in 1944, argued that Ch'ü Yüan had actually been a slave whose glory was the self-liberation through which he became simultaneously a human individual and an artist. This dramatic assertion was consonant with Kuo Mo-jo's historiography, but its picture of Ch'ü Yüan was one that Kuo never supported. There were other contemporaries of Wen who, in effect, did support his thesis by arguing similarly that during the ancient Warring States period there were "radical" schools of thought whose memberships were of slave origin.[66] For Wen I-to, Ch'ü Yüan's biography was a specific instance of history's most general trend, humanity's struggle for liberation from slavery.

He explained that slaves like Ch'ü Yüan who served at court were only quantitatively different than those who served elsewhere throughout the society. The intensified interdependence of the master and slave relationship at court had advantages for the slave, but disadvantages as well. Court slaves had to submit directly to the personal whims of the king and the sometimes demeaning intimacies he demanded of them, and it was the king's personal servants that were the last to be set free. Ch'ü Yüan himself had the responsibility at court for literary amusement—he was a kind of sophisticated "court jester." The crucial point for Wen I-to was that the court's protection and demands made it possible for Ch'ü Yüan the artist to emerge: out of the court amusements came "literature"; out of the court jester came the true poet. If the slave's spirit and hope for freedom could remain alive, Wen said, there was a chance that the slave could avoid becoming a wasted sacrificial victim and be turned into something precious for future times.[67]

Slavery and art thus had a dialectical relationship. The former made the latter's existence possible, but art, once extant, both signified and was a means of liberation from slavery. Wen explained that:

> The slave system not only produced the literary arts, it also produced humans (*jen*). In the beginning, Shang Ti did not create masters and slaves, he only created humans. Ch'ü Yüan and King Huai were not of different blood types (they did have the same surname). It was only that a human-made system placed them in their shameful relationship. And Ch'ü Yüan's "human determination" could not "overcome destiny."[68]

On the contrary, he was moved as if by a heavenly plan. His slander, banishment, and suicide were all signs of the weakness of the slave. But "when we have seen the weakness of the slave, we also will have seen the dignity of the human. . . . We ought to be sympathetic with his inability to escape slavery completely (that was because he was bound by his time); and we ought to respect his ability to escape to the extent that he did."

Thus, said Wen I-to, Ch'ü Yüan was not like the long-lived ancient characterization—"naturally talented," "loyal and virtuous," "pure and honest of heart." However, Wen did agree with the classical picture of Ch'ü Yüan as the self-serving egotist. This was precisely the point, he argued, this was what made Ch'ü Yüan special, for these traits were symptoms of his liberation from the anonymity of slavery and his emerging individuality. He was an "independent, radical slave" and this was why the medieval Confucian historians did not write a biography for him; they hated Ch'ü Yüan because such a slave is a bad slave. But a bad slave is a good human, and Ch'ü Yüan's development from a cultured slave to a politician shows immense progress. Although he may have suffered defeat in the latter role, nevertheless his transformation represents a real "*fan shen*" (here Wen uses a term popularized by the Communists and meaning for them the "turn-around" in all areas of the life of the oppressed that results from successful class struggle).

To the degree that Ch'ü Yüan fulfilled the role of a loyal minister in his political life, Wen concluded that he was a "man of his times." But beyond that, there was another Ch'ü Yüan for all times. This was the genius, the fighter, the fiery poet. This was the person who drowned himself. This was the Ch'ü Yüan who ranks among the greatest of those who struggled for the liberation of mankind.[69]

Writings from the Han dynasty, during the formative stages of the Ch'ü Yüan myth, had described him as the entangled, the bound one; this was seen as the informing feature of his life and the cause of his suicide. Wen I-to tried to bring this tradition to an end when he saw Ch'ü Yüan's life and death as a process of loosening, if not completely throwing off his bonds altogether.

4

Rites of Summer:
Ch'ü Yüan in the Folk Tradition

Tungting Hill floats on the lake. At its foot are hundreds of gilded
halls where the jade virgins dwell, and music in every season carries
to the crest of the hill. King Huai of Ch'u made talented men
compose poems by the lake . . . [and later he] gave ear to evil
ministers and all the good men fled. Ch'ü Yüan, dismissed for his
loyalty, lived as a hermit among the weeds, consorting with birds
and beasts and having no traffic with the world. He ate cypress nuts
and mixed them with cassia oil to cultivate his heart until, hounded
by the king, he drowned himself in the limpid stream. The people of
Ch'u mourned his loss bitterly and believed he had become a water
saint. His spirit wanders through the Milky Way, descending on
occasion to the River Hsiang. The people of Ch'u set up a shrine for
him which was still standing at the end of the Han dynasty.
   Forgotten Tales (Shih i chi),
   Fourth Century A.D.

D URING the first half of the twentieth century, the intelligentsia's reverence for Ch'ü Yüan was interwoven with their
growing awareness and appreciation of folk culture. A characteristic of the new literature written about Ch'ü Yüan was an

argument for his close association with the common people. This was true even of those who saw him as a transcendent superman, or a prophet without honor in his own land. The legitimacy and value of his example were argued on the basis of his understanding of the people's suffering and his desire to help them. For those intellectuals who depicted Ch'ü Yüan as a commoner himself, it was that much easier to link his politics and art to folk culture. In either case, the same datum was repeatedly adduced to demonstrate that he was indeed a people's poet. This was the central role he played, reputedly since the time of his death in the third century B.C., in the cluster of customs and festivals celebrated throughout south China in early summer. Here was irrefutable evidence, it was argued, that the masses themselves recognized Ch'ü Yüan's association with their lives and interests, and that ultimately he was one of them.

Though it will mean stepping back in time, I explore the folk cult of Ch'ü Yüan at this point, in the midst of our discussion of twentieth century China, for a number of reasons. First, because I have wanted to develop an uninterrupted narrative of the lore as it has evolved in the literary tradition up to this point. Second, because it is not until this time in history that Chinese intellectuals show a sustained consciousness of folk culture and make it a basic category of Chinese civilization. The entire tradition of Ch'ü Yüan is transformed by this new consciousness which, among other things, results in the idea of Ch'ü Yüan as a revolutionary people's poet.

One of the signal features of the intellectual tradition of modern China is its claim to the discovery of an indigenous folk tradition in China's past. Once having made the discovery, many prominent intellectual leaders have then gone on to conclude that this was the "true" and essential tradition of Chinese culture, and that it, in its contemporary forms, must be the inspiration and point of departure for China's new culture. Thus, beginning in the 1920s, some of China's most prominent scholars and poets devoted themselves to recon-

Plate 7. "The Lady of the Hsiang River"

structing one or another aspect of China's past folk cultures, laying particular emphasis on folk poetry, song, and story. Much effort was spent to learn which of the most ancient and venerated literary monuments (like the Odes and the Ch'u Tz'u) were in fact records of the oral tradition, or at least were inspired by it. And fruitful results were obtained by applying to these efforts newly learned Western techniques and concepts of mythography and folklore.

However sophisticated these endeavors were, and whatever useful knowledge they imparted, they nearly all shared a common sociological theme which often served to obscure more than it revealed. This was the theme of the antithetic "two cultures"—of the "people" and of the "aristocracy"— locked in a perennial adversary relationship. Even before the application of a Marxist dialectical approach to the role of "the people" in Chinese history, it was being argued that the people's culture was the source of all progressive cultural innovation in China. What had been innovative and of value for China in the aristocratic (read: ruling class) tradition was considered to be merely "imitative" and derived from the folk. When we consider the relationship of the Ch'ü Yüan folk and elite traditions, these generalizations may be found simplistic and misleading.

My goals in this section are first to provide a detailed analysis of the evolution of the Ch'ü Yüan folk cult so that we may further appreciate how the myth as a whole was conveyed and what it conveyed. In this way we can see more precisely what legacies were available to the modern intelligentsia for its populist transformation of Ch'ü Yüan. Then, on the basis of these details, I want to speculate briefly how the so-called elite and folk traditions of Ch'ü Yüan might be related to each other. And finally, the details of the folk cult will provide material for indicating some of the broad continuities and changes which have occurred in the Ch'ü Yüan lore up to the time of the People's Republic. Though we will go back in time to the formative period of the myth, we shall be talking about the folk tradition in familiar terms. The themes we have seen emerge from Han times through the modern Republic will structure our discussion here, albeit changed into forms that have had immediacy to the lives of Chinese from all walks of life. Central among these are the themes of sacrificial death and regenerative power, the passage of time and cosmic order.

As early as the second century A.D., in the last years of the Han dynasty, the image of Ch'ü Yüan was becoming closely associated with a number of the folk customs of south China. Around the figure of the "loyal and pure" minister who drowned himself there coalesced celebrations of the summer solstice, and a variety of festivals and rites associated with water. All of these customs originally had been independent of one another, yet by the sixth century they had become linked together and with the classical myth of Ch'ü Yüan. This chain comprised the summer solstice festival known best as Tuan Wu, the eating and offering as a sacrifice of the *tsung-tzu* rice dumplings, the use of long-life threads (*ch'ang-ming-lü*) to ward off evil influences, and the Dragon Boat Festival (*Lung-chou-chieh*).

These folk customs and the Han myth of Ch'ü Yüan provided reciprocal services one to another. The customs, still practiced throughout the Chinese-speaking world, served to bring Ch'ü Yüan beyond the confines of official literary culture and to make him a very familiar and sympathetic figure in the oral tradition of south China, a principal in one of China's three or four most important calendar festivals. In turn, the Ch'ü Yüan lore of Han provided a logic, a force around which there arranged themselves disparate and sometimes seemingly contradictory elements of folk culture. The logic which informs the political mythology of Ch'ü Yüan in the Han is continuous and apposite, if not identical, with the logic of these united customs. Reconstructing it will help us to understand how Ch'ü Yüan came to be the center of independent customs and festivals with which he originally had no relation and indeed which often first celebrated some other figure. And we shall see how customs and festivals from different regions of south China conflate in Ch'ü Yüan's home territory of Ch'u (today's Hunan and Hupei provinces).

The Summer Solstice and Evil Days

There are two clusters of customs which are associated with Ch'ü Yüan: those of the summer solstice,[1] and those concerned with boat festivals and making sacrifices related to water. On the lunar calendar, the fifth day of the fifth month is the conventional date for celebrating as a whole, and on Ch'ü Yüan's behalf, these originally independent customs. We shall consider first the solstice customs and the sense of danger associated with them. The Fifth of the Fifth, the day of Ch'ü Yüan's drowning, has been considered an evil day since the Warring States period (fourth century B.C.),[2] and has typically been treated as a time for the exorcism of harmful influences since Han times. All customs of the festival, W. Eberhard's research shows, "were to provide protection against poisonous animals of darkness, or they were to utilize the forces emanating from the battle between animals of darkness and animals of the sun (fire). [And] the customs were to protect people from war . . . which is male and fire."[3] Very prominent in the lore is the belief that a child born on this day or even in this month would kill its father or both parents.[4] So it is a time to exercise precautions: the home is swept clean; amulets are worn or hung from the doorways; baths are taken and special foods are eaten.[5] Already in Han times, red and multicolored silk was hung from doors for the protection it was believed to provide against evil forces at this time of the year.[6]

The special power, and danger, assigned to this day comes from the achievement of fullness of the cosmic principle of *yang*, the sun (light, maleness). Though the sun will imminently yield to its alternating and complementary principle, the *yin*, for the moment it is at its fullest strength, and humans must take compensatory actions. Thus, a child born at this time would be super-charged with "maleness" and hence be of danger to the parents. "People such as these," Eberhard notes, resemble in their actions the owl Hsiao, [an animal of darkness], whose young kill their mother. This owl was used to make broth which was consumed on that day. The owl, furthermore, steals children's souls; therefore one must not put bedding [i.e. accoutrements of the night] out into the sun on this day which is the owl's day. Around this day the souls of [humans] are undergoing changes, and therefore it is particularly easy for the owl to steal the soul. For the same reason one must not climb on the roof on this day. This taboo [fits] with the concept of "calling the soul to return" *(chao-hun)* [associated with Ch'ü Yüan].[7]

We shall see that Ch'ü Yüan is very much associated with the complement of the *yang* principle, that is, with *yin* — femaleness, the moon, darkness, and water. And by way of transition to a fuller consideration, let us look at two bits of lore which are perhaps only intelligible in the context of Tuan Wu. In an eclectic little T'ang dynasty treatise called the "Unofficial Biography of Ch'ü Yüan" the putative author, Shen O-chih, retells the story of how Ch'ü Yüan came to write his poem *Heavenly Questions.* Drawing inspiration from the iconography of the king's temple, Ch'ü Yüan began to compose his poem, and then "bright day turned into darkest night and remained so for three days." Shen relates (with charming precision) another anecdote that also seems to make some sense in our present discussion. A man of the Tsin period (ca. A.D. 371) by the name of Yen Yü of Wu (the lower Yangtze Valley) was sitting in a boat anchored near the shore of the Milo River (in which Ch'ü Yüan drowned). One moonlit night he heard someone singing a phrase from Ch'ü Yüan's poem about the fall of the capital of Ch'u. What he saw was "weird" and he called out to the singer, "Are you Ch'ü Yüan?" The singer suddenly disappeared.[8]

Water Rites: Sacrificial Drowning

Tuan Wu, or the Fifth of the Fifth, originally had nothing to do with water rites. Indeed, up to recent times, some people have celebrated the former independently of the latter. However, sometime in the period of Northern and Southern division, fourth to sixth centuries A.D., old traditions of sacrificial drowning came to be associated with Tuan Wu. Accounts of the sacrifice of human beings to the rivers of China can be found in Han texts. In the following summary of such accounts, north China is the focus, but the roles of the shaman and the female sacrificial bride-victim are of special importance to the Ch'ü Yüan lore which developed in the South.

> The River God had to be appeased by giving him "wives." We read that at Yeh, in the extreme north of Honan, it was the custom c. 400 B.C. to give the god a wife every year. The shamans went round from house to house looking for a particularly pretty girl. When they found her they gave her a good bath, dressed her in the finest silks and housed her in a special "house of purification" on the river bank, where she lived in seclusion behind red curtains. After ten days or more they powdered her face and decked her out as a bride and set her afloat on a thing shaped like a bridal bed. After drifting some 10 *li* (five or six miles) down stream the bridal-raft sank and disappeared. "People with handsome daughters," we are told, "fearing that the shaman would take them to 'marry' to the River God, used to flee with their daughters to distant parts." The place where the victims were launched was still shown in the sixth century A.D. It was on the banks of the River Chang which now flows into the sea, but may then have been a tributary or sub-tributary of the Yellow River. Sometimes these sacrifices were made to appease the god when his waters were tampered with.[9]

Whether or not this particular form of mock-wedding sacrifice took place in the South, there is ample evidence from the lower Yangtze Valley and down into the southern Yüeh region (Kwangtung, Kwangsi) for a tradition of sacrificing women by drowning or making sacrifices to drowned women. For example, "sacrifices were made to drowned women by sinking into water fruit wrapped in orchid or other leaves and tied with colored ribbons, as protection against the Chiao [malevolent] dragons."[10] Additionally there are the Hsiang River goddesses to whom temples were built in Yung chou,

Plate 8. "The God of the Yellow River," fourteenth-century illustration for the *Nine Songs*

Hunan. They were said to live in Tung-t'ing Lake and were considered to be moon goddesses as well.[11] Eberhard's classifications show that actually there are two myth cycles on the theme of the drowned woman, only one of which is connected with the festival of the fifth day of the fifth month:

> One [features] the idea—which belongs to the Yao culture—of the drowned women who became the patron goddesses of the river festivals; the other one—which belongs to the Thai culture—[links] the concept of the fifth day of the fifth moon with the sacrifices that must be offered to the evil demons living in the rivers.[12]

Edward Schafer's pursuit of these goddesses, in his study *The Divine Woman*, has demonstrated how the popular cult of the "deified drowned woman, often a suicide"—as well as many prominent female water deities of the southern rivers—were by T'ang times either forgotten or lost through masculinization.[13] His sensitive reconstruction of the lore of these goddesses, of their expression of the female quintessence, and of their cosmic significance provides us the best available key to the legacy which the figure of Ch'ü Yüan inherited when it became a principal in the river sacrifice cult. Life-giving water is of course central to the chain of symbols linked to the ancient notions of women, "who represented metaphysical water in human form"[14]—rain and rainbows, rivers, lakes, and tidal flows, and by extension the moon which regulated the flow from above, and the dragon which often exercised its control from its abode below the water's surface.[15]

In the literature explored by Schafer, as with the customs we are presently discussing, the dragon symbol is often ambivalent and its sex ambiguous. For example, the fifth moon water sacrifices and rites associated with Ch'ü Yüan implicitly distinguish between the good dragons *(lung)* and the bad ones *(chiao)*, who must be propitiated or diverted lest they devour the drowned corpse.[16] Though the dragon had begun to take on masculine attributes by T'ang times, Schafer shows that "in China, dragon essence is woman essence."

The connection is through the mysterious powers of the fertilizing rain, and its extensions in running streams, lakes, and marshes. In common belief as in literature, the dark, wet side of nature showed itself alternately in women and in dragons. The great water deities of Chinese antiquity were therefore snake queens and dragon ladies. . . . Despite their natural affinity to women, dragons appear in many tales as fertilizing males and sometimes as powerful dragon kings. But these too were part of the rain cycle. The women . . . were the repositories of moisture—the cool, receptive loam, or the lake or marsh; the virile dragons were the active, falling rain. Both were manifestations of the infinite transmutations of the water principle.[17]

It was this female water principle which was at the heart of the combined solstice and water rites festival celebrated on the Fifth of the Fifth.

Who Drowned on the Fifth of the Fifth?

Ch'ü Yüan was not the only and probably not the first male figure to supplant the female drowning suicides and the goddesses of the southern water cults. In the oldest records, a number of drowning victims, most of them suicides, are associated with the Fifth of the Fifth, the day on which Ch'ü Yüan was supposed to have drowned himself.[18] Before considering other features of the water rites, we should meet some of the most prominent of these figures.

The earliest example available is that of the shaman Ts'ao Hsü and his daughter Ts'ao O (or Ts'ao Yü). This is important for having both a male and female drowning victim associated with the Fifth of the Fifth, and for the suggestion that shaman practices are related to these. The main source tells us:

The filial daughter, Ts'ao O, was a native of Shang-yü in Kuei-chi [the Wu region, present day Chekiang]. Her father, Ts'ao Hsü was a skilled musician and shaman. On the fifth day of the fifth month of the year Han-an [A.D. 143] he was drowned while rowing out towards the oncoming bore to meet the god with dancing in the Shang-yü river, and his body was never recovered.[19]

耳冀吹黄搜蟬搜損我残陰忘焉兮
洲兮不蔡遺兮遠少捐余袂兮员不
兮澧蒼兮采芳兮願荬荐行
柱上兮不兮子兮顧望兮
若水若是荐兮孔孔蔡渥油兮
鹏鹏牽兮兮鹏荬兮孔荬兮荐
兮荐兮兮乩蔡兮珹黠氣兮兮
潠堂兮不荐薄薛兮荐兮荐潠
宮兮下湘兮细荐孔兮珹荐水兮
兮纷疑湘兮兮孔荐湘遺兮中
女余蔡麝荐兮荐遺兮湘湘荐兮兮
兮珹兮荬荐兮中荐兮荐兮珹
天兮荐麝荐荐荐兮兮荐荐兮荐
兮兮兮顧兮兮荬兮兮荐子兮
再荐兮兮顧荬兮荐孔兮荐兮
褐兮兮顧兮荬荐荐兮兮荐荐
聊荐荐兮兮荐荐荐和兮荐荐兮荐
潠兮兮荬兮荐荐兮兮荐荐兮
荐兮兮荐兮兮兮兮今世兮兮荐兮荐
寄天喜兮荐荐荐兮荐荐荐兮

Plate 9. "Lady of the Hsiang River" (left) and "Lord of the Hsiang River" (right), from fourteenth-century hand-scroll of the *Nine Songs*

湘君
湘夫人

Plate 10. "Lord and Lady of the Hsiang River," from seventeenth-century woodblock illustration of the *Nine Songs*

An elaboration of the story describes the daughter, a mere fourteen years old, searching into the darkest night for her father and then giving up and throwing herself into the river and drowning. The two corpses, intertwined, appeared a few days later.[20] A cult and temples were later dedicated to Ts'ao O, and these seem to have become centers for a cult of female deities or saints, all of whom sacrificed their lives.[21] In recent centuries, at least one local tradition, from northwest Hupei, attributed the origins of the Tuan Wu water festival to the "loyal Ch'ü Yüan and the filial Ts'ao O."[22]

The story of Ts'ao O and her father implicitly contains within it the next, and very important, figure in the history of the transmutation of the river goddesses. The god of the bore whom Ts'ao Hsü sought to meet was none other than Wu Tzu-hsü. We have seen him frequently paired with Ch'ü Yüan as an ill-fated minister. In Wang Ch'ung's compendious *Lun Heng* (first century A.D.) we read that Wu has already become a water god to be reckoned with:

> It has been recorded that the king of Wu, Fu Ch'ai, put Wu Tzu-hsü to death, had him cooked in a cauldron, sewed into a leathern pouch, and thrown into the River. Wu Tzu-hsü, incensed, lashed up the waters, that they rose in great waves, and drowned people. At present [first century A.D.], temples for him have been erected on the Yangtze on Tan-t'u [near Chinkiang in Kiangsu] as well as on the Chekiang river of Ch'ien-t'ang [in Hangchow prefecture of Chekiang] for the purposes of appeasing his anger and stopping the wild waves.[23]

There is further evidence from the fourth, sixth, and ninth centuries of temples devoted to Wu Tzu-hsü in the lower Yangtze Valley and even north into Shantung province.[24] It is very fortunate that the first record of Ch'ü Yüan's association with the rites is careful to point out that originally they were an Eastern Wu custom celebrated on behalf of Wu Tzu-hsü and were not related to Ch'ü Yüan.[25] Thus, by the first century A.D., Wu Tzu-hsü had become a central figure in water-related sacrifices in the lower Yangtze Valley. By the third/fourth centuries, Ch'ü Yüan had begun to replace him in that role throughout the Yangtze Valley.[26]

I want to cite a few more examples of minor figures associated with either the water cult and/or the Fifth of the Fifth to add some useful detail to our understanding of the rich customs which clustered entirely around Ch'ü Yüan by the sixth century. The figure of Fan Li (fifth century B.C.) illustrates the regional qualities of this lore. His biography in the *Historical Records* is intimately related to Wu Tzu-hsü's, for they were chief advisors of rival kings—Fan Li from Yüeh and advisor of Kou Chien (fl. 496 B.C.), Wu Tzu-hsü from Wu.[27] In addition to being a successful military strategist, Fan Li was something of a natural philosopher specializing in irrigation.[28] It seems that he (or his legend) moved north, into Ch'u and the heartland of the water cults around Lake Tung-t'ing and the Hsiang River, "where many natural features bore his name, and it was said that he dwelt in the midst of the lake, transformed from a semi-legendary philosopher of nature and advisor of kings into a kind of water deity."[29] A corollary to his story, preserved in a Ming text, has a touch of regional chauvinism. Here it was argued that Kou Chien, king of the Yüeh state, and not Ch'ü Yüan, was truly the original figure whose death was memorialized by the Tuan Wu festival.[30]

Chieh Tzu-t'ui (ca. seventh century B.C.) is another victim of the Fifth of the Fifth. According to the *Chuang-tzu*, "he was a model of fealty, going so far as to cut a piece of flesh from his thigh to feed his lord, Duke Wen [of Chin]. But later when the Duke [failed to reward him] he went off in a rage. [He withdrew to a forest and when the king tried to smoke him out] he wrapped his arms around a tree, and burned to death."[31] According to later tradition, this was supposed to have occurred on Tuan Wu. The Ch'ing scholar Ku Yen-wu (1613–1682), whose opinion is always worthy of consideration, understood Chieh Tzu-t'ui to be a cognate of Wu Tzu-hsü and noted that the Five Elements system (alternation of the cosmic elements: water, wood, fire, metal, earth) may be at work here, structuring the legend and linking it systematically to Wu Tzu-hsü.[32]

A final illustration is Chung K'uei, a multi-purpose

fellow—star god, patron of literature, and exorcist of evil spirits—who is said to have committed suicide by drowning on Tuan Wu.[33] He seems to have originated in T'ang times. In the nineteenth century he was serving the people of Peking in a useful fashion on Tuan Wu. A book on calendar customs records that "every year at Tuan Yang [alternate name for Tuan Wu] shops have yellow streamers a foot long, covered with vermilion seal impressions, or perhaps painted with figures of the Heavenly Master or Chung K'uei, or with forms of the five poisonous creatures. . . ."[34] These streamers could be purchased to be posted on home portals to ward off evil influences.

Long-life Threads

The protective streamers may have a very ancient heritage that began in the Wu-Yüeh regions and made its appearance at the same time as Tuan Wu. The modern poet and mythologist Wen I-to explains the origins of what came to be known as long-life threads in terms of the special characteristics of the culture of Wu-Yüeh. Wen argued that a prominent feature of the area was the use of the dragon as a totem. In order to incorporate personally the qualities of their totem, these "dragon children," as they called themselves, cut their hair and tattooed their bodies so as "to look like dragons."[35] The body tattoos, especially those on the arms, evolved into customs such as binding the forearms with multicolored silk threads.[36] Five was a common number of strands, and Wen argues that this number is of special significance to the Wu-Yüeh culture. In particular, the number is persistently associated with the dragon. This in turn Wen adduces as external proof for his philologic demonstration that the name "Tuan Wu" (correct center) is an ancient lexicographical misrecording of the original "Tuan Wu" (correct five).[37] With the advent of the Five Elements systemization during the Han, he concludes, the associations of the number five, especially with the dragon, became fixed.

A second century A.D. encyclopedic work on popular customs already treats the use of long-life threads as a commonplace. However, its explanations are less complex than the modern scholar's: why, it asks, are multicolored silks bound to the forearm on the Fifth of the Fifth to ward off evil influences? "This is done because of Ch'ü Yüan," is the simple answer.[38] As we shall see momentarily, these threads were used to bind the *tsung-tzu* rice dumplings thrown into water as a sacrifice to Ch'ü Yüan on Tuan Wu. However, there was at least one pre-Han water rite that used the threads in the same fashion but had nothing to do with Ch'ü Yüan: "Fresh plants, or colored ribbons in a bag or objects made of metal were let down into the river because the Chiao [malevolent] dragons were afraid of these things and in this way the sacrificial offering would be protected from being devoured by the dragon."[39]

These explanations and illustrations of the threads are all quite consistent with each other and apposite with the main themes and motifs we have been laying out. However, if we go beyond these and ask what the threads have to do with "long life" and look to the shamanistic ritual which frequently accompanied the water rites, we shall have a fuller explanation that at least complements the sometimes tenuous arguments of Wen I-to. The modern folklorist Chao Wei-pang has made the astute observation that the threads are indeed related to the soul of the dead. To substantiate this, he cites some vivid evidence from the Miao tribespeople who formerly lived in southern Hunan.[40] Chao reminds us that part of the Dragon Boat Festival is the calling back of Ch'ü Yüan's soul. This calling back is of course the job of the shaman, and in the *Ch'u Tz'u* poem "The Summons of the Soul" (Chao-hun) we have a dramatization of the shaman conducting the ritual and using "silk cords."[41] However, I believe Chao Wei-pang is incorrect when he suggests that these threads and cords are probably a symbol of the soul of the dead. Instead, M. Eliade's description of shamanistic ritual seems to provide the correct interpretation: "This [thread] is the 'road' along which the spirits will move," this cord is "the road by which the shaman will reach the realm of the spirits, the sky."[42] Whatever the ultimate origin of these magical filaments, it seems most useful to think of them, in the context of the Tuan Wu rituals, as having the function of clearing away malevolent influences so that the soul (or its escort, the shaman) can make its necessary progress.

Tsung-tzu

By the same token, it is well to keep in mind that on Tuan Wu, when the *tsung* rice sacrifices were thrown into the water, they were intended to benefit the dead, not the dragons. Such sacrifices predated Ch'ü Yüan's putative death in the third century B.C., and came to be associated with him no later than the first century A.D.[43] A sixth-century text preserves the lore of Ch'ü Yüan's association with the *tsung-tzu* and the five-colored threads. It says that the people of Ch'u, upon the death of Ch'ü Yüan, and thereafter on every Fifth of the Fifth, made a sacrificial offering to his memory with rice put into bamboo tubes which they threw into the water. But then, in the first year of the Eastern Han (A.D. 25), a man from Changsha by the name of O Hui had a dream in which Ch'ü Yüan appeared to him and said: "I appreciate your yearly remembrance of me; but the rice you throw in the water is being grabbed away by the malevolent dragons (*chiao-lung*) who eat it all up. Please seal up the mouths of the tubes with melia leaves, and then bind around them five-colored silk threads, because the dragons are afraid of such things."[44] As with much of this lore, the dating seems oddly precise but it is in keeping with the date of Ch'ü Yüan's association with the custom of binding one's forearms with five-colored threads in order to ward off evil forces on Tuan Wu. Just how the *tsung-tzu*, bound with the magic threads, relates to the dead soul, and recalling the soul, is a question we shall take up after considering the Dragon Boat Festival.

The Dragon Boat Festival

No later than the sixth century A.D., the Yangtze Valley saw the complete melding of solstice and water rite customs around the figure of Ch'ü Yüan. By this time, the most dramatic element was incorporated, the Dragon Boat Festival (*Lung-chou-chieh*). For the reader unfamiliar with the essentials of the colorful and often fractious festival in its competitive aspect, this is a brief description by James Legge, translator of the Chinese classics. He is here recording his first encounter with the festival, around 1855, in the interior of Kwangtung province near the East River. These details substantially agree with those we have from over a thousand years earlier, as well as with the performance of the festival today. Legge saw:

> Two boats, long and slender, each built to represent a dragon, the head of which rose high and formed the prow. A man sat upon it with a flag in each hand, which he waved to direct the movements of the crew, and with his face turned towards the helmsman who stood near the stern. Midway in the boats were two men beating with all their might, one a gong, the other a drum. The crew in each boat could not have been fewer than thirty men, each grasping a short stout paddle, and all with quivering eagerness and loud cries, racing towards a certain point.[45]

The races, apparently of pre-Han origin in regions close to where Legge witnessed this spectacle, originally were associated neither with Tuan Wu nor Ch'ü Yüan.[46] They never seem to have been associated with Wu Tzu-hsü. The original function of the festival was "to sacrifice humans to the river in order to ensure fertility." The boat race was in effect a fight for survival, for the losing boat crew (originally there were perhaps only two boats with crews of fifty) would be toppled or beaten into the water and drowned, thus becoming the sacrificial victims.[47] The violence of the races was repeatedly attested to in the reports of local officials who tried unsuccessfully to proscribe them altogether.[48] Officialdom had become quite ambivalent toward the Ch'ü Yüan cult by the tenth century. On one hand, officials supported the construction of public temples to Ch'ü Yüan's memory and they participated in the Dragon Boat Festival. On the other, the mayhem of the competing dragon boat crews troubled their law-and-order mentality and eventually led them to try to control this aspect of the celebration. The great popularity of the racing events in many Dragon Boat Festivals made it very difficult for the officials to achieve this control. Thanks to a Ming scholar, Yang Ssu-ch'ang (1588–1641), from the lake region northwest of Changsha, there is preserved and collated an invaluable body of data on the Dragon Boat Festival as it was understood and practiced in the modern Hunan-Hupei area going back to the sixth century.[49] For our purposes, the most important feature of this material is its description of the festival's relationship to Ch'ü Yüan. Fundamentally, the festival had great significance as a ritual to insure fertility and good health in the ensuing growing season; but by the sixth century it had come in some locales to be understood simultaneously as a memorial reenactment of the events surrounding Ch'ü Yüan's death.

The boats on the water were understood to be searching for Ch'ü Yüan's body. From the boats, *tsung-tzu* were thrown into the water (a prevalent tradition has it) in order to feed the malevolent dragon and thereby divert him and keep him from eating Ch'ü Yüan's corpse before the boat crew had an opportunity to retrieve it. In the meantime, Ch'ü Yüan's soul was called back (*chao-hun*) by way of the song, dance, and drumming by various members of the crew. It was common for a shaman or some kind of sorcerer to perform this ritual, either in the boat and/or from the shore. And, whether the participants addressed themselves to Ch'ü Yüan or not, it was common for the shaman or sorcerer to prognosticate about the future abundance of the harvest before the boats were actually launched.

Yang Ssu-ch'ang provides us with some of the early illustrations of the form of this tradition. Here he cites the sixth-century *locus classicus* of Ch'ü Yüan's association with the festival:

> "We are going home no matter whether we have found him or not. Don't wait until the cold wind blows over the river." This sentence originated very far in the past. According to the *Geographical Treatise* of the *Sui History*, on the [5th] day of the 5th [moon], Ch'ü Yüan went to the Milo river. The na-

tives pursued him to the Tung-t'ing Lake but in vain. The lake was vast, the boats small and no one could cross it. They all sang "How can we cross the lake?" Then on the way back they started racing to gather together at a pavilion. From that it comes that the people sing "We come back no matter whether we have found him or not."[50]

Yang also brings to our attention the writings of Liu Yü-hsi (772–842), who for a decade performed his official duties in Yang Ssu-ch'ang's home town, Wu-ling (now Ch'ang-te), Hunan. Liu was fascinated by southern customs and he recorded observations such as his belief that the Dragon Boat Festival originated right there in Wu-ling. "Even nowadays," he notes, "the rowers, lifting up their oars and singing together are shouting: 'Who is here?' They are calling to Ch'ü Yüan."[51] Liu provides evidence of Ch'ü Yüan's popularity when he notes that Wu-ling had a "Recalling Ch'ü Yüan Pavilion" (Chao Ch'ü T'ing) near which Liu at one time resided.

And there is even an earlier tradition, noted by Yang Ssu-ch'ang, that Wu-ling, in the vicinity of the pavilion, once had a street called "Ch'ü Yüan Lane," near which was a small river called the San Lü (that is, named after Ch'ü Yüan's formal official title: San lü ta-fu). "Probably," Yang nostalgically concludes, "Ch'ü Yüan often walked there and enjoyed himself during his lifetime."[52]

Finally, Yang brings us back to the problematic nature of the Dragon Boat Festival by citing a Sung dynasty (960–1127) source which chastises Ch'ü Yüan for his alleged predilection for boat racing. Because of this, "boat racing was made a custom of the people; some were wounded and drowned in fighting. And if it were not held for one year, plagues would be sent down." Yang Ssu-ch'ang notes that another Sung writer responded to this charge and defended Ch'ü Yüan, saying that "the boat race was not Ch'ü Yüan's idea."[53]

It is a rather striking note the Sung writer makes when he suggests that a natural catastrophe would ensue were the Dragon Boat Festival not celebrated annually. Evidence supplied

拍千歡為奇觀適時擬船近年
天之使王一人怨誤入江心比及救
趙則已进深屈大夫
奥水懦祈民郴
雨琉之和多
尤馬謀我

Plate 11. "Searching for Ch'ü Yüan," nineteenth-century graphic of Dragon Boat ritual on the Fifth of the Fifth (Tuan Wu), in Anhwei province

追蹤屈子

芜湖端陽節有龍舟競渡し
舉爭先鬥捷各奏爾能時
適有湖南煤船泊扗此舩中
東影十餘人蒲觴醉後逐
興逸飛載以刘舩裝作龍
舟模樣相随大隊容與中
流不料一轉側间竟作繁蔔
翻芽し慾兩幸眾人熱扵水
性如熱水蜻蜓然兔赴岸両有
兩人賣其餘勇躍登舩背若無
兩頭敗興也者觀者無不相與

by such sources as Yang Ssu-ch'ang make it possible to conclude that, at least in the central Yangtze Valley, there has
been an intimate relationship between the agricultural cycle
and the lore of Ch'ü Yüan, Tuan Wu, and the Dragon Boat
Festival. Göran Aijmer has convincingly demonstrated that
what we see here, in the heart of the rice growing region, is
"the ceremonialism of the transplantation of rice." Tuan Wu,
that time when Ch'ü Yüan and the festival are of importance, is a critical time in the agricultural calendar and the
ecology of this region—the summer solstice marks the time of
rice transplanting and the hiatus in the agricultural work
schedule just before the summer heat and rain which will
make the rice plants grow. Here is Aijmer's summary description of the critical part of the cycle:

> Rice [in Hunan-Hupei] is usually sown towards the end of
> April on special plots, and the young plants are moved to the
> large fields after thirty or forty days. During the period be-
> tween sowing and planting, the farmers are busily engaged in
> preparing the soil and flooding the fields. The winter wheat is
> harvested at about this time. The transplanting of the rice
> plants, which is usually done around the end of May or the
> beginning of June, is a period of intense work. It is followed
> by a time with relatively little work in the rice fields,
> . . . weeding . . . and keeping water at the right level.[54]
> [Dragon Boat Festivals take place after this transplantation.]

Whatever its variations in ritual details or time of performance, the Dragon Boat Festivals all over south China have
had the common denominator of an expression of hope for
rain and a good harvest.[55] But in Hunan-Hupei in particular,
Aijmer suggests, "the essential thing in the Ch'ü Yüan
tradition . . . [is that] every year after the transplantation of
rice, a drowned person's *hun* [soul] was called back."[56] In the
agricultural context of the tradition, Ch'ü Yüan connoted
rice. Thus, Aijmer writes, "young rice plants are transplanted
in the large flooded fields under water, that is to say, they are
'drowned.' By this, the rice, probably considered collectively,
was thought to have lost its *hun*. To me it seems feasible that
it was the *hun* of the rice that was recalled in order to restore

the growing strength of the uprooted and transplanted rice plants."[57] We can buttress Aijmer's perceptive conclusions with structurally similar ones from the customs of the Karen of Burma. Long ago, Frazer noted their ceremonial recalling of the rice soul.[58] More recently, and even more to the point, is Eliade's observation of the shaman's role in the ceremony. The shaman, who is instrumental in calling back the soul of a sick person, employs "a similar treatment for the 'sickness' of the rice, imploring its 'soul' to return to the crop."[59]

I, too, would like to return for a moment to that useful collection of anecdotes about Ch'ü Yüan, the "Unofficial Biography of Ch'ü Yüan," for two more of its gems which reflect the themes of fecundity and rice. The first, which I have seen repeated nowhere else, says that after Ch'ü Yüan composed his poem "The Mountain Spirits" (Shan kuei), the spirits of the hills cried out and could be heard for miles; and this caused all the vegetation in the environs to decay and wither. The second story, which many texts repeat, accentuates the positive. We are told that in the *Chiang ling Gazetteer* there is mentioned a certain "Jade Rice Field." The field originated in this way. After Ch'ü Yüan was slandered and banished, he sadly returned home and plowed his fields. One day, while chanting the *Li Sao*, he leaned on his plow and wept aloud to heaven. At that time, there was a great drought and famine in Ch'u, but in the very spot where his teardrops had fallen there grew rice white as jade.[60]

Clearly then, where the Ch'ü Yüan lore intersected Tuan Wu and Dragon Boat customs there was a central concern being expressed for a successful rice crop. In this context the *tsung-tzu* rice dumpling should be understood as a kind of ritual shorthand—a minor plot which contains within it all of the important themes. Like Ch'ü Yüan and the young rice sprouts, it too is "drowned," and it too requires protection of its soul with the multicolored threads which, accordingly, are wrapped around it. We should not ignore the fact that apparently from the beginning of Ch'ü Yüan's association with the Dragon Boat and *tsung-tzu* customs, the *tsung-tzu* were eaten by the celebrants as well as thrown into the water as an offering. If the identity of Ch'ü Yüan with rice—a rice god—is accepted, then the consumption of the *tsung-tzu* must appear to us as the familiar ritual incorporation of the god. However, the Chinese, true to their gustatory predilections, were quick to proliferate the varieties of *tsung-tzu*— stuffing them with delicacies other than rice (strawberries or turtle meat for example). The next step, naturally, was to consume them straightaway on Tuan Wu with no thought to wasting any of the tasty morsels by throwing them into the river.[61] So much for ritual and symbol.

In sum, the conflation of solstice and water sacrifice customs around the figure of Ch'ü Yüan which occurred during the sixth century A.D. had special regional associations and a set of clearly recognizable functions. In general geographical terms, this is a southern phenomenon. Professor Wen Ch'ung-i's exhaustive reading in local gazetteers from all over China, and dating back to the sixteenth century, makes clear that once we leave the wet rice cultivating regions of China, this cluster of customs and demigods can no longer be found. Nor indeed is the most dramatic element, the Dragon Boat Festival, to be found in the north.[62] One does find that Tuan Wu and the eating of *tsung-tzu* are customary in northern settings, like Peking, but they seem to have nothing to do with any of the water-associated customs and lore.

In studies of the local cultures of China, distinctions can be made within the South concerning the practices we have examined. While Ch'ü Yüan is celebrated along the full length of the Yangtze Valley, the epicenter of his cult, and perhaps the only area where the cluster as a whole was operative, was in present-day Hunan-Hupei. Thus, using the local studies of scholars like Eberhard and the eyewitness accounts of people like Yang Ssu-ch'ang, it is possible to conclude that Ch'ü Yüan appears in his rice-god mask only in this area of China where he was a principal in the ceremonialism of rice transplanting. Down river, Eberhard suggests, in the Wu region, there is no evidence of the Dragon Boat Festival serving that ceremonial function.[63] By no means is this to say, however, that Ch'ü Yüan was incapable of stirring up the devotion of the folks of Wu. In Anhwei Province, Hui Prefecture, for example, there was a Ch'ü Yüan temple (San Lü Tz'u) which housed an idol of him. It is said that on the Fifth of the Fifth the idol was carried aloft in a procession from the temple to the docks, where it was placed on a boat in preparation for the ritual search and recalling of his soul.[64]

All in all, the development of the cluster of customs around Ch'ü Yüan gives evidence of the movement and interpenetration of the major southern local cultures. The recurrence of figures such as Wu Tzu-hsü, Fan Li, and Kou Chien along with Ch'ü Yüan dramatizes this. As for the functions of the combined solstice and water rites lore, they were so clearly recognized by Yang Ssu-ch'ang that modern scholars able to draw on wider evidence find little to add. Yang said that the customs surrounding the Dragon Boat Festival and Ch'ü Yüan were meant to avert natural calamity and to exorcise all manner of evils; they were also meant to provide means of foretelling and guaranteeing a productive harvest.[65]

Conclusion: Ch'ü Yüan in the Folk and Elite Traditions

To conclude this discussion and as a prologue to considerations of Ch'ü Yüan in the People's Republic, I want to speculate from a number of angles on how the folk and elite lore are related. I see them as complementary parts of a mythology that addresses itself rather comprehensively to basic concerns of human life, in the realms of polity and society, sacred and secular, cosmos and history. Approaches that rely on notions of "big and little traditions," "elite and folk," or "aristocratic and peoples" often suggest antagonism or mutual exclusiveness. In the Ch'ü Yüan lore we have an example apparently spanning these categories. We could simply dismiss this as an illusion, and argue that it is only the name of Ch'ü Yüan that links the two categories in which very different kinds of things are going on. But I ask that we defer that judgment while we consider a series of questions about the lore which I will discuss with some assumptions in mind. The first is that it is analytically more useful here to employ the categories of "written and oral traditions" and "cosmopolitan and regional cultures" than the other paired categories. The second assumption is a corollary. Perhaps the use of these latter categories will help us to see and remember that China's poet-officials who created and participated in the political and literary traditions of Ch'ü Yüan were also (and necessarily) participants in the oral traditions. By the same token, if we consider the "rites of summer" lore an important feature of Yangtze Valley regional culture, then there is no reason to doubt that some individuals who participated in the essentially literary, cosmopolitan culture also participated in it. In China, as in any other society, becoming literate, educated, and even literary did not necessarily mean abandoning religion, ritual, local custom, or regional culture.

The last assumption is that the relationship between any of these sets of categories will be understood differently depending on whether they are viewed as static entities or as part of a dynamic process. If we adopt the latter perspective, then we see not only that the content of the categories is often changing, but that the changes often result from cycling and recycling of the contents from one category to the other, from "big" to "little" tradition, if you will, and back again; from cosmopolitan to regional, and back again. In the instance of the Ch'ü Yüan lore, historical perspective reveals greater interdependence of these categories than might be evident from juxtapositions made without any sense of the preceding and subsequent developments.

These considerations enter into the first question I want to raise, if not answer, here. Why did Ch'ü Yüan in particular become associated when he did with the "rites of summer"? The modern Chinese explanation is the one that has prevailed since at least the sixth century, and I am treating it as part of the myth itself. This is the story that the association began immediately after the death of Ch'ü Yüan in the third century B.C., when the rites were initiated spontaneously by the common folk of Ch'u, specifically as a memorial to him.

The special modern addition to this story is that Ch'ü Yüan endeared himself to the folk with his patriotic fervor, and hence earned this memorialization, when he wandered among them during his banishment. The extant evidence, however, suggests that all aspects of the summer rites predated Ch'ü Yüan's association with them and were in some cases originally associated with other figures. Actually, the evidence first associates him with an element of the summer rites only in the first century A.D., three centuries after the surmised date of his death. Thus it must be concluded that Ch'ü Yüan did not become part of the summer rites, and perhaps was completely unknown by the common public, until after he gained his preeminent position within Han literature. And further, it seems certain that the figure of Ch'ü Yüan only became part of the summer rites and known to the general populace of the Yangtze Valley through the determined efforts of the educated elite.

Now the questions are changed. Why did officials and notables introduce their Ch'ü Yüan into the general culture of the Yangtze Valley? How did they do it? And finally, why did they do it when they did? Let us take the question of timing first. The literature we have reviewed consistently shows the formation of the Ch'ü Yüan folk cult over the centuries, starting with the disintegration of the Han polity, and ending with the initial stages of political reunification in the sixth century. This span of time is marked by the collapse of the Han, the first of the great waves of nomadic invasions of north China, the sacking of the capital, and the fragmentation of the polity into a series of northern and southern dynasties. All this has resonance with the story of Ch'ü Yüan in Han literature; but I am venturing that the events most relevant to our questions are the migrations of populations south, to the refuge of the Yangtze, in the wake of the invasions. There the emigrants set up colonial regimes, microcosms of northern cosmopolitan society. Periodically they revealed their obsession to return north by their costly attempts to reconquer it and reunite the country.

Because of his prominence in the Han literary tradition,

Ch'ü Yüan was surely well known to these settlers in the South who devoted themselves to perpetuating Han literary culture. How much more meaningful and immediate to them must have been his experience, now that they themselves, or their parents before them, had witnessed the destruction of their state and had been forced into exile in the South.

Conquering or colonizing peoples, like these émigrés to the South, quite regularly bring with them their gods and heroes and establish them, if they can, alongside or in place of indigenous ones. The fact that Ch'ü Yüan was a Southerner may have made it seem even more reasonable to these émigrés that they should put him in the place of the various local cult figures. That effort also entailed the substitution of Wu Tzu-hsü by Ch'ü Yüan. The former figure seems to have initiated the process of replacing local goddesses and saints with male political figures who were prominent within the northern literary tradition. The process of supplanting indigenous cult figures has the appearance of an effort by the Northerners to use southern "native sons" as a medium for conveying the civilized political values of the North. The rivalry between the figures of Ch'ü Yüan and Wu Tzu-hsü may reveal the social complexity of the southern migrations. Perhaps it reflects tension and rivalry between the older northern Chinese settlers in the Yangtze Valley and the émigrés of the fourth century and later.

Let me summarize my speculations. First, officials and/or local notables were necessary for establishing the southern popular cult because only they could command the resources necessary to build and maintain temples, shrines, and dragon boats; and only through them could a figure like Ch'ü Yüan come to prominence in the oral tradition. Only they could have provided the impetus and the coordination that resulted in the substitution of a melange of cults and customs by a regularized calendar festival whose parts were linked together with a single, pedigreed figure. Secondly, the fact that Ch'ü Yüan should be the single figure must be a function not only of his southernness (Wu Tzu-hsü was a prominent Southerner too), but of his name being associated with a corpus of poetry, and concomitantly, the unmatched adulation which he received in Han letters.

The central role which the classes played in bringing Ch'ü Yüan to the masses during this formative period should not be taken as a confirmation of the modern Chinese claim that the lore of Ch'ü Yüan was created merely as a medium for the "aristocracy" (that is, the ruling class) to broadcast a notion of compliance to authority, and as a device for obtaining popular respect for bureaucrats. Given the personal political and social situations of the émigrés we have been discussing, I believe that they were motivated by a desire to use Ch'ü Yüan to represent their own political despair and their undying loyalty to a lost homeland. Moreover, the evidence we have about the practice of the Ch'ü Yüan cult, especially the Fifth of the Fifth, suggests that the story of Ch'ü Yüan's political life and the details of his loyalty were at best superficially conveyed to the general public, and were all but absent from the most important rituals.

Taking the long view, from the earliest elements of the Ch'ü Yüan lore down to the formation of the popular cult, what we see is a cycling of symbols, motifs, and attitudes between the oral and regional and the literary and cosmopolitan sectors of Chinese culture. Schematically, we begin with the oral traditions of Ch'u culture (shaman lore, water deities, water sacrifices) drawn into literature like the *Li Sao*. Here they were used to convey ideas and sentiments that found appreciative audiences within Han official culture. Only within the latter cosmopolitan, literary tradition does the figure of Ch'ü Yüan emerge. And once having achieved prominence there, he is then introduced into the regional, oral traditions where the cycle first began.

Related to this cycling process is the structural kinship between the content of the literary and oral traditions of Ch'ü Yüan. The Han literary lore and the oral tradition of Ch'ü Yüan appear to have congruence and overlap because the former develops its political themes with a sense of cosmic order and time, the alternation and balance of cosmic forces, and the relationship of these to human powers, productivity, and mortality. Not only does the oral tradition share these grand themes, it also employs similar motifs and symbols, which revolve around the complementary primal forces and a concern over the danger of their potential or actual imbalance.

The sacrifice motif is also prominent throughout both traditions. And in both, I believe that the result of the sacrifice is understood to be a renewal of life and fecundity. Just as future health and an abundant crop are the expected results of the Tuan Wu and Dragon Boat sacrifices, so literature (Ch'ü Yüan's poetry, Ssu-ma Ch'ien's history) is the product of the officials' ordeal and sacrifice, the ultimate source of their potency and immortality.

A final illustration of the resonance between the Han literary tradition and the summer rites is in the use of shaman lore to achieve this renewal of productive life. Where the shaman journey might empower the poet-official, the shaman's summons and guidance of the soul is the means for periodic regeneration. Shaman lore provides a way to cross sacred, hence dangerous, boundaries. It is a device to mediate between complementary forces at critical times of transition or imbalance: between light and darkness, water and fire, life and death, minister and king. Thus, the linkages between the Han literature of the loyal official and the summer rites are made both at the level of a concern with cosmic forces and at the level of ritual, which is meant to comprehend and control those forces.

By the time we come to the treatment of Ch'ü Yüan in the exile poetry of the eighth century, most of these grand themes and dramatic motifs are missing. Cosmic orientations, shaman motifs, and sexual symbols do not inform the literary tradition about Ch'ü Yüan from this point on. Though the theme of sacrifice and ordeal persist in the exile poetry, they are quite refined and sedate vestiges of the raw and earthy lore of the Han. However—and this is my point—despite the narrowing of the scope of Ch'ü Yüan literary tradition after the Han, the power and appeal of the myth as a whole remained intact and was broadened. This is so because the main structures of the Han lore were displaced into the oral tradition, which I see as a strong complement to the literary tradition, and continued down to modern times.

In the twentieth century, we see for the first time that the lore of Ch'ü Yüan itself begins to encompass the question of the relations between the oral and literary traditions. In spite of insistence on the fundamental categories of "people's" and "aristocratic," the tradition of Ch'ü Yüan is considered to be wholly within the former. It is perceived as a single unit with no distinctions, invidious or otherwise, between an oral, folk, or regional Ch'ü Yüan lore, and a literary, elite, and cosmopolitan one. The basic reason for this perception is the modern insistence on finding in the lore important sources for the transformative power of Chinese history. It is valued as a classic instance of that power, which can be taken as a model for modern times.

In the twentieth century, we seem to be witnessing another cycle of interaction between literary and oral traditions. The former has co-opted the latter and informed it, explicitly, with new meanings. The newly evolved lore of Ch'ü Yüan is concerned not with cosmos but with history; not with alternating and complementary seasons and elemental cosmic forces, but with progressive, linear history propelled forward by the clash of antagonistic human forces. No longer is the problem one of crossing sacred boundaries, but rather of crossing the secular boundaries that divide historical epochs and social classes.

5

A Touch of Class:
Ch'ü Yüan in the People's Republic

In their own time, each ruling class was revolutionary.
    Mao Tse-tung

IT is appropriate that extraordinary developments of the Ch'ü
Yüan lore should occur at a time when Chinese society was
dominated by an extraordinary Madman of Ch'u. During the
1950s, the lore reflects changing images of political leadership projected by Mao Tse-tung—from superpatriot in the
early 1950s to Promethean emancipator during the Great
Leap Forward at the end of that decade. However, it is that
"mad ardour" of Mao that seems most resonant with the lore.
Many of Mao's contemporaries were disturbed by, and even
hostile to his excessive ardour, his sense of continuing revolution, his great leaps beyond the confines of history and social
realities. So also they had qualms about using as a cultural
hero or political exemplar the Republican era Ch'ü Yüan—
that romantic poet and genius whose zeal and sense of self
threatened to separate him from the masses and from the
realities of history.

Still, in Mao's China as in the Republic before it, the lore of Ch'ü Yüan conveyed the ambivalence of China's intellectual community about their relationship to the masses, about their place as creative individuals in a collectivist society. The lore acted as a forum for confronting the relations of creative will and the restrictions of history and social structures. Thus, in the late 1950s, Ch'ü Yüan and Mao Tse-tung were depicted respectively as forerunner and foremost contemporary practitioner of something called "revolutionary romanticism"—an idea that tried to integrate the individualism and voluntarism of New Culture days with Marxist historicism and class consciousness. Contributors to the new Ch'ü Yüan lore hence became preoccupied with vexing questions about his suspect class origins; the individualistic and personal stamp of his art; his true relationship to the common people; if and how he represented the "progressive forces" of his times.

In the literature surveyed in this chapter, there are persistent efforts to play down or eliminate the romantic image of Ch'ü Yüan—to mitigate his individualism, his willfulness, his role as southern visionary and prophet. This is done with characterizations that make him into a mere conduit of collective, popular sentiment and an instrument of anonymous historical forces. Nevertheless, the post-1949 literature on Ch'ü Yüan reveals strong differences of opinion, and a continuing ambiguity. This is to be expected in a society where, for example, the personality cult of Mao was promoted in tandem with a celebration of anonymous, mass creativity.

In the People's Republic, Ch'ü Yüan lore is tightly interwoven with the monumental task of establishing new criteria for political judgment and its counterpart in China, historical judgment. The fact that these tasks were actually begun during the Republic should indicate that the historiographic polemics and sociological discourses are not mere codes for policy statements. Nor can they be dismissed as epiphenomena of factional struggle and power plays. No less than in the Han dynasty or in the Republic, polemics about Ch'ü Yüan in the PRC can provide insights into fundamental and long range cultural problems.

The most obvious function of the lore since 1949, as in all

previous periods, has been to provide a means for the intellectuals, especially creative writers, to evaluate their place in the polity and society. From the old regime to the present, though the lore suggests a continuity of concerns in this respect, there has been a significant reversal of sensibilities. This is illustrated by the reversal of attitudes about the metropolis and the countryside. Into recent times, a major strand of the lore has been the sentiment that to leave the former for the latter, to lose touch with high culture and become immersed in nature and folk culture, is to abandon public service, to lose hold of reality and reason, to risk impotence and death. By the early 1950s, the lore conveys the very Maoist notion that associates wholly negative feelings with cosmopolitan culture. It suggests that only in the countryside and among the people is reason, power, and life to be found. Once, the countryside of Ch'u had been the setting of Ch'ü Yüan's punishment and the symbol of his failure. Now, the Hunan countryside has become the scene of his greatest success and the source of his ultimate reward by current standards—the respect and following of the people.

The 1953 Commemoration

In Hunan province, on the banks of the Milo River during the early summer of 1953, Ch'ü Yüan formally became a patriotic model for the still-young People's Republic. In remembrance of the 2,230th anniversary of his death, a great convocation was held at the newly renovated Ch'ü Yüan shrine on a hill overlooking the bank from which, a historical marker now explains, he threw himself to his death. Peasants who lived along the river gathered with officials to watch the long procession of dragon boats sweep past on the Milo. "Throughout the land," according to reports, "people honored the annual Tuan Wu festival . . . and this year as in the past the people held the traditional dragon boat races."

The following month brought new and peculiarly modern forms of tribute: a convention, a flood of scholarly papers, exhibitions, radio broadcasts, standing committees. On June 15, a commemorative meeting of the All-China Federation of Writers and Artists opened in Peking. The general topic of discussion was how to proceed with the study of Ch'ü Yüan's poetry in the light of historical materialism. Major poets and critics lectured on how Ch'ü Yüan's life work voiced demands of the people of his time; how it mirrored the irreconcilable conflict between the people and the feudal lords. Literary historians reported on cultural relics from the time of Ch'ü Yüan which had been collected for public display. Kuo Mo-jo, who was behind most of these proceedings, also saw to it that there was a new production of his 1942 play *Ch'ü Yüan*, featuring carefully authenticated settings and costumes, as well as most of the original cast. The celebration was rounded off with new textual studies and editions of the *Ch'u Tz'u*. The National Peking Library put on a special exhibition of various editions of Ch'ü Yüan's poetry, notably including foreign translations. Peking Foreign Languages Press published two English language works for the occasion: translations of the *Ch'u Tz'u* and Kuo Mo-jo's play.[1]

The timing of this commemorative effort, and perhaps its inspiration, came from the PRC's active participation in the World Peace Congress, founded in 1949 in Paris. Among other things, the Congress acted as a sympathetic international forum through which the PRC could assert its national identity in the hostile post-war world. Here it could gain at least moral support and a medium for anti-American propaganda during the Korean war.[2]

The Chinese delegation to the congress was led by Kuo Mo-jo. In 1953, it sponsored a special commemoration of "Four Giants of World Culture" which either determined the timing or was planned as an extension of the Ch'ü Yüan celebration. This provided a cosmopolitan setting for Ch'ü Yüan, who was China's representative to go along with the odd mix of Copernicus, Rabelais, and the Cuban poet José Marti. The PRC issued a set of four postage stamps bearing the likenesses of these four giants, and, in the thick of the commemorative festivities for Ch'ü Yüan, a multilingual booklet was published in their honor. Then a special issue of *Wen-i pao*, the premier literary journal, was devoted to them under the general title "They Struggled to Protect the Advance of Mankind's Cultural Traditions." Generally, the effect of celebrating the quartet was to show that the PRC possessed a world-class culture hero who had all of the best qualities of the other three combined. All four of the celebrities were described as having had a high degree of populist sentiment, a spirit of realism, patriotism, a deep love of truth, and the ability to renew the cultural traditions of their respective countries.[3]

The bulk of the special *Wen-i pao* issue was devoted to describing the uniqueness of the three giants against whom Ch'ü Yüan was to be measured. First there was Rabelais, the great humanist who fought the darkness, superstition, and the religious enslavement of the European dark ages with his independence and sense of justice. He was described glowingly as a polymath and scientist whose literary works drew on the spoken language of the masses, a leader of the new thought of his age and a representative of the rising bourgeoisie. Copernicus was the revolutionary who combined scientific and philosophic thought, while struggling for the independence of science and his country. And finally, Marti—martyred in 1895 during Cuba's war of independence—was a leading promoter of anti-imperialism, national independence, and autonomous native culture. Though not a socialist, we are reminded, he was a member of the advanced section of the petty bourgeoisie.

In spite of Ch'ü Yüan's international company in the foursome, *Wen-i pao's* purpose was not to promote an international culture or cosmopolitanism, but rather to emphasize "national culture" and the Chinese variants of those qualities attributed to the three foreign giants. The special issue's lead essay said that China's former cultural traditions must be used as a basis for the new ones. While China should be aware of the best of world culture—and learn from the experience of the USSR—the basic cultural foundations must be indigenous. Current Chinese literature did not enjoy a high level of accomplishment, the essay complained, nor were the talents of writers coming forth. One reason was that writers were not

Plate 12. "Four Giants of World Culture," 1953

assiduously studying their own ancestral land's best literary heritage. Especially among the young writers and poets there prevailed a downright ignorance of the heritage. This often led to bad consequences, such as anti-patriotism, making light of the heritage, or a lack of information about key figures in the tradition—such as Ch'ü Yüan.

Evaluating Historical Individuals

In the PRC, Ch'ü Yüan lore developed within broader processes of rethinking the study and evaluation of all historical figures. Sometimes, as in the famous case of General Ts'ao Ts'ao (third century A.D.), this process resulted in reassessing and reversing long-standing judgments of the old regime.[4] In the case of Ch'ü Yüan, it brought subtle shifts of emphasis, or the development of themes first formulated during the New Culture era. Invariably, the process meant coming to terms self-consciously with the criteria for making historical judgments, with the fundamental problems of historical relativism, contextualism, and the relationship of historical forces to individual will.

The problem of selecting historical figures for study was often expressed as a need to find new heroes for China. In 1950, the literary critic Huang Yao-mien expressed concern that writers were still failing to recognize and celebrate "the new hero": the masses, and workers. He particularly objected to the "individualism and defeatism" which seemed to be current. Granting that some individuals could still be used for contemporary heroes, he preferred literature like Ch'ü Yüan's poem "The Spirits of the Fallen" (Kuo shang) which had an anonymous and collective hero—in this instance, valiant warriors who nobly defended their homeland. By 1953, during the height of the Ch'ü Yüan commemoration, Huang had come to approve of Ch'ü Yüan himself as a model poet and a worthy subject for historical study. He was a hero of sorts, if evaluated in his historical context. Huang said that Ch'ü Yüan could be used as a positive historical example inasmuch as his poetry was inspired by folk culture; moreover, his failure to appreciate and use the political

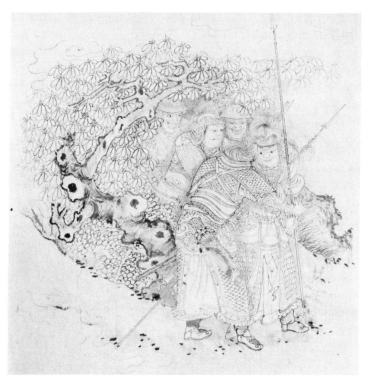

Plate 13. Fourteenth-century illustration of poem from the *Nine Songs*, "Spirits of the Fallen" (Kuo shang)

power of the masses could serve as a useful negative example and deserved further study and discussion.[5] Huang's casual judgments reflect the trends of the more extensive and rigorous "historical personages debate" of the early 1950s. Its guiding principle—"it is not heroes that create history, but history that creates heroes"—is borrowed from Soviet historiography.[6] Participants in the debate understood this to mean "that the laws by which society progressed cannot be produced or changed by an individual or group of individuals." There is no sage who is fated by heaven, nor any tiny minority who foreknow the future. In effect, a "hero" or "advanced person" is merely one "who completely understands the factors of social progress, and how and when to advance these factors. Only then can they accomplish great things in society." Analysis of such persons must be based on the historical factors of the subject's time and not the historians' own time. Additionally, historical individuals must not be judged solely on the basis of their personal lives. Rather, they must be placed in historical context, and their function or role in the class struggle of their time must be determined.[7] This highly relativistic mode of evaluation, which the Chinese have come to call "historicism" *(li-shih chu-i)*, was already a standard approach to Ch'ü Yüan by 1953.[8]

Broadly speaking, between 1953 and the eve of the Cultural Revolution more than a decade later, the historical understanding of Ch'ü Yüan was caught up in the polemical debates which resolved themselves into questions of individual creativity and class association. Where Ch'ü Yüan was concerned, the creativity problem was approached positively by the poet and critic Ho Ch'i-fang during the 1953 celebration:

> In short, Ch'ü Yüan's main contribution to literature lies in the fact that he was the first to write poetry expressive of the individuality of the author. He thus greatly extended the possibilities of poetic expression and opened a new stage in literary creation. Of course, in the *Odes*, which precedes Ch'ü Yüan, there are beautiful compositions, and we cannot say

that they are entirely without the stamp of an individual creator, but we are justified in saying that they do not contain poetry which, like that of Ch'ü Yüan, is clearly stamped with an individuality that is the very incarnation of one's ideas, one's life struggle for those ideals and the ardour of self-sacrifice, in short, one's whole personality. This is why we can say that poetry before Ch'ü Yüan was a collective folk product and that with Ch'ü Yüan we came to the creative activity of an individual author.[9]

This emphasis on Ch'ü Yüan's individualism was not only reversed within a few years, literary individuality itself became an embattled value. Thus, by 1957 Chou Yang (hatchet man of Party literary policy) declared pointedly to the Chinese Writers Union: "[In the 1920s] we revered Ibsen and cherished his famous dictum: The strongest man in the world is he who stands most alone. [But now] bourgeois individualism and proletarian collectivism are irreconcilable."[10]

In the second problem area, the relativism of the "historicist" approach was opposed by a "class" approach, which evaluated historical actors according to their *place* in the society and polity, and not according to what they did or thought. The former approach has been more resilient, and has provided greater opportunity to make positive evaluations. Thus, in an excellent 1958 study of the *Ch'u Tz'u*, admiration for Ch'ü Yüan was expressed while pegging him straightforwardly as both a member of the upper class and an official: "In the context of Ch'ü Yüan's society and era his political thought was advanced."[11]

Some historians took an intermediate position, as in this discussion of the patriotism of figures such as Ch'ü Yüan and Yüeh Fei:

Their patriotic thought is melded with their feudal political loyalty. . . . We must not confuse their patriotism with ours today, for what they loved was a feudal kingdom, while what we love is the socialist ancestral land. And moreover, we promote proletarian patriotism together with internationalism. Thus, although we recognize that their patriotic thought is valuable, that we must praise them for it, and that

historically it has its necessary place, we must not take them
as our models. The only models [we should have] are proletarian patriotic heroes.[12]

Finally, there was the extreme "class" approach which expressed itself most vividly in attacks on the notion that "in
feudal times" (read: ancien regime) there could be "incorrupt
officials" and "good officials." This was not possible, the at-
tackers claimed, because the interests of the ruling class and
the people were irreconcilable. Indeed, so-called good officials were merely creating a false consciousness in the people
by appearing to take their side; they masked the realities of
class conflict and thereby "prolonged the supremacy of the
feudal ruling class. A 'good official' was a contradiction in
terms."[13]

Under the pressures of the historical debates and particularly in response to the extremities of the "class interpretation," how was it possible to retain Ch'ü Yüan as a contemporary hero? Before 1949, the writings of Kuo Mo-jo and
Wen I-to had anticipated and tried to solve some of the interpretive problems growing out of Ch'ü Yüan's apparent
high-born background and his official position. During the
1950s, a number of similar strategies were followed by the
many writers, critics, and historians who seemed compelled
to make Ch'ü Yüan's image suitable for the new communist
society.

Populism and Popularization

The first strategy was to develop new arguments to demonstrate more fully the popular quality of Ch'ü Yüan's
thought and art. These arguments were then made accessible
to a mass audience. The initial claim was that Ch'ü Yüan
fought on behalf of the suffering masses and used his poetry
as a conduit for their grievances and aspirations. Then it was
pointed out that Ch'ü Yüan's success in the latter undertaking
was a function of his studies leading to the incorporation into
his poetry of folksong, popular legend, the colloquial language, and the Ch'u dialect.

The cornerstone of this populist argument was the claim that the poetry of the *Nine Songs* was written by Ch'ü Yüan, inspired by folk culture. Debate on this subject had begun in the early 1920s and was comparable to folklorists' arguments about the relation of the *Odes* to the oral tradition. Quite early, some scholars had rejected the idea that Ch'ü Yüan authored the *Nine Songs*, and attributed the work to an anonymous, folk religious tradition, long antedating him. Major *Ch'u Tz'u* scholars of the Republican period similarly concluded that it was written much earlier than Ch'ü Yüan's time and was, at most, an inspiration for the *Li Sao*. None denied that the *Nine Songs* had strong folk connections: by the late 1920s, it was being mined by folklorists and budding mythographers quite independently of any considerations of Ch'ü Yüan and the *Ch'u Tz'u*.[14] In the 1940s, the eminent *Ch'u Tz'u* scholar, Yu Kuo-en, concluded that the *Nine Songs* derived from southern Ch'u folk art and was written by an anonymous "people's poet," but certainly not by an "aristocratic poet" like Ch'ü Yüan. Yu determined that the *Nine Songs* in its present form in the *Ch'u Tz'u* already had evolved some distance away from an earlier and less formal folk song form.[15]

The position of scholars like Yu Kuo-en was flatly rejected after 1949. A strong consensus now supported the authenticity of Ch'ü Yüan's authorship of the *Nine Songs*. Widely read literary historians broadcast the theory that Ch'ü Yüan based the *Nine Songs* "on the religious songs of the people of Ch'u and intended them for ritual use."[16] Even the more cautious and independent *Ch'u Tz'u* scholars, and those intent on demonstrating Ch'ü Yüan's autonomy of vision and personal genius, nevertheless acceded to Ch'ü Yüan's authorship. However, they sometimes restated Wang I's classic theory which was unflattering to the folk. This depicted Ch'ü Yüan in exile, receiving inspiration for the *Nine Songs* from folk religion. Wang had said that when Ch'ü Yüan fortuitously came into contact with common art forms he was offended by their crudeness and vulgarity, and so hastened to secularize, polish, and raise them to a formal, sophisticated, and respectable level of art.[17] Although as late as the 1960s there were still prominent holdouts to the contention that Ch'ü Yüan directly authored the *Nine Songs*, their voices were muted by the appearance of nationally circulated literary histories and college textbooks which without hesitation presented the contention as a fact. Most of the space such texts devoted to Ch'ü Yüan was filled with examples of his poetry from the *Nine Songs*, specifically to illustrate his popular affinities.[18]

Ch'ü Yüan's intimacy with the people was regularly depicted as a function of his oppression by his government, his subsequent banishment, and his wandering through the countryside of Ch'u. Never was this inadvertent association with the folk depicted as a fall in status, as in the self-pitying, resentful exile literature of T'ang times. Very differently, this pat formula of Ch'ü Yüan biographies was clearly meant to point out a parallel with the purifying and democratizing "downward transfer" (*hsia-fang*) of intellectuals, cadres, or bureaucrats, as periodically carried out in the PRC to bring these elements of society into contact with the realities of the working masses of the countryside. It was said that Ch'ü Yüan's rustication developed within him a sympathy and love for the people. But it was not a one-way affair, for they likewise grew to love and revere him. Biographical accounts tell how "children rushed to hold his hand" wherever he went. In one prose portrait of Ch'ü Yüan's bucolic last days in the Ch'u (Hunan) countryside he is depicted as "always aiding the people," sharing his poetry with them, and weeping with them over the destruction of Ch'u by Ch'in.[19]

The sentiments of the people toward Ch'ü Yüan after his death were adduced as equally strong evidence of his true populist spirit. The festivals devoted to him over the millennia, such as the Tuan Wu and Dragon Boat, were universally attributed to the efforts of the people of Ch'u to commemorate him immediately after his drowning. These accounts of his relationship to the folk rituals completely ignore the body of earlier scholarship which established its complex evolution.[20] For example, one of the simply written popular biographies of Ch'ü Yüan, published in Hupei province in 1956, explained that to the people the death of this poet was like the death of a parent. It went on to date his drowning, the search for his corpse, and the use of the ceremonial *tsung-tzu* dumplings as May 5th, 278 B.C. Finally, it made a novel addition to the lore of Tuan Wu. It said that the exorcism of evil influences on this day (sweeping the home, hanging leaves of sweet flag on doors or lintels, etc.) is a custom derived from the Ch'u peoples' desire to be rid of the evil spirits of those traitors who were responsible for the death of Ch'ü Yüan.[21]

Although Peking promoted both Ch'ü Yüan and the festivals for purposes of "national culture," regional interests and pride were likewise stimulated. School children of Hunan and Hupei provinces were given special lessons in the meaning of the poet-patriot and his festivals, which apparently were a regular part of their lives after 1949. On occasion, however, local cultural organizations self-consciously expressed some ambivalence about such popular lore and customs. In 1958, for example, Hupei province published a child's book called *The Story of the Tuan Wu Festival.* It is rare for its special focus on the festival and Ch'ü Yüan's relation to it, leaving out any discussion of his literary role. The short text is remarkable for its caveats against perpetuating the "superstitions of former days" and at the same time suggesting, with a tolerant relativism, that such customs had been functional and made sense "in their times." It also deplored the exploitation of popular festivals like Tuan Wu by the "ruling classes and the Kuomintang" who took advantage of these occasions "to plunder the working people." At such times "they pressed for rents, claimed indemnities, demanded presents, and thereby blemished the festival day." Thus, a bit of local cultural pride was displayed for the lore of Ch'ü Yüan; but there was also some apprehensiveness about its "un-scientific" qualities, and the bad associations it brought to mind from the bad old days.[22]

Ch'ü Yüan was established as a populist and his lore was popularized through official sponsorship of the festivals as well as a broad range of literature, including textbooks, comic

A. Cover illustration of *Ch'ü Yüan*

子蘭等人曾勸懷王赴秦，既怕懷王回來問罪，又怕得罪秦國，屈原的話只引起他們的煩惱，因此不但不聽，而且不許他再到郢都。

B. Ch'ü Yüan is refused access to king

他掛念着郢都，因此到一處就敬幾天，遊歷一番，有一天，在一座古廟裏的牆壁上，看到了豐富的天地神靈和古代瑰麗的故事。

C. Temple iconography inspires Ch'ü Yüan to write *Heavenly Questions*

Plate 14. Scenes from Ch'ü Yüan comic book, 1955

然後，他恭恭敬敬的立在神位面前，吟着新做的一篇「國殤」詩。吟到沉痛地方，百姓都流下淚來，屈原也放聲痛哭。

D. Ch'ü Yüan reads "Spirits of the Fallen" to the masses

他用盡力量，跳進江裏，清澈的水波抱住了他。愛國詩人帶了楚國的乾淨土地，很快沉了下去。這天是五月五日。

E. Ch'ü Yüan commits suicide

百姓相信愛國詩人是不會死的，每年五月五日，他們搖着龍船，到處去尋覓詩人。他的愛國精神，已經在中國人民心中生了根。

F. The Dragon Boat Festival

books, and vernacular renditions of his poetry.[23] Equally important for popular tastes was official interest in Ch'ü Yüan monuments, another palpable expression of his importance. Since Han times, gazetteers and encyclopedias had created a lore about Ch'ü Yüan's birthplace. The earliest accounts located it in Lo-p'ing Li, in modern Szechwan, thirty-odd miles north of Tzu-kuei district in Hupei. Some accounts also said that in the same place there was a votive temple to his sister (Nü Hsü of the *Li Sao*).[24] Modern researchers claim to have confirmed this birthplace and thus assert another support to Ch'ü Yüan's historicity.[25] Today it is officially maintained that he was born near the Hsiling Gorge of the Yangtze at Tzu-kuei in Hupei province. Here a traditional-style memorial gate marks the entrance to an area of the village where a cottage like the one in which Ch'ü Yüan was born is on display. The village also features a Ch'ü Yüan temple and a fictive burial site.[26]

Burial sites, memorial mounds and markers have also been associated with Ch'ü Yüan since at least Sung times. In the eleventh century, Su Shih noted that while the real burial site was in Tzu-kuei, there were many fictive sites throughout the central Yangtze Valley so that people who wanted to pay their respects to Ch'ü Yüan would not have to travel inconveniently long distances.[27] Since 1949, it has been officially decided that Ch'ü Yüan is buried in a memorial mound in Hsiang-yin county, Hunan, near the spot where he drowned himself in the Milo River. A bit of local lore claims that this mound is actually one of twelve in the area. The others were decoys, raised by the people to confuse the "traitors of Ch'u and the troops of Ch'in who would have desecrated the corpse of Ch'ü Yüan."[28] The claim that the site actually contains his remains is at odds with the tradition of the Dragon Boat Festival which has it that his corpse was never recovered. But there is a local account that some time after his drowning, and the failure to recover his body, Ch'ü Yüan's sister was washing clothes in the Milo River. She saw a "spirit fish" bearing toward her his corpse, which she then buried.[29]

Near the official burial mound there is also a stele which

Map 2. Ch'ü Yüan Monuments and Other Sites Mentioned in the Text.

KEY

1. Tzu-kuei, Hupei Province: Birthplace and burial site memorials; Ch'ü Yüan Temple.

2. Chiang-ling, Hupei Province: Site of Ying, the ancient capital of the kingdom of Ch'u.

3. Ch'ang-te Hunan Province: Formerly Wu-ling. Site of temple and other memorials to Ch'ü Yüan reported by Liu Yü-hsi in the eighth century.

4. Wuchang (Wu-ch'ang), Hupei Province: Ch'ü Yüan Memorial Hall and statue in Eastlake Park, constructed or renovated around 1953.

5. Milo River, Hsiang-yin county, Hunan Province: 1953 official burial site and memorial stele marking site of Ch'ü Yüan's drowning suicide.

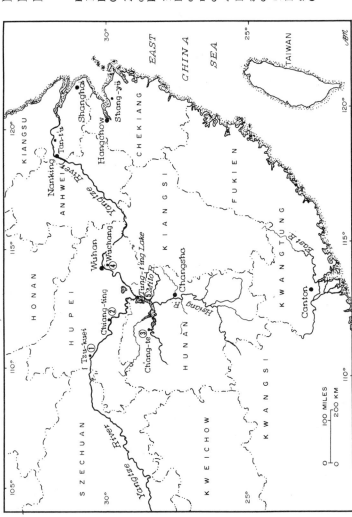

marks the spot where Ch'ü Yüan lived in banishment and
wrote the *Li Sao*. In the same neighborhood, there is an official Ch'ü Yüan temple. It is supposed to be on or near
the site where an ancient temple once stood to commemorate a visit from him during his banishment. This temple
was replaced by another built for him "by the people"
near Yü-hsün mountain on the Milo; but the Kuomintang purportedly destroyed it during the civil war. It was
restored, again "by the people," for the occasion of the 1953
commemoration.[30]

Sometime between 1950 and 1953, the most imposing of
all the Ch'ü Yüan monuments was erected. This is the Ch'ü
Yüan Memorial Hall located in the East Lake Park of
Wuchang city. It features a monumental outdoor statue of
the poet in an area where the annual chrysanthemum exhibition is held.[31] In 1975, a Western journalist described its
striking setting as he viewed it from atop the library of
Wuhan University: "You see Wuchang nestling on a dozen
peninsulas, like fingers pushing for respite into the water.
East Lake's thirty-five square kilometers lie on three sides, a
sapphire rug tossed between the university and the chimneys
of Green Mountain to the east. On one bank stands a
monument to Ch'ü Yüan."[32]

A Touch of Class

However successfully the lore of Ch'ü Yüan was popularized and however well he was depicted as a people's
poet and pro-people official, there still remained a series of
questions about the credibility of these characterizations for
an apparent upper-class aristocrat. Throughout the 1950s
there were prominent analyses of Ch'ü Yüan's behavior
which emphasized the severe limitations placed upon him by
his class origins. It was argued that his critical challenge of
the old society was made from within the aristocratic camp.
Although ultimately sympathetic with the people, he could
not operate from their ground. He hated the current regime
of Ch'u and predicted its demise, but he had to depend on
the king and was therefore helpless to save the people. His

class affiliation prevented him from melding with the people and fully understanding them: "He could have led the masses in a struggle, but coming from his class as he did, he could not conceive of himself doing this kind of thing."[33] And finally, though his banishment brought him closer to the people, his failure to appreciate their potential power and his continued separation from them "caused him unresolvable contradictions which were the source of his pessimism" and his lonely desolation.[34]

Those who wished to turn the argument about class limitations into a positive or less damaging statement relied repeatedly on Lenin's apologies for the contributions to populism and revolution made by Russian aristocrats and high-born intellectuals. One line was to compare Ch'ü Yüan to Herzen. If the latter was not a revolutionary in the 1840s, Lenin had said, it was not his *sin* but his *misfortune*. Likewise, if Ch'ü Yüan did not stand completely within the people's camp, this was a function of time and circumstances which he could not overcome. There was thus no question of willful resistance to popular revolution, and the pair could be praised for their efforts.[35]

Another favorite for comparison was Tolstoy. In the 1940s, his example had been used to suggest the "backwardness" of Ch'ü Yüan's thought; but in the fifties, the purpose was to explain that class origins could prevent populists from becoming true revolutionaries.[36] Most important for appraising Ch'ü Yüan was Lenin's description of the leadership sequence of the Russian revolutions. The initial contributions came from the aristocracy (such as the Decembrists), then from commoners who were closer to the people, and by 1905 from the people themselves. By the same token, an aristocrat like Ch'ü Yüan had his place in the revolutionary process and positive, if limited, contributions to make.[37]

The arguments of those who were concerned with Ch'ü Yüan's class limitations were overwhelmed by the dominant theme in the analysis of his social position. Somewhere between the extremes of Wen I-to's claim that Ch'ü Yüan was of slave origin and the "class limitations" position was the prevailing notion that Ch'ü Yüan's family and he himself were technically not aristocrats and, in effect, were commoners. It is an argument which Kuo Mo-jo and others revived in the early 1950s. At the commemoration, for example, Kuo had made a point of finding a new way to present this case:

> Although of noble background, Ch'ü Yüan says that he was poor. This was because, according to the law of Ch'u, feudal princes' fiefs were granted them only for two generations, after which they reverted to the crown. Hence, although he was related to the king of Ch'u, he was in actual fact just like any other common citizen of the realm. Because of this, he knew all the people's difficulties. . . . He seems to have had a special sympathy for the peasantry.[38]

Ch'ü Yüan was a "fallen aristocrat" in the sense that the entire aristocracy in his day was already fragmenting and being challenged by the monarchy. It was argued that although his power originated within the aristocracy, it was a residual power dependent on his intimacy with the court. Further, the king entrusted Ch'ü Yüan to draft a new set of laws inimical to the old aristocracy; and his poetry strongly reflected his anti-aristocratic promotion of government by the virtuous and talented.[39]

It was only rarely that all these arguments were dismissed as ill-founded and irrelevant, on the grounds of the class analysis ordinarily associated with Maoism. The critical issue here was the relationship of class origins to revolutionary consciousness or to "thought" (szu-hsiang). In explicit opposition to rigid class analysis, it was claimed that there is no predictable, simple, one-to-one relationship between thought (read: political values, art, etc.) and class origins or social position. Thus, Ch'ü Yüan most assuredly could have felt a high degree of sympathy for the people even as an actual member of the aristocracy. Additionally, his high social and political positions should not automatically be assessed as a liability to this sympathy, but on the contrary, they should be understood as valuable strategic means for him to implement his advanced political ideals and to help the people of his country.[40]

Realism and Romanticism

However diversely Ch'ü Yüan's class status might be viewed, there was agreement on the characterization of his art. If he was considered a populist, then it was asked how his art both responded to and served the common people (that is, how did it follow the "mass line")? How did it have revolutionary force? If he were a representative of another class, such as the new landlords, it still remained important to know how his poetry was both a reflection of their lives and an impulse to progressive action. The fullest evaluations of Ch'ü Yüan's art claimed that it carried out these dual functions because it was of a "revolutionary romantic" quality. It combined a realistic and probing portrayal of contemporary social problems with personal, imaginative, and visionary qualities that were revolutionary in implication. Because of this, his art was considered in effect to be an ancestor of and model for the socialist realism in China of the 1950s.

The idea of Ch'ü Yüan's "revolutionary romanticism" began to be formulated in Kuo Mo-jo's writings of the 1930s, when he claimed that his hero had a dual intellectual heritage of northern rationalism and southern romanticism. This characterization was standard in the Ch'ü Yüan lore of the 1950s. It took on special importance in 1958 when the Great Leap Forward was launched and "revolutionary romanticism" was emphasized as an orientation that was essential to the progress of the Chinese communist revolution. Ch'ü Yüan became not only the outstanding exemplar for the orientation but, because of his place at the beginning of Chinese literary history, he was considered to be the very source of China's revolutionary romantic tradition. In contrast to interpretations informed by the "historicist" and "class" positions, characteristic literature of the Great Leap years emphasized the force of human will instead of the constraints of history. Imagination and creativity were stressed in preference to the limitations of time, context, or even class. Once again, the Promethean image of Ch'ü Yüan which had been played down during the early 1950s was revived, if only briefly. As the chains of class and history fell from him, he was never closer to becoming a mythical alter ego for Mao Tse-tung.

To the dismay of the Chinese, foreign Marxist critics linked the emphasis on revolutionary romanticism to the "political" or "psychological" attitudes that made the Chinese stress the uninterrupted character of their revolution.[41] In 1960, CCP spokesmen explicitly said that Mao had put forward the theory of the combination of revolutionary realism and romanticism "on the basis of the Marxist idea of combining the theory of the uninterrupted revolution with the theory of the development of the revolution by stages."[42] But foreign critics felt that the more compelling sources of revolutionary romanticism were the "economic subjectivism and the voluntarism which were the result of the socially active factor of the [Maoist] personality cult."[43] One Western observer suggests that revolutionary romanticism was "probably prompted by a wish to stress the continuity of Chinese literary history and to outline a literary policy which at least in emphasis was different from the Soviet program."[44] Soviet literary policy, it is suggested, did provide a precedent for the combination of realism and revolutionary romanticism in order to "represent a reality not in stasis but in motion." But this was merely another way of formulating "socialist realism," and the Chinese in their emphasis on romanticism went far beyond the Soviet intent.[45]

This emphasis was regularly expressed through the figure of Ch'ü Yüan. For example, there is the 1958 *Hung Ch'i* (Red flag) policy statement on the subject:

> One of the greatest poets in the history of our nation, Ch'ü Yüan, was a very great romantic, while among later poets it was Li T'ai-po who achieved remarkable results as a romantic. In their works both show close relations to folk literature. When more than a thousand years ago [a famous critic] commented on Ch'ü Yüan's style by saying that a true poet "dips into the marvelous without losing the truth and appreciates the fanciful without sacrificing substance," it was, one could say, the very first simple idea of the combination of

fantasy [*huan-hsiang*] and reality [*chen-shih*] in the literature in our country.[46]

Later that year, it was Kuo Mo-jo who made the main policy statement.[47] Although his essay called for the synthesis of revolutionary realism and revolutionary romanticism into socialist realism, he argued that the Chinese synthesis would be different from (read: better than) Soviet socialist realism, because, *inter alia*, "Chinese romanticism never lost its revolutionary character, . . . Chinese realism remained uncontaminated by the decadent influence of the West, and early acquired a revolutionary soul." These facts were demonstrated earlier, he added, by Mao's 1942 *Talks at the Yenan Forum on Art and Literature.*

The theoretical heart of Kuo's essay was the idea that "truly great writers invariably make a synthesis based on life itself, in order to create typical characters in typical circumstances; and since this creative process involves fantasy, we should also be justified in calling it romantic." He then turned to Ch'ü Yüan with gusto:

> Our great ancient poet, Ch'ü Yüan, looks like a romantic. His *Li Sao, Nine Songs*, [etc.] draw heavily on the supernatural. He speaks of riding on the clouds, the rainbow, the dragon and the phoenix, of urging on the sun and moon, the wind and thunder, and wandering ceaselessly through the sky. He ascends to Paradise, returns to remote antiquity, soars to the roof of the world, or descends to the bottom of Tung-t'ing Lake. He caresses the comet in outer space, and talks of love to goddesses in the clouds. . . . Surely here we have an out-and-out romantic. But Ch'ü Yüan makes no attempt to escape from reality in order to satisfy his personal desires, or to create art for art's sake. He seeks an ideal and an ideal ruler in order to save his country and its people and help to unify the China of his day. He sets out from completely realistic premises and finally returns to reality. Moreover he sets no store by his own life and death. He takes an interest in everything under the sun. Some of the questions about the universe he poses in the *Heavenly Questions* have not been answered to this day. We cannot, therefore, but admit that at the same time he is a great realist.[48]

The bulk of Kuo's essay, we should note, was devoted to demonstrating that Mao's recently published nineteen poems in classical style were "now generally agreed to be our finest examples of a synthesis of revolutionary realism and romanticism." For the remainder of the Great Leap years, Ch'ü Yüan's prestige continued to lend authority to policy statements on the Chinese version of socialist realism. In turn, these statements augmented the place of Ch'ü Yüan in the Chinese literary tradition, whatever questions might be raised about his class background. In 1960, party policy again relied on his image to describe to the Third Congress of Chinese Literature and Artistic Workers the correct "Path of Socialist Literature and Art in China."[49] This policy statement was also structured by the issue of integrating romanticism and realism. It alluded, as a matter of course, to the *Li Sao* and how it showed Ch'ü Yüan's "concern for his country, his love for the people, his deep hatred for evil, and his sublime, magnificent vision which combined to make it an immortal work."[50] Then, remarkably, Ch'ü Yüan's contributions were set in relief by listing native and foreign literary artists and works making similar contributions. The drama of Kuan Han-ch'ing and the novel *Water Margin* spoke to the brotherhood of man. Dante's *Divine Comedy*, many of Shakespeare's plays, Goethe's *Faust* "all show a wonderful combination of fantasy and reality." Some of the work of Gorky and Lu Hsün show "sober attitudes towards reality and critical spirit as well as the fervent aspirations of a revolutionary idealist." The coda of the statement once again placed Ch'ü Yüan in, indeed at the head of, a proud national tradition:

> We are living in a country with an ancient cultural tradition. The nation that has produced Ch'ü Yüan, Ssu-ma Ch'ien, Tu Fu, Kuan Han-ch'ing, Ts'ao Hsüeh-ch'in, and Lu Hsün.[51]

In addition to these rather histrionic policy statements, the issue of realism and romanticism was used to explore "the Ch'ü Yüan problem" in a number of ways. Feng Hsüeh-feng, a leading literary critic before his 1957 purge in the aftermath of the Hundred Flowers campaign, emphasized the realist facet in order to elucidate the problematic relation of ruling class poets and popular sentiment. He wrote that the principle of realism (*hsien-shih*) in literature makes it possible (and even inevitable, he implied) that writers and poets of ruling class affiliation will reflect contradictions in their own society. Therefore, if they are realists, even though they employ ruling class forms and values, they will also show contradictions between the oppressed and the ruling class, and they will show the "weak, rotten, oppressive" elements of the upper class and the feelings which the people have about them. Regarding Ch'ü Yüan in particular, Feng wrote:

> Although his thought and principles were from the orthodox tradition of feudalism, his realistic attitude acted as a kind of combative [force]. The wants of the contemporary masses were included within his desire to implement humane government [*jen cheng*], within his dissatisfaction with the king of Ch'u, and within his personal attitude of noncompliance. Therefore his thought and sentiment were in opposition to the purposes of the king of Ch'u and the ruling circle, and they contained revolutionary elements.[52]

Feng applauded poets like Ch'ü Yüan for not idealizing the old regime and not prettying it up, for being the kind of artist who turned his dissatisfaction into an exposé of the system and a revelation of the people's problems, and hence aided historical progress.[53]

Another tack was the one pursued by Ho Ch'i-fang. Like Feng Hsüeh-feng, he emphasized Ch'ü Yüan's works as "masterpieces of realism" which expressed the people's spirit. But he was concerned with the relationship of their strong romantic coloration to their realism and so he drew upon a formulation made by Gorky which appeared repeatedly in the literary debates of the 1950s:

> As Gorky has well said, a distinction should be made between negative and positive romanticism. Negative romanticism is unrealistic because it uses imagination, allegory, and myth to distort and falsify reality, thus leading people to flee from real-

ity or to compromise with its irrational aspects. Positive
romanticism, although it is also coloured with imagination,
ardent language, and fantasy, is fundamentally a reflection of
reality. It leads people to a correct understanding of reality or
inspires them to struggle against the irrational phenomena of
reality. Thus the fundamental spirit of positive romanticism is
realistic.[54]

Ho Ch'i-fang of course concluded that Ch'ü Yüan's poetry
was a form of "positive romanticism."

Gorky's positive and negative distinction for romanticism
prevailed during the evaluations of Ch'ü Yüan's art during the
1950s; but it was felt by many critics that details and refine-
ments were needed to understand more fully the nature (positive or negative) of romanticism's qualities. Some tried to iso-
late the special literary devices which were part of the romantic
approach, such as simile, the use of the pathetic fallacy, myth
and legend. Some argued that the use of shaman motifs was a
special quality of the romanticism of the Li Sao.[55]

It was only rarely however that the delicate subject of Ch'ü
Yüan's individualism was acknowledged to be the essence of
his romanticism. An outstanding 1958 commentary on the
Ch'u Tz'u remains the best formulated statement of this position. It was not an easy one to maintain during the Great
Leap years when Kuo Mo-jo, on one hand, praised the personal artistic creations of Mao Tse-tung, and on the other,
encouraged mass, collective, and untutored literature. The
commentary took the position that the presence of an individual personality in the Li Sao and other poems was not an
issue since that was merely a function of the creative process
itself. Rather, the problem was the special quality of the
poetry which resulted from contexts—such as southern
culture—in which the personality found itself. However, "the
means whereby a great author creates a great work resides not
only in the mutual interaction of thought and feeling with the
flesh and blood of the people and the ancestral land, but also
there must be the appropriate literary training and artistic talent." The Ch'u Tz'u poetry written or inspired by Ch'ü Yüan
is realistic where it mirrors the objective situation of the folk;

but it goes beyond this and is romantic where it uses simile and metaphor. It is realistic where it portrays the corruption of the aristocracy, but it carries this forward to romanticism and is "more important where it takes individual aspirations and puts them in the forefront." The commentary stressed that it is not the basic realities of life that are most essential here, but the poet's emotional reactions to and feelings about these things.[56] This was a conception of romanticism which Kuo Mo-jo would certainly have recognized as his own from the 1920s. But in the late 1950s, discussions of romanticism virtually avoided these questions of personal emotions and feelings and emphasized instead the conformity of artistic vision to the "objective world."

It is appropriate then that we conclude this section with a brief consideration of how the poem *Heavenly Questions* was increasingly used as evidence that Ch'ü Yüan was ultimately a "realist" in spite of his romantic style. Generally, the strategy was to take the list of questions which comprise the poem ("What manner of things are the darkness and light?" "When P'ing summons up the rain, how does he make it come?" "When the lords of the centre ruled together, why was the king angry?". . . .) and use them for evidence that Ch'ü Yüan employed legend, myth and fantasies only as literary devices to accomplish his fundamentally realistic and iconoclastic purposes.

The authenticity of Ch'ü Yüan's authorship of the *Questions* had been hotly debated throughout the Republican period. Challenges were made specifically of Wang I's ancient explanations of their origins. He had said that Ch'ü Yüan, in banishment and standing before a state temple, was inspired by the iconographic wall decor depicting all manner of cosmology, legends, and so on, which he recreated in his poetry. Few modern critics who challenged this explanation of the *Questions* did so to discredit the authorship of Ch'ü Yüan. Instead, the main reason for discrediting Wang I on this point was to strengthen the credibility of the *Questions* as a legitimate part of the Ch'ü Yüan corpus.[57] In the PRC, there were still some who publicly doubted Ch'ü Yüan's au-

Plates 15 and 16. Seventeenth-century illustrations of the *Heavenly Questions*

15. "When Yi shot down the suns, why did the ravens shed their feathers?"

16. "What manner of things are the darkness and light? . . . How does Heaven co-ordinate its motions? . . . What is the peculiar virtue of the moon?"

thorship of the *Questions*, but they were very much in the minority of published opinion.[58] By the late 1950s, the *Questions* were regularly indicated to be his creation and there was hardly a trace of controversy left. Further, the *Questions* had become the most favored work of Ch'ü Yüan to receive scholarly attention.

What do the *Questions* tell us about Ch'ü Yüan? Kuo Mo-jo's answer was this:

> Although he accepted popular beliefs, Ch'ü Yüan did not actually believe in spirits. He doubted or even hated what was felt to be supernatural. In the *Heavenly Questions*, the questions [he asks] prove that he did not always weave a poetic web of fantasy over the natural universe, but sometimes probed into truth like a scientist.[59]

In another statement, Kuo again conjured the poet into the scientist when he wrote that the most noteworthy questions in the *Heavenly Questions* are those about the structure of the universe. These are very rational and reveal Ch'ü Yüan's concern with nature. "Chinese science," Kuo reminded the reader, "had in Ch'ü Yüan's time reached great heights."[60]

After Kuo's association of the *Questions* with science, some writers chose to speak of Ch'ü Yüan as a "pioneer of materialism," a precursor of the great skeptic Wang Ch'ung (A.D. 27–100).[61] Others, borrowing the terminology of the New Culture iconoclasts, depicted Ch'ü Yüan of the *Questions* as a true "antiquity doubter."[62] And in the post-Cultural Revolution years, Ch'ü Yüan became a materialist pure and simple. His romantic qualities were ignored altogether and he was grouped with other great ancient "materialists" such as Han Fei and Hsün-tzu. The *Questions* were now adduced not only as the foremost expression of his materialism, but they had come to replace the *Li Sao* as the foremost expression of the man.[63]

From Confucianist to Legalist

The *Heavenly Questions* was also presented as evidence of Ch'ü Yüan's affiliations with Legalism, the statist political philosophy which guided the unification of China under the Ch'in kingdom in the third century B.C. Conventionally, it was interpreted as the major rival of the Confucian schools. For those shaping the modern Ch'ü Yüan lore, it was important to determine which, if any, of the ancient Hundred Schools of philosophy most informed his thought. The Warring States period of antiquity in which these schools flourished and competed with one another remained of critical importance to the reevaluation of Chinese history by the moderns. So it was not enough to establish Ch'ü Yüan's class, his popular sympathy, and the nature of his art. These could not logically be judged acceptable by Chinese Marxist standards if Ch'ü Yüan remained tainted by an association with the wrong philosophic tradition. The literature on this aspect of Ch'ü Yüan's biography comprised a full spectrum of opinion. It ranged from a refusal to place him in any school, to an eclectic designation, to the majority opinion (the best formulated and by far the most detailed) that he was in the Legalist tradition. The gradual association of Ch'ü Yüan with the Legalists paralleled a general trend in the PRC to transvalue the Legalists and ultimately to assign them the role of the most progressive forces of antiquity.[64]

The problem of making Ch'ü Yüan into a Legalist was doubly complicated. On one hand, since the days of Wang I in the Han dynasty a ponderous tradition of criticism had created an interpretation of the *Ch'u Tz'u* that placed it within a "Confucian" lineage. On the other, during the Republican period when all aspects of the Confucian philosophic heritage were targets of iconoclasts, Kuo Mo-jo's formidable studies had concluded that ancient Confucianism was revolutionary (hence respectable) and that Ch'ü Yüan's thought was Confucian (hence revolutionary).[65] It was not until the late 1940s that important *Ch'u Tz'u* scholars began to challenge Kuo Mo-jo directly on this point. It was argued that, at best, Ch'ü Yüan's ideas had some resonance with later Confucians, like Mencius; but too much of his poetry and life were incompatible with earlier Confucians. He lacked their conservatism; he promoted progressive legal reforms, like the early

Ch'in political philosophers; and his suicide violated Confucian values.[66]

During the 1953 commemoration, Kuo Mo-jo showed no sign of changing his position, and only suggested that Ch'ü Yüan's interest in the unification of China reflected his respect for and influence by the Legalists.[67] Kuo's original position, however, was restated and elaborated at length by scholars who argued for the Confucian essence of Ch'ü Yüan's political thought on the basis of its anti-aristocratic values, and its promotion of government by the talented as sanctioned by the model of an ancient Golden Age.[68]

More common than this picture of Ch'ü Yüan was one that attempted to depict him as a "self-made and unique" thinker who belonged to no school but showed similarities with many, simply because they all were responding to the same social environment. This kind of argument regularly cited the *Heavenly Questions* as evidence that Ch'ü Yüan was basically a challenger to what in his day could be considered Confucian thought; however, the argument noted, it was not necessary to conclude that he was therefore a Legalist.[69] Some writers explored the possibility of linking Ch'ü Yüan with the proto-Legalist tradition of reform. Here, his work for the king of Ch'u was compared to the abortive reforms of the famous Shang Yang (c. 390–338 B.C.) and the lesser known Wu Ch'i (fourth century B.C.) of Ch'u. It was correctly pointed out by others that there are no details at all about Ch'ü Yüan's reforms, and thus no way to evaluate the reality of this linkage.[70] It was further pointed out that the Legalist anti-historical orientation was strongly at odds with Ch'ü Yüan's thought where it clearly relied on precedent and examples of the ancient sages.[71]

Ch'u Tz'u scholarship by the late 1950s had begun to draw some conclusions about the Ch'u polity which are still generally accepted, in and out of China. Prototypical changes in the political economy, considered to be the substance of Legalist policy, were very early (perhaps first) developed in the kingdom of Ch'u (for example, the *hsien* geopolitical unit and bureaucratization).[72] The effect of this scholarly activity was to give heart to those who argued for the incorporation of Ch'ü Yüan into the Legalist tradition of Shang Yang, thereby making him less a maverick and more a "transmitter." Their argument had to confront a number of anomalies, such as Ch'ü Yüan's very hard-to-place loyalty to his kingdom. As critics had pointed out decades earlier, that kind of loyalty seemed to be anachronistic for the fourth century B.C. Discussion in the People's Republic further admitted that it was not sanctioned in either Confucian or Legalist schools. No one said it, but there could be only one conclusion: Ch'ü Yüan must have invented this new kind of loyalty. Polemicists were satisfied, however, simply to say he was "unique" in this behavior, and leave it at that.

In this new interpretation of Ch'ü Yüan's political strife, his loyalty and conflict with the Ch'u traitors had become a negligible factor. The heart of his problem was now depicted as the battle of the old feudal nobility against Ch'ü Yüan's new legal code, which was aimed at severely restricting their power. This explanation did away with the notion that his political behavior could be explained by his membership in a dissolving aristocracy, for that group was considered to have been still so active and prominent that new laws were needed to control it. Furthermore, this approach asked that Ch'ü Yüan's troubles with the great aristocratic families be understood as more than just an expression of their envy of his powerful position; they were afraid of the damage his new legal code would do to them.[73]

By the end of the 1950s, some rather imposing polemics had painstakingly stripped away all association of Ch'ü Yüan with Confucianism and placed him squarely at the early stages of the Legalist tradition. Sometimes this meant setting Ch'ü Yüan against himself by arguing that Confucian-like beliefs which he expressed in the *Li Sao* were repudiated by the "materialist" skepticism which he later expressed in the *Heavenly Questions*. On other occasions it meant adducing the "Contre Sao" Confucian bias against Ch'ü Yüan as further evidence that he was no Confucian. He was now the aggressive reformer guided by the Legalist motto of "wealth and power" for the kingdom, and using as his instrument the politics of law (*fa-chih*) and not the Confucian politics of moral suasion (*hsin-chih*).[74]

Ch'ü Yüan vs. The Ch'in

In the light of this compulsion to remake Ch'ü Yüan into a Legalist, there is a detail in Ch'ü Yüan's classical biography which has been the source of embarrassment and confused apology. In the *Historical Records* account, Ch'ü Yüan's self-destruction was ultimately brought about by his opposition to the state of Ch'in. But conventionally, Ch'in has been considered to be the ultimate practitioner of the Legalist philosophy. During the 1950s it had also become routine to consider Ch'in as the leader of the "progressive tendencies of its age." In the *Historical Records*, Ch'ü Yüan suffered initial banishment because he was slandered by high officials at court who envied his power and his proximity to the king. Additionally, and quite independent of this, the biography also tells us about his consideration of whether Ch'u should ally itself with the state of Ch'in in the interstate struggle for hegemony. Ch'ü Yüan was depicted as uncompromisingly opposed to Ch'in and the proffered alliance. Traitorous courtiers and villainous spies from Ch'in countered Ch'ü Yüan's policy. They led his king, a victim of greed and stupidity, to his death while a humiliated prisoner in Ch'in; and soon they led the entire state of Ch'u to absorption into the Ch'in hegemony. Ch'ü Yüan killed himself, in many versions of his biography, after hearing the news that Ying, the capital city of Ch'u, had fallen under the sword of the advancing Ch'in armies, an event supposedly recorded in the *Ch'u Tz'u* poem "Lament for Ying" (Ai Ying). The problem in the PRC, then, was how to reconcile Ch'ü Yüan's new image as a Legalist, in the forefront of the "progressive tendencies" of history, with this dramatic stance against Ch'in.

First, some observations on the image of Ch'in. Conventional historiography of the old regime depicted the Ch'in as an archetype of despotism and the arbitrary use of power (especially its first emperor, Ch'in Shih Huang-ti, 221–209

B.C.). Ch'in became notorious for the excesses it employed to achieve unification and centralization of the states, like Ch'u, still independent in the fourth to third century B.C. Its methods were heavy-handed, its demands on mass labor oppressive, its treatment of ideological adversaries murderous and destructive (the infamous "burying of scholars and burning of books"). In the *Historical Records*, Ch'ü Yüan's oft-quoted evaluation of the Ch'in was simple and clear-cut: "They are a nation of tigers and wolves and cannot be trusted." The First Emperor, himself, was seen as an embodiment of the Ch'in despotism, and became a political bogeyman with a popular lore to match. For example, as recently as the early twentieth century the "people living in the immediate vicinity of [the First Emperor's tomb, in northwest China] still used his name to frighten their children into good behavior, and as a term of abuse in scoldings and quarrels."[75]

The bad image of the Ch'in was nurtured in the earlier PRC lore of Ch'ü Yüan, even by writers who cannot have been unaware of the problem of interpretation this created. In Kuo Mo-jo's well-circulated history of the age of slavery, the Ch'in are depicted as just one more of the uncivilized northern barbarians who regularly invaded and pillaged China.[76] In popular narratives of Ch'ü Yüan's life, the ruthlessness of Ch'in has been a favorite subject and much attention has been lavished on how Ch'in killed tens of thousands of ordinary innocent people during its invasion of Ch'u.[77] Typical is a pivotal scene in a 1957 dramatic narrative "The Milo River." It shows Ch'ü Yüan in banishment among the common people, receiving news from a band of maimed warriors, returned from the front where Ch'in decimates Ch'u. They tell of the failure to defend the capital of Ch'u and, in counterpoint to the wails of the villagers and Ch'ü Yüan's weeping, they recount how murderous and destructive Ch'in has been, killing indiscriminately old and young, men and women.[78]

It was thus an anti-popular image of Ch'in that was exploited in this kind of literature. No interest was displayed in Ch'in, the "burier of scholars and burner of books." Ch'in was used instead as a vague and nightmarish symbol for an outside enemy (Japan? the United States?), the galvanizer of patriotic sentiment. Closely related to this sentiment, but more pretentious, was that element in the modern Ch'ü Yüan lore which suggested that the example of his life and/or the inspiration of his poetry led to the revolt in 207 B.C. against Ch'in and the First Emperor. This in turn was supposed to have provoked universal rebellion throughout China and eventually the overthrow of the Ch'in.[79]

In sum, the lore of Ch'ü Yüan, from the early fifties through the Cultural Revolution, created a double image of the Ch'in. There was the positive one: the instrumentality of progressive historical forces moving toward unification and a non-aristocratic polity. Rarely was this explained in detail. From this point of view, the pro- and anti-Ch'in alliances had the same purposes: to destroy the old aristocracy and to unite all of China. Ch'ü Yüan in this context only hated Ch'in because he loved Ch'u, which he believed was just as capable of carrying out the unification. The other, negative image of Ch'in was based on the traditional criticism distinguishing ends and means. Ch'in's goals were approved because they were potentially beneficial to the common people; but Ch'in accomplished these with brutal conquest, harsh laws and punishments, and severe demands on the people's labor. When Ch'ü Yüan opposed Ch'in on these grounds, he was "correct and progressive."[80]

Conclusion: History, Will, and General Will

By the mid-1960s, on the eve of the Cultural Revolution, Ch'ü Yüan's appearance in published materials available to the West had dwindled to occasional scholarly pieces on the *Ch'u Tz'u* and chapters in literary histories. The image of Ch'ü Yüan which prevailed was that of the "progressive" Legalist statesman, the "realist" spokesman for the new landlord class in their war against the old slave-owning aristocracy. The emphasis was decidedly on that aspect of the lore which shows Ch'ü Yüan in office, practicing the art of politics, promulgating laws and statutes. Obscured is Ch'ü Yüan in exile, playing the role of poet, performing artistic political acts. In part, this emphasis reflects reactions to the "excesses" of revolutionary romanticism during the Great Leap Forward. What had Ch'ü Yüan come to represent? How was his image used a decade and more after his grand commemoration in 1953? One answer is suggested by the famous Wu Han affair in the early 1960s that heralded the Cultural Revolution. An academic historian and vice-mayor of Peking, Wu Han had been a long-time critic of the Communist Party's management of China, particularly its control of intellectual life—its doctrinaire narrowness and sometimes oppressiveness. He came into open conflict with the regime in 1961, when he made public a historical drama he had written about the figure Hai Jui, an important official of the Ming imperial court. Hai Jui was celebrated by Wu Han for criticizing his emperor at the cost of his own life when he disagreed with him on public matters. In this thinly disguised commentary on contemporary politics, Wu Han placed "explicit stress on the value of personal integrity and the courage to act on one's own convictions. Wu wrote that although Hai Jui lived in such a difficult time, he 'still steadfastly clung to his own belief, and without bending or giving in struggled on until he died.'"[81] These of course were some of the main traits for which Ch'ü Yüan was celebrated right into the twentieth century. But Ch'ü Yüan is never mentioned.

From the New Culture period, the nature of Ch'ü Yüan's steadfastness and struggle was shifted gradually from a confrontation with the embodiments of political authority to a more generalized confrontation with society's restrictions on personal autonomy and free expression. Typically, he was depicted as clashing with inherited art forms of the old society. During the Anti-Japanese War years and in the early People's Republic, his lore depicts the object of his conflict to be "national" enemies and class enemies. But just a decade after the great Ch'ü Yüan commemoration, it would have been difficult to invoke Ch'ü Yüan for Wu Han's purposes of criticizing party and state, for Ch'ü Yüan was no longer conspicuous as a symbol of "resistance" or individualistic revolt. He was now a personification of class revolution within the rather strict confines of particular historical contexts. Additionally, for a critic like Wu Han, Ch'ü Yüan lore may well have become too closely associated with the regime he wished to criticize; and perhaps the lore had by the mid-sixties become too routinized, its political cutting edge blunted by the historiographic niceties of Chinese Marxism.

In the post-Cultural Revolution years, Ch'ü Yüan has appeared only briefly. As an exemplar for modern leadership he would seem to have been set aside in favor of the new kinds of proletarian heroes called for in the 1950s and spawned in numbers by the Cultural Revolution.[82] The historicist emphases of 1970s historiography suggest that all figures from the past, no matter how highly evaluated as "progressives," are to be held at arm's length and clearly marked as historical actors, relevant for their time at best, but not desirable or acceptable as models for today.[83]

The reappearance in the early 1970s of national publications concerned with Chinese history had the anti-Confucius, anti-Lin Piao campaign for its context. The campaign simultaneously promoted the progressiveness of Ch'ü Yüan's old nemesis, the Ch'in state, and the Legalist political economy. The reign of the First Emperor of Ch'in was considered to be the critical time for the implementation of Legalism and the class war between the ruling groups representative of the old (slave owning) and new (landlord feudal) stages of history. His regime was considered to be the force that realized the first stages of the anti-aristocratic, pro-landlord values, and actually fought the old aristocracy on behalf of the new landlord class. Following generally the historicist mode of analysis, and guided by Mao's dictate that "in their own time, each ruling class was revolutionary," the reevaluation of the First Emperor and Legalism reversed many of the traditional clichés and stereotypes.

The most recent understanding of Ch'ü Yüan is bound up with the appraisal of the First Emperor and his regime. Characterizations of the First Emperor now make it clear that to receive the appraisal of "progressive" does not mean that a historical figure also warrants the rank of hero, or is worthy of contemporary emulation. The First Emperor is depicted during the 1970s with his faults quite conspicuous, and on the whole is not a very attractive figure for all his progressive contributions. Indeed, he is shown to have been fatally flawed through his failure to consolidate his political power and fully purge his class enemies. (Here were lessons for the CCP, which seemed to be living in constant dread of "restoration" of the power of contemporary class enemies.) Even in his most flattering portraits during the 1970s, the First Emperor appears at best merely a vehicle of progress, the rather wooden instrument of mechanical historical forces.[84]

The recent fate of Ch'ü Yüan is parallel to that of the First Emperor. Building on the legacy of the earlier PRC lore, he is depicted unequivocally as a staunch Legalist with no Confucian connections. (Confucianism, because of new historical periodization, was gerrymandered into the slave stage of history, and Confucius was considered a "restorationist" apologist for slavery.[85]) His anti-Ch'in diplomacy was glossed over as an expression of his patriotism, and as a kind of loyalty which was vestigial of his high-class origins and connections with the old order. Within his state of Ch'u, those who opposed him are said to have done so because they objected to his reforms, and no mention is made of his rivals who chose to support the Ch'in alliance. His enemies were "anti-people," "anti-revolutionary," and "anti-true reforms." They are compared to Tz'u Hsi, the Manchu Empress Dowager who died in 1908, to Yüan Shih-k'ai (d. 1916), the general who served the Manchus and then became the first president of the Republic, and to Lin Piao himself. Ch'ü Yüan was now considered to be a spokesman solely for the new landlord class, and not at all connected with the common people. Like the First Emperor, he was absorbed into the great forces of history and he was explicitly denied the characterization of hero or genius. Coolly, he is described as "a great personage who at that time led the epoch's progressive wave," and as one who "suited the needs of historical progress."[86]

A diffuse notion of "general will" has been central to Ch'ü

Yüan's role in the PRC from the beginning, and what we see in the 1970s is an expression of the reappraisal of that notion. The most recent portrayal of Ch'ü Yüan may appear to be a reversal or repudiation of the lore of the 1950s, especially where it denies Ch'ü Yüan the glorious role of people's poet. But the post-Cultural Revolution historiography is really aiming at a reappraisal of the historiographic premises of the lore rather than of the lore itself. The issue has been whose "will" or "consciousness" Ch'ü Yüan (or the First Emperor) has been expressing. To be truly "progressive," to be considered a true leader of revolution and participant in the advance of Chinese history from one of its stages to another, figures like Ch'ü Yüan must "reflect" or speak for representatives of the most advanced stage of history, that is, for the ruling class of the newest or forthcoming stage. To speak on behalf of the common masses in Ch'ü Yüan's time is not to speak for the most progressive forces, since (according to this historicist approach) the masses only began to develop and represent an advanced revolutionary consciousness in modern times and under socialism.[87]

The apparent abrupt reevaluation of Ch'ü Yüan in the 1970s is actually a clear expression of a political and historical position argued throughout the PRC years. Its central questions are these: Which social group(s) or class(es) are the revolutionary forces at a given stage of history? And which leaders will embody, reflect, build on those forces? When Ch'ü Yüan was considered a people's poet, he was personifying an idea that the Chinese masses are somehow the ultimate source of revolutionary momentum at all times in history. Somehow, no matter what the mode of production or stage of history according to Marxist categories, the masses have a revolutionary consciousness and will that transcends historical specifics. This view was consonant with that Promethean picture of Ch'ü Yüan and that mad ardour which were so prominent during the late 1950s.

However, if Marxist historiography is to be applied seriously to China—the historicists argued—then surely it must be conceded that the revolutionary consciousness of the masses is secondary to that of the dominant class of each epoch preceding the socialist revolution. If Ch'ü Yüan lived during the critical transition years between the slave and feudal stages of Chinese history, the main conflict or contradiction would therefore be between the old, slave-owning aristocracy and the new, and hence progressive, landowning class.[88] In this scheme, if Ch'ü Yüan is to be considered in the front ranks of progress, his life work has to be seen as an embodiment of this latter class. His relationship to the common folk thus becomes of secondary importance.

This scheme is an expression of one of those competing modes of analysis which have shaped Ch'ü Yüan lore in the People's Republic: the historicist as opposed to the class viewpoint. Through historicist reconstruction of the past, figures like Ch'ü Yüan have ironically been rescued from the depredations of the extreme class viewpoint at the price of becoming entangled once again in the overpowering if benevolent forces of time and circumstance.

To get to this point, Ch'ü Yüan and the First Emperor have both traveled a very long road. When Ch'ü Yüan set out in the Li Sao, he was a soaring spirit, the cosmic voyager, transporting himself across the universe with an act of will. As for the awesome First Emperor, his classic portrait shows him "cracking his long whip and driving the universe before him." Now, History wields the whip and drives before it the Revolution. The First Emperor and Ch'ü Yüan, both of them, are just along for the ride.

Conclusion

To conclude this study, I want to touch first on a few methodological points. Next, to summarize the evolving pattern of the myth of loyalty and dissent, I have chosen the problem of "self and individuality" which is so prominently associated with Ch'ü Yüan lore. Finally, I want to suggest that for all the emphasis on conflict or excess, and on the extremes of behavior and sentiment, this myth and lore are also informed with structures that connote mediation. These structures may be the ones that have extended the appeal of the Ch'ü Yüan tradition so far in space and time, and have made it so integral a part of Chinese civilization.

Form, Content, and Context

The Ch'ü Yüan tradition has served the modern Chinese as a medium for grappling with problems in the transformation of twentieth-century Chinese society. The lore and the myth have focused on the role of the new intellectuals in these changes, and have provided a linkage with the past for their artistic and political experiences. In order to increase our understanding of these phenomena, I have taken the whole Ch'ü Yüan tradition as a context for understanding any one part. If the tradition had only been examined as a sequence—one strata of mythology covering another, one stage of the lore superseding its predecessor—then it could appear to us that the tradition lacked any coherence or consistency. It might appear, contrary to the reality, that symbols were used arbitrarily and that Ch'ü Yüan was a man for any and all seasons.

Viewing a segment of the myth in light of the whole is the prerogative (and obligation) of the intellectual historian. In this case, it was also regularly the fashion in which the Chinese themselves understood and used many of the symbols in question (in the interminable "Contre Contre Sao" dialogue, for example). This leads us to see this myth not as a medium for asserting a monolithic position, but rather as a forum for discourse, a stage for dramatically posing and answering questions, for expressing dilemmas. The lore, from its outset, derives its drama and dynamism from the premise that there are optional solutions to the dilemmas, and that choosing among them is difficult and sometimes dangerous. Only a superficial understanding of the premodern lore will conclude that it asserts some kind of pure loyalty. More truly, it asks how to remain loyal to temporal expressions of political legitimacy and still be true as well to a set of absolute values. Or it asks how we can remain politically loyal when we feel compelled to dissent.

My presentation has tried to make it possible for the questions and discourse to reveal themselves by "reading" the lore horizontally as well as vertically, by seeing the long, thin filament of the myth in a series of relations with cognate literature and lore from various periods in Chinese history. This provides a series of changing contexts for evaluating the significance of the lore in time. Typical contexts have been the king/minister lore of the Han, the recluse/hermit lore and loyalty literature of the post-classical period, and the historical personages debates of the 1950s.

The lore of Ch'ü Yüan has absorbed and reflected interests and problems from each of the epochs through which it has passed. However, this is not simply to say in the fashion of those arch-relativists, the Chinese New Historians, that "each age has its own Ch'ü Yüan." For those iconoclastic scholars of the 1920s and 1930s, that formula was meant to debunk tradition and to expose and destroy false gods and heroes. But the worthiness or historicity of Ch'ü Yüan has not been at issue in my analysis. He and the symbols associated with him have been considered here as means, not ends. The issue has not been that each age of Chinese culture has its own version of Ch'ü Yüan, but rather that each age has the problem of how to relate its educated elite to political power, to ultimate values, to art and literature. And we may understand through the lore of Ch'ü Yüan (or of others, like Confucius) how this problem has been formulated and what answers have been put forth.

The abstract goal of this study has been to precipitate out of premodern political mythology one particular tradition—a chain of symbols that has had coherence and was obviously significant to the old regime, that has reached into the twentieth century, and that is capable of providing a context for talking about intellectual change or continuity. In addition to deciding what changed, I have sought something beyond the usual clichés to convey the subtleties of the change and to provide a sense of how the change was mediated intellectually. My object in dealing with the Ch'ü Yüan story has been to take seriously all cultural forms (symbols, myths, rituals). I have tried to avoid looking through or past the "mere" forms to get at "real motives" or "underlying realities." Rather, it has been a matter of asking: What has this or that form meant in Chinese society up to now? Why did these people choose a particular form and choose it when they did? This has required a detailed scrutiny and appreciation of the forms themselves.

A Changing Pattern of Self and Individuality

The problem of "self" or "individuality" seems to be the one most fitting to summarize and conclude this study of Ch'ü Yüan, as well as the interpretive question of continuity and change. The pre-twentieth-century lore has provided modern intellectuals with a language to express the dilemmas of a kind of individuality that excludes anarchism and a kind of dissent or revolt that excludes nihilism. It has also acted as a medium for the shift from China's rich tradition of individuality to the modern and truly novel ethos of individualism. It follows then that the lore should have continued to be used in formulations of the new social and historical philosophies which challenge basic assumptions of that ethos. Perhaps with more strain, the lore has also been a medium for introducing the question of the role of individuals (or a class of individuals) in social transformation.

If we begin with the sense of self that is initially evoked by the lore and then follow along its full transference into modern times, we see "self" as a product of conflict. The conflict was expressed in complex emotions like resentment, moral outrage, frustration, and in a form of political behavior which we call dissent. Before modern times, this self was not perceived apart from society. If uprooted or *dépaysé*, this self was not alienated, nor did it turn to anarchism, espouse nihilism, or defect, although these were available options. Even self-destruction (Ch'ü Yüan's suicide) was conceived of as socially concerned, an act of commitment. Before modern times, the foundation of this self and the source of this kind of individuality was moral insight. Failure to implement the insight was the initial source of the conflict, which in turn enhanced and developed the peculiar features of individuality and self.

This kind of self and individuality in the lore of Ch'ü Yüan has passed through four broad phases, characterized by four symbolic relations: the self and the king, the self and "mind," the self and society, and the self and history. In the classical phase of the lore, the confrontation of the king and the official dramatized a predicament of separation between moral insight and sovereign power. Here, the self was distinguished by that insight and it required reintegration with the king for its fulfillment. Though it struggled with the king to achieve that end, the struggle drove it further away from integration and toward an isolation that resulted in fuller self-expression and individual development.

The post-classical lore of Ch'ü Yüan moved away from an expression of the initial "predicament" through the symbols of king/official conflict. The conflict was turned inward; it became ethically sufficient to purify the self and achieve moral insight. The lore now celebrated Ch'ü Yüan for his moral integrity, achieved not by any outward political success, but by a dedication to inner "self-cultivation." This was a reflection of the gradual shift within some Neo-Confucian traditions from outer concerns (court politics, institutional reform) to an emphasis on inner ("mind") cultivation. The enemy for the classical Confucian was the bad king, unwilling to use good men to institute good policies. However, the enemy for some prominent Sung and Ming Neo-Confucians was the "'inner' force within 'the mind' of the Confucian subject leading to moral corruption."[1] The Ch'ü Yüan lore of the classical period conveyed the idea that the king and institutions were prime forces for benevolent transformations of society. The post-classical lore dramatized the Neo-Confucian idea that the mind of the self had the most significant transformative power. Notwithstanding this shift, there continued from the earliest phases of the lore through the entire post-classical period a growing concern with the artistic expression which mediated the inner and outer self. Closely accompanying this concern, there also developed a stress on the solitary isolation of the self. On one hand, this represented the punishment suffered as a result of outer conflict. On the other hand, it came to symbolize the "critical moment," the test of the self's moral integrity and authenticity.

For the moderns, during the New Culture era, the self became a unit of social discourse. In a social philosophy informed initially with late nineteenth-century social Darwinism and vestigial utilitarian atomism, liberating the "true self" from the inhibitions of false (read: anachronistic) norms and institutions became the explicit goal. Liberating individual sentiments was good because it was considered to be the initial stage in liberating individual genius and talent. New notions of collective welfare and a progressive sense of history were active here. It was thought that to liberate the self was ultimately to liberate national talent and energy, and to give them an opportunity to develop. This would provide the wherewithal to bring China out of its decline and eventually would lead to the advancement and progress of its civilization. In the twentieth century, "romantic" individuality has been portrayed in the role of Ch'ü Yüan as the heroic genius, a role that harked back to the classical literature where it emphasized the "outer" confrontation with authority in its various forms, and where it in effect argued for the co-optation of the sovereign's role (Ch'ü Yüan as the national leader, or the prophet). But an essential factor changed, for the modern sense of individuality was shifting toward one of atomistic individualism which was not premised on a basic linkage of self with absolute values. Instead, the new sense of self was tied to history. It suggested the optimistic view that the self is a creative historical force, at once the product and cause of historical progress. Beginning as a notion of isolated genius, it ends up pointing to the creation of a society of liberated individuals.

The "minority of one" politics emphasized in the post-classical Ch'ü Yüan lore was easily transformed into the messianic politics of liberation fostered by the romantic generation. The post-classical and the New Culture Ch'ü Yüan additionally had in common a sense of frustration and a lack of fulfillment, as well as separation from common humanity and a self-conscious aloofness. The first modern adaptation of this aspect of the lore came with the idea of the self as an embodiment of a general popular will, and the self as necessarily a part of society if successful action were to be taken. There is a movement from inner to outer, from singleness to collectivity. The final step has been to absorb this self into history, either as an agent of anonymous historical forces, or as the embodiment of a general will which itself is the product of historical forces. Thus the long-range tendency of the lore of Ch'ü Yüan in the twentieth century has been to relativize the values and the ideals which are the motivating force of the self; and to historicize the will and creative power of that self, making it contingent on but fulfilled by history. How is this problem of self and individuality expressed in the three major themes which were indicated at the outset of this study, namely, time, place, and madness?

Modern scholarship suggests that the origin in a culture of a distinctive sense of self is tied to the development of a sense of objective time. It has recently been argued that in the *Li Sao*, that poem so fundamental to the Ch'ü Yüan lore, there occurs the genesis of a sense of objective time and of self in Chinese literature.[2] If this is true, then the myth of Ch'ü Yüan begins with a sense of time generative of self and individuality, and comes, in its recent developments, to employ a sense of time (historicism) which diminishes if not destroys these.

When Ch'ü Yüan comes closest to representing the autonomous self, for example in the Republican period when he is the superman-genius, he is thought to have transcended time, to be outside of its influence and beyond its reach. Here, an apocalyptic mood prevails. In the writings of Kuo Mo-jo we see the continuous flow from this position to one which demands that the individual must develop in rhythm with "the times." Time becomes a progressive, teleological process, and self-fulfillment becomes a function of understanding and working with and within that process.

This study has given many examples of how Ch'ü Yüan lore linked individuality (or eccentricity and deviance) with the South. To these must be added the linkage between the South and barbarianness and individuality. This barbarian quality attributed to the South is consonant with the lore's sense of the South's "otherness" to the conventions of northern cosmopolitan literary culture. The barbarian motif is used to depict Ch'ü Yüan standing on the border between styles of behavior within one culture, or perhaps even straddling two different cultures.

There is a relationship in the lore between this notion of space and that of time which deserves special attention here, even though it will momentarily take us away from the issue of individuality. In Western history, there have been notable occasions when the encounter of Western European civilization with "barbarians" has produced conflated notions of time and space. For example, movement to the West (the New World) was also considered by some as going back in time (in a Biblical sense, to Eden; in a classical sense, to Arcadia). The meeting of Europeans with the indigenous inhabitants of the West was sometimes understood as a meeting with an earlier or younger people, enviable and exemplary in their purity and innocence.[3] In the post-classical lore of Ch'ü Yüan, one has no sense that the people of the South are similarly perceived by exiled poet-officials, or that their primitiveness is thought to be of any potential value to the culture of the Han people. Rather, the prevailing idea was the one argued by Wang I in the classical period: Ch'ü Yüan's contact with the primitive peoples of Ch'u had the potential of benefitting them (by refining their folk art, for example).

In the modern period, a new point of view emerges. The South in Ch'ü Yüan lore is historicized, and time and space conflate. From a state-of-being, the South is transformed into a process-of-becoming. Earlier associations of southern culture with individuality are reformulated into the idea of a dynamic force in the creation of Chinese culture. In particular it is thought to have been a source of those values which the moderns hold in esteem. Part of this new conception of the South contains ideas borrowed from European romantic historiography. The ancient southern kingdom of Ch'u comes to be conceived of not only as a geographical entity, but a chronological one as well. It is thought of as younger than the decrepit North; its culture is likened to "the song of a child." Therefore, it was in a position to reinvigorate the North, to bring "new youth" to it. Eugenic and organismic theories of history and society were common in the Republican period, and to this extent these treatments of Ch'ü Yüan's South together with its and his barbarianness were not unusual. The moderns who used this notion of the barbarian

Ch'ü Yüan and his South meant to demonstrate with it that the ethos of individualism advocated in the twentieth century has deep roots in true Chinese culture, i.e., the culture which resulted from the amalgamation of the North and South and was dramatically expressed in the life and art of Ch'ü Yüan. By the same token, they were arguing that the moderns should call forth the "southern" qualities of the Chinese cultural personality; for, just as these had resuscitated China in Ch'ü Yüan's time, so could they rescue China from its current decline.

Madness has been the most dramatic metaphor for self and individuality throughout the Ch'ü Yüan lore. In addition to linkages with the South and southern individuality, in retrospect we can add a final link here with the notion of the barbarian. The antithesis of both kinds of madness we have discussed in this study is not "reason" or "the rational" in an eighteenth-century European sense. It is rather comprised of notions like restraint, moderation, and normativeness. The idea of madness which developed in the lore is evocative of wildness, eccentricity, and nonconformity. Its opposites are cultivation, civilization, and conformity. Could we not say that to be mad, in the manner suggested by the Ch'ü Yüan lore, is to be like a barbarian? In the early stages of the lore, when an official behaved in a "mad" fashion, he was treated (punished) accordingly by being transported to live with or like the barbarians in the South. The punishment recapitulated the crime. If one transgressed (went beyond the boundaries of the cultivated, civil, ordered polity or society), one was sent across the boundaries of civilization to barbarian realms. If one behaved like a wild person, one was sent to the wilds.

This barbarianlike alienness of Ch'ü Yüan's individuality made him attractive to poet-officials who themselves were driven to extremities. In the twentieth century, it was all the more attractive to the self-proclaimed *deraciné*, those intellectuals who saw themselves as "superfluous," and "made useless by the times"—those "imitation foreign devils" who had travelled in and learned from the barbarian West.

Modes of Mediation

Throughout the Ch'ü Yüan lore, whether in the expressions of self and individuality, or in the motifs of time, place, and madness, varieties of extremism often prevail. Ch'ü Yüan was both praised and blamed for his irreconcilability, for example. His art and politics have been perennially characterized as excessive and imbalanced. His personality is described as dissonant, and it is at times of chaos, in various forms, that Ch'ü Yüan is recalled: when the moral order is "topsy-turvy," when there is conflict at court; when northern nomads wreck northern Chinese society and drive it south; or when the good official is forced into exile. Yet, however compelling and dramatically seductive these themes are, it is doubtful that they would have been so successful at capturing the imagination and attention of Chinese intellectuals, and plain folk as well, had there not been imbedded within the structures of the Ch'ü Yüan lore some sense of mediation, some indication that the figures, experiences, and emotions that fill the lore comprehend the full round of life—order as well as chaos, some kind of balance as well as excess. Let me conclude with some suggestion of how the lore does in fact do this.

In the folk cult devoted to Ch'ü Yüan, he is transformed into a water symbol, an expression of one of the two primal cosmic forces (the *yin* and *yang*). However, the Fifth of the Fifth rites are not emphasizing the extreme quality of the symbol, nor even primarily the complementarity of the two forces. The significant point is that Ch'ü Yüan is of prominence at a time of critical *transition* from the preeminence of one primal force to another. The purpose of the rites in which he plays a rice or fertility god is to insure the successful transition from one cosmic phase and one season of agricultural production to another. Ch'ü Yüan, the drowned poet, like the shaman who haunts his poetry and who presides at the rites, is in effect a mediator between life and death, dormancy and productivity. In addition to the Dragon Boat rituals, think of the beautiful little anecdote about Ch'ü Yüan the farmer, tilling his fields during a drought in Ch'u. It concludes: "And where his tears fell, there grew rice, white as jade."

The very prominent north/south motifs in Ch'ü Yüan lore perform a number of exemplary mediating functions. A simple and literal example of this is found in the basic biography of Ch'ü Yüan the official. This is his role as a diplomat. He was desperately concerned with forging an alliance between northern and southern states, and even engaged in a kind of shuttle diplomacy between them. We tend to forget this when we encounter the later and more dramatic aspects of his story. This north/south mediation stays with the lore from the earliest times to the present. Looking again at the formulation of Wang I about the relation of northern and southern culture, we recall that he perceived Ch'ü Yüan as a mediator of refined northern civilization and the barbarians of the South. In the twentieth-century Ch'ü Yüan lore, this kind of mediation becomes a central issue. Kuo Mo-jo, for example, viewed the life and work of Ch'ü Yüan as the beginning of an essential synthesis of northern and southern culture. And Kuo Yin-t'ien, while describing Ch'ü Yüan as a transcendent prophet, nevertheless depicts him at the same time as a cultural synthesizer whose special genius was. to avoid the extremes of the northern and southern cultures of his day.

When the figure of Ch'ü Yüan is viewed alone, qualities of extremism and imbalance can be striking. But I have illustrated how the juxtaposition of Ch'ü Yüan to other poet-official types can reveal some of the mediating qualities of the overall myth of loyalty and dissent. From the point of view of Chinese bureaucratic norms, Ch'ü Yüan can be said to mediate between the extremes of the Li Po type and the T'ao Ch'ien type. The former refuses to participate in the polity; the latter abandons the polity and eventually abandons faith in its legitimacy. However, Ch'ü Yüan was a participant, and though forced to leave the polity, he continues to support its legitimacy and to desire reinstatement. It should be noted here that Ch'ü Yüan was regularly described as "sober" precisely because the extremes represented by Li and T'ao are intimately associated with an escapism symbolized by wine and inebriety. It is rather striking to have the lore depict Ch'ü Yüan as both sober and wild. This underlines my point that Ch'ü Yüan's wildness (or madness) is not to be mistaken as a metaphor for the extremes of escapism or defection.[4] A final set of examples comes from modern Chinese historiography. Even though the revolutionary or novel qualities of Ch'ü Yüan may be stressed, his effectiveness is said to come from his mediation of classes (the aristocracy and the people), of stages of history (slave and feudal), and of aesthetic modes (romanticism and realism).

The mediating structures which have evolved throughout the long history of the myth of loyalty and dissent are singularly appropriate expressions of the old regime's bureaucratic elite, which ideally functioned as brokers between state and society. For the moderns, these structures suggest not merely roles that they would like to play in the new society, but the new wholeness and comprehensiveness which they envisioned for the new state and the new culture.

We are left with two sets of after-images of Ch'ü Yüan: the aloof and isolated, uncompromising, mad-genius poet; and Ch'ü Yüan the sober, diplomat-lawmaker, friend of the people. These seem to be equally appropriate expressions of the tensions and ambivalent aspirations of the modern Chinese intellectuals as they have gradually and painfully transformed the legacies of their bureaucratic predecessors.

Those familiar with the lore of Ch'ü Yüan from other sources are no doubt unused to thinking of this "madman of Ch'u" in the light of mediation. But the process of mediation may begin from either extreme, from both sides. Thus, if Ch'ü Yüan has managed to maintain his appeal down through the generations and into modern times, it may be because there has been a constant need in Chinese culture for those madmen who mediate reason with passion, and temper public service with private sentiment; who confront reality with vision, and history with will.

Notes

Abbreviations

CTSM   *Ch'u Tz'u shu-mu wu-chung*, Chiang Liang-fu.

CTYCL   *Ch'u Tz'u yen-chiu lun-wen chi.*

HSWC   *Han shih wai chuan*, James R. Hightower, trans.

W:RGH   *Records of the Grand Historian*, Ssu-ma Ch'ien.

A prefatory word on sources: two publications have been of special help with this study. The first, Chiang Liang-fu's *Ch'u Tz'u shu-mu wu-chung* (1961), is basically a critical bibliography of all aspects of *Ch'u Tz'u* and Ch'ü Yüan studies. Of particular value are the short critical essays which Chiang has reprinted in the volume. In this fashion, he makes many obscure materials easily available, and with them he also provides a panoramic view of attitudes toward Ch'ü Yüan and criticism of the *Ch'u Tz'u* from antiquity to the twentieth century. The second publication is the three volume *Ch'u Tz'u yen-chiu lun-wen chi* (1957–1970). In its eight hundred pages it reprints, in full, seventy essays published in the People's Republic of China in a broad range of periodicals between 1951 and 1963. This provides a thorough sampling of changing and conflicting attitudes about Ch'ü Yüan and about all aspects of *Ch'u Tz'u* poetry. In my notes, I cite these two publications respectively rather than the specific works which are reprinted in them.

Introduction (Pages 1–15)

1. In addition to my own reading of Aeschylus' *Prometheus Bound*, my use of the Promethean imagery here and later in the text draws upon Richard H. Cox, "Ideology, History and Political Philosophy: Camus'

L'Homme Revolté," 69–97; and Karen Hermassi, *Polity and Theatre in Historical Perspective.*
   2. I have written about one of the major New Historians in *Ku Chieh-kang and China's New History.* Of special relevance to this study of Ch'ü Yüan are the mythological researches of Ku Chieh-kang and his associates published in the *Ku-shih pien* [Critiques of ancient history]. Their experimental studies of the legends of Lady Meng-chiang and of Confucius are exemplary: Ku Chieh-kang, ed., *Meng-chiang ku-shih: yen-chiu chi* [Legend of Lady Meng-chiang: anthology of studies]; idem, "Ch'un-ch'iu te K'ung-tzu yü Han-tai te K'ung-tzu" [The Confucius of the Warring States period and the Confucius of the Han period], in *Ku shih pien,* 2:130–138.
   3. Leslie Fiedler, *Return of the Vanishing American.* "Literary anthropology" is Fiedler's description of his own scholarship. I have taken additional encouragement for my study from some recent studies of Chinese myth. Sarah Allan's excellent analysis of ancient sage-king lore employs Levi-Strauss' structural analysis much more formally than Fiedler does. The effect is to reveal some fascinating patterns in the recalcitrant material scattered throughout many difficult early texts. See Sarah Allan, "The Heir and the Sage: A Structural Analysis of Ancient Chinese Dynastic Legends" and "The Identities of Taigong Wang in Zhou and Han Literature." Ralph Croizier has followed the development of the legend of a famous anti-Manchu loyalist, the military hero Cheng Ch'eng-kung, in *Koxinga and Chinese Nationalism: History, Myth, and the Hero.*
   There have been a number of recent historical studies which attempt to determine a culture's fundamental character through the analytical use of concepts like "conflict," "predicament," and "paradox." They argue that a culture may be understood by laying bare its conflicts as opposed to dealing with it as if it were monolithic and in a state of quiescent equilibrium. For examples, see Michael Kammen, *People of Paradox: An Inquiry Concerning the Origins of American Civilization;* J. C. Heesterman, "India and the Inner Conflict of Tradition"; Thomas A. Metzger, *Escape From Predicament. Neo-Confucianism and China's Evolving Political Culture.*
   4. Aeschylus, *Prometheus Bound,* trans. Philip Vellacott, p. 20.
   5. See Etienne Balazs, *Chinese Civilization and Bureaucracy,* p. 237. Balazs raises the question of madness in his discussion of the poet Juan Chi (210–263), whose "contemporaries often called him a madman." Balazs says that the expression here for madman *(ch'ih)* "was used to describe a simple minded person — an idiot in the same sense as Dostoevsky's Prince Mishkin. 'Madmen' frequently cropped up during troubled periods of Chinese history." In the same source, Balazs, still talking about the troubled times of the third century, cites another figure who was called "the madman" *(k'uang sheng).* Originally, Balazs says, "it meant a mad dog, but had come to mean a crazy fanatic, excitable and tempestuous, an extremist, a visionary. . . . Perhaps the best translation would be 'noncon-

formist.'" (p. 214) The two "madmen" examples cited by Balazs had in common their refusal to serve in public office.

Also see Julia Ching, *To Acquire Wisdom*, pp. 25–27, 52–53, for discussions of "madness" (*k'uang*) from the point of view of Confucian learning, and for the notion of "mad ardour."

Chapter 1 (Pages 17–47)

1. Our epigraph, relating the anecdote about Chieh Yü and Confucius, is taken from Arthur Waley, trans., *The Analects of Confucius*, chap. xviii.5, p. 219.

In the *Ch'u Tz'u* poem, "Nine Declarations" (Chiu chang), this madman appears by name along with a group of exemplars which my text discusses below:

> Chieh Yü shaved his head;
> Sang Hu [a recluse] naked ran;
> So a loyal man is not certain to be used;
> Nor a wise man certain to be employed.
> Wu Tzu-hsü met a bad end;
> Pi Kan was cut up and made into pickles.

See David Hawkes, trans., *Ch'u Tz'u: The Songs of the South*, p. 62.

From later epochs, there are examples such as Li Po, the seventh-century poet, who identified himself as "basically a madman of Ch'u / madly singing and laughing at Confucius." See Li Po's poem "Lu shan yao" (Song of Lu Mountain) in Shigeyoshi Obata, trans., comp., *The Works of Li Po*, pp. 162–163. The fourteenth-century poet Kao Ch'i, in political self-exile, wrote about his rustic locale where he endured the ridicule of the locals who called him a "muddle-headed scholar of Lu [Confucius' state]" and a veritable madman of Ch'u. See Frederick Mote, "A Fourteenth Century Poet: Kao Ch'i," p. 243.

2. See "Biographies of Ch'ü Yüan and Master Chia," in Ssu-ma Ch'ien, *Records of the Grand Historian of China*, 1:499–516. This 2 volume translation is hereafter referred to as W:RGH.

3. Ibid.

4. Ibid., p. 516.

5. Ibid., p. 508. Cf. Burton Watson's biographical study, *Ssu-ma Ch'ien, Grand Historian of China*, pp. 63–65, 217.

6. See Watson, *Ssu-ma Ch'ien*, p. 65. Here Watson translates biographical materials about Ssu-ma Ch'ien from the *Han shu* (History of the Han dynasty, *chüan* 62) by Pan Ku.

For other opinions that Ssu-ma Ch'ien identified with Ch'ü Yüan see: Fu Ssu-nien, "Lecture on Chia I," in *Fu Meng-chen hsien-sheng chi* [Fu Ssu-nien's collected works], 3:107; Yu Kuo-en, *Chung-kuo wen-hsüeh shih* [History of Chinese literature], 1:93; Liu Ta-chieh, *Chung-kuo wen-hsüeh fa-chan shih* [Development of Chinese literature], 1:158; Todo Akiyasu, "Kutsu Gen to Shiba Sen" [Ch'ü Yüan and Ssu-ma Ch'ien], pp. 85–98.

7. *W:RGH*, 1:509.

8. Translation by David R. Knechtges, "Two Han Dynasty *Fu* on Ch'ü Yüan: Chia I's *Tiao Ch'ü Yüan* and Yang Hsiung's *Fan-sao*," pp. 8–9. Knechtges cites the second century *Feng-su t'ung-i* [Rules for public morality] as the source for this passage. Also see the translation of this passage by Burton Watson, *Chinese Rhyme-Prose*, p. 25.

9. Knechtges, "Two Han Dynasty *Fu*," pp. 10–13.

10. Translated by James R. Hightower, "The *Fu* of T'ao Ch'ien," pp. 200–203. Also prototypical of this genre of poetry are these examples: Ssu-ma Ch'ien's "Lament for an Unemployed Gentleman," translated by Hightower in this same essay; and Chia I's "*Fu* on Dry Clouds" (Han-yun fu) translated by Hellmut Wilhelm, "The Scholar's Frustration: Notes on a Type of *Fu*," p. 317. Hightower and Wilhelm present excellent analyses of the political sentiment of the Han era through these studies of poetry.

11. The translation is from Knechtges, "Two Han Dynasty *Fu*," pp. 17–28. For another translation of the same passage and further commentary on it, cp. Chan Ping-leung, "The *Ch'u Tz'u* and Shamanism in Ancient China," p. 61.

12. Knechtges, "Two Han Dynasty *Fu*," p. 29. Also see David R. Knechtges, *The Han Rhapsody: A Study of the Fu of Yang Hsiung*, pp. 97–103. In a separate communication to me, Professor Knechtges also cites this example: in a piece written by Liang Sung (?–83 A.D.) titled "Lamenting the *Sao* Rhapsody" (Tiao sao fu), Chia I and Yang Hsiung are singled out for criticism: "It was Tutor Chia who missed the point/Why was Scholar Yang deceived from the truth?" Liang wrote this poem on his way to exile in Chiu-chen (Vietnam). "As he went to the south, he crossed the Yangtze and the lakes (of the south), traversed the Yuan and Hsiang (rivers). He was moved to lament for Wu Tzu-hsü and Ch'ü Yüan because they drowned themselves though guilty of no crime. He then composed the 'Lamenting the *Sao* Rhapsody,' and tying it to a black stone he sank it in the river." Professor Knechtges cites his source as Li Hsien, *Hou Han shu* commentary (Peking: Chung-hua, n.d.), *chüan* 34.1171.

13. Pan Ku's "Preface" to the *Ch'u Tz'u* is translated in Liu Hsieh, *The Literary Mind and the Carving of Dragons*, p. 27.

14. Ibid.

15. See James Legge, *The Chinese Classics, The She King*, 4:543. This is the "Ta ya," sec. III.3.6.4:

> Most dignified the king's charge. And Chung Shan-fu carries it into execution. . . . Intelligent is [Chung Shan-fu] and wise, Protecting his own person; Never idle day or night. In the service of the One Man.

Punctuation is Legge's. The implication of this passage is that he serves his king best who keeps himself intact.

16. Wang I, *Ch'u Tz'u chang chü*, pp. 19–21.

17. Ibid., p. 69.

18. Ibid., p. 71. "Feigning stupidity" is a reference to Chi-tzu, one of the three wise ministers of the Shang dynasty who were persecuted by evil King Chou. See chapter one below.

19. Ibid., pp. 71–72. Arthur Waley's translation is used here for lines one through three. See Arthur Waley, *The Book of Songs*, p. 302. Legge's translation of the last line seems to convey the strength of Wang I's message best, so I use it. (Legge, *Chinese Classics*, 4:517.) Wang I himself did not cite the second line of the original passage in the *Shih ching*.

20. See chapter three and chapter four below.

21. An important formulation of this position was made by Chung Hung (fl. fifth century) in his *Shih p'in*. See E. B. Brooks, "A Geometry of the Shī p̆in."

22. For an example from Sung times, see Chiang Liang-fu, *Ch'u Tz'u shu-mu wu-chung* [Five-fold bibliography of *Ch'u Tz'u*, hereafter, *CTSM*], p. 28. Also see examples from Ming times in ibid., pp. 22, 80.

23. See Liu Hsieh, *Literary Mind*, p. xxxvi. Cp. criticism from eighth century in William H. Nienhauser, ed., *Liu Tsung-yuan*, p. 22.

24. Hawkes, *Ch'u Tz'u*, pp. 150–169.

25. Cf. Lu Ch'in-li, *Ch'ü Yüan Li Sao chien-lun* [Short discussion of Ch'ü Yüan's *Li Sao*]; Arthur Waley, trans. *The Nine Songs: A Study of Shamanism in Ancient China*; Chan Ping-leung, "*Ch'u Tz'u* and Shamanism." Chan Ping-leung's study is by far the most extensive review of the role of shamanism in the *Ch'u Tz'u* poetry, especially in the *Li Sao*. In spite of its gratuitous bellicosity and hasty judgments, it is a good introduction to a fascinating anthropological subject.

26. Arthur Waley, trans., *A Hundred and Seventy Chinese Poems*, p. 13; Arthur Waley, trans., *The Temple and Other Poems*, pp. 20, 26. For an excellent analysis of the love metaphor in the *Li Sao* from the vantage of comparative literature, see Chen Shih-hsiang, "The Genesis of Poetic Time: The Greatness of Ch'ü Yüan, Studied with a New Critical Approach." Also see Wang Ching-hsien, "Sartorial Emblems and the Quest: A Comparative Study of the *Li Sao* and the *Faerie Queen*." The Chen and Wang essays broach the problem of comparing the allegorical structures of Dante's *Divine Comedy* and the *Li Sao*. Yu Kuo-en's controversial study of female symbolism in the *Ch'u Tz'u* poetry has some insights relevant to this problem. See "*Ch'u Tz'u* nü hsing chung-hsin shuo," [Centrality of feminine qualities in *Ch'u Tz'u*], in Yu Kuo-en, *Ch'u Tz'u lun-wen chi* [Anthology of *Ch'u Tz'u* studies], pp. 191–204. Cp. Hawkes, *Ch'u Tz'u*, pp. 213–214, for the allegory of poet as woman and the poet's prince as the woman's lover.

27. Arthur Waley remarks that "love-poetry addressed by a man to a woman ceases after the Han dynasty; but a conventional type of love-poem, in which the poetry [of either sex] speaks in the person of a deserted wife or concubine, continues to be popular. The theme appears to be almost an

obsession with the T'ang and Sung poets. In a vague way, such poems were felt to be allegorical. Just as in the Confucian interpretations of the love-poems in the Odes . . . the woman typifies the Minister, and the lover the Prince, so in those classical poems the poet in a veiled way laments the thwarting of his own public ambitions." A Hundred and Seventy Chinese Poems, p. 20.

· Explicit use of this imagery of king-husband, minister-wife, goes back some time before the Li Sao. For example, see H. G. Creel, Shen Pu-hai: A Chinese Political Philosopher of the Fourth Century B. C., p. 45. For the cosmologic equation minister: female: yin, see discussion of the Chou li in Yu Kuo-en, Ch'u Tz'u lun-wen chi, p. 191, and also the Sung dynasty commentary on the I Ching in Richard Wilhelm, trans., The I Ching or Book of Changes, 1:9. Not quite as explicit as these texts, but still contribut-ing to the development of the micro-, macro-cosmic linkage of yang, king, and husband is the philosophic system of Tung Chung-shu in the Han dynasty. See Fung Yu-lan, A History of Chinese Philosophy, 1:42–44.

28. For P'eng Hsien, see Lin Keng, "P'eng Hsien shih shui?" [Who is P'eng Hsien?], in Lin Keng, Shih-jen Ch'ü Yüan chi ch'i tso-p'in yen-chiu [Study of Ch'ü Yüan and his works], pp. 63–77. The essay is dated 1948. Lin's argument is solid. Among other things, he points out that Wang I was the first to identify P'eng Hsien as a suicide. Lin thinks that Wang reasoned backward from the accepted fact of Ch'ü Yüan's suicide to that position. Wang did not know himself who P'eng Hsien was, and therefore, accepting Chia I's belief that Ch'ü Yüan drowned himself, Wang concluded that P'eng Hsien did likewise because Ch'ü Yüan seemed to say he was using P'eng Hsien as a model. Some scholars suggest that P'eng Hsien was perhaps a shaman priest, or some kind of Taoist adept. For example, see Lin Keng, Shih-jen Ch'ü Yüan, p. 71; Chan Ping-leung, "Ch'u Tz'u and Shamanism," pp. 132–136; Lu Ch'in-li, Ch'ü Yüan Li Sao chien-lun, p. 26.

29. David Hawkes has written two brilliant essays about the quest theme and the nature of the magic journey: "The Supernatural in Chinese Poetry," and "The Quest of the Goddess." In the latter essay, Hawkes says "the idea of the progress, the ritual journey—usually a ritual circuit . . . postulates a symmetrical cosmos whose various parts are presided over by various powers. These powers can be induced to give either their submis-sion or their support to the traveler who approaches them with the correct ritual. A complete and successful circuit of the whole cosmos will therefore make him a lord of the universe, able to command any of its powers at will, if he is a wizard; to move in it with utter freedom, if he is a mystic; to rule by divine right and title with the allegiance of both temporal and spiritual powers, if he is an emperor."

In his analysis of the Li Sao journey theme, Etienne Balazs says that "The soul's voyage of discovery through the landscape of the self was pro-jected onto the natural landscape." See Balazs, Chinese Civilization and

Bureaucracy, p. 181. Henri Maspero sees Ch'ü Yüan's journey in the poem "Yüan yu" (Distant journey) no longer directed toward a search for the prince as in the *Li Sao*. Instead it is directed "to the search for unity, the First Principle with which he wished to unite." Maspero argues that Ch'ü Yüan is herein seen gradually converting to Taoism. See *La Chine antique*, p. 500. Cp. Wang Ching-hsien, "Sartorial Emblems and the Quest," and also Chen Shih-hsiang, trans., *Essay on Literature, Written by the Third Century Poet Lu Chi*, pp. 28–29, 49–50.

30. H. Wilhelm, "The Scholar's Frustration," pp. 316–317.

31. This theme is strongly emphasized in Chen Shih-hsiang, "The Genesis of Poetic Time."

32. Hawkes, *Ch'u Tz'u*, p. 22.

33. Ibid., p. 24.

34. Ibid., p. 160. For the obsessive concern of Han literature with death or a means of obviating death and achieving immortality, see Yü Ying-shih, "Life and Immortality in the Mind of Han China."

35. F. S. Couvreur, *Dictionnaire classique de la langue Chinoise*, p. 19.

36. James R. Hightower, trans., *Han shih wai chuan: Han Ying's Illustrations of the Didactic Application of the Classic of Songs* [hereafter, *HSWC*], p. 191. Han Ying (fl. B.C. 150) has anthologized in this handbook an entertaining melange of anecdotes, parables, and plagiarisms from countless pre-Han philosophic texts. Professor Hightower explains that the book's intended function was no doubt broader than acting as a guide to the classic *Odes*. It was apparently meant "to demonstrate the practical use of the Classic" as well. The many stories it relates "were preserved not as a record of events, but as themes illustrative of ritually prescribed conduct. As such, they could be applied to any person, historical or fictional, whose activity fitted a given role" *HSWC*, pp. 2–3.

Han Ying seems to have drawn quite a bit of his material from the philosopher Hsün-tzu (third century B.C.), whose career was known to have suffered in a fashion similar to those described repeatedly in the *HSWC*. A probable disciple of Hsün-tzu summed it up this way: "Critics say: 'Hsün Tzu was not as great as Confucius.' This is not so. Hsün Tzu was harassed by disordered times, and constrained by severe circumstances; when on the one hand there were no worthy lords and on the other there was the aggression of Ch'in . . . Hsün Tzu, who cherished the heart of a Sage, but which could not express itself as such, hid it under a manner of feigning to be mad, and so appeared to the country to be stupid. . . . The country was not well governed and Hsün Tzu missed his time." See Homer Dubs, trans., *The Works of Hsuntze*, pp. 319–320.

37. *HSWC*, pp. 126–127.

38. Burton Watson, trans., *Records of the Historian*, pp. 16–29.

39. Burton Watson, trans., *The Complete Works of Chuang Tzu*, p. 191.

40. Wang Ch'ung, *Lun Heng*, 2:92.

41. *HSWC*, pp. 34, 336.
42. Hawkes, *Ch'u Tz'u*, p. 139.
43. Ibid., p. 145.
44. Ibid., p. 64.
45. Watson, *Chuang Tzu*, pp. 78–79.
46. Ibid., p. 329. Cf. Wang Ch'ung, *Lun Heng*, 2:248.
47. *HSWC*, p. 34.
48. See Allan, "The Heir and the Sage," p. 144.
49. *HSWC*, p. 228.
50. Creel, *Shen Pu-hai*, pp. 84–85.
51. Marcel Granet, *Danses et légendes de la Chine ancienne*, 1:79, 82–83.
52. Allan, "The Heir and the Sage." Also see Allan, "Identities of Taigong Wang," passim.
53. Hawkes, *Ch'u Tz'u*, pp. 145–146.
54. Ibid., p. 178.
55. *HSWC*, pp. 228–229. Cp. these important discussions of "timing": J. I. Crump, *Intrigues–Studies of the Chan-kuo ts'e*, pp. 24–26, and passim; T'ao Ch'ien's "Lament for Gentlemen Born Out of Their Time," translated in Hightower, "The Fu of T'ao Ch'ien," p. 208; Wang Ch'ung's discussion of "proper time" in *Lun Heng*, 1:140, 2:31.
56. Granet, *Danses et légendes*, 1:169–170.

Chapter 2 *(Pages 48–86)*

1. The formulation is that of the French politician Alain (Emile Chartier, 1868–1945), a leader of the so-called Radicals.
2. For an evaluation of this situation in Sung dynasty politics see James T. C. Liu, *Ou-yang Hsiu, An Eleventh Century Neo Confucianist*. Professor Liu writes: "Whenever a leading official became more influential than usual, others would insinuate that he was verging on usurpation of power, if not exactly disloyalty. Whenever a group of officials remained in power for a considerable length of time, those out of power would begin to accuse them of forming a faction, monopolizing access to the emperor, misleading him and preventing better advice from reaching his ears. . . ." (pp. 16–17). For the late Ming through the nineteenth century, see Frederic Wakeman, Jr., "The Price of Autonomy: Intellectuals in Ming and Ch'ing Politics."
3. W. T. de Bary, *Self and Society in Ming Thought*, p. 7.
4. Ibid.
5. Ibid., p. 8. Also Wakeman, "The Price of Autonomy," pp. 37, 41.
6. See particularly my discussion in the first section of chapter four.
7. Ching, "Wang Yang-ming: A Study in Mad Ardour."
8. W. T. de Bary, *The Unfolding of Neo Confucianism*, pp. 27–28.
9. See Jao Tsung-i, *Ch'u Tz'u yü tz'u ch'ü yin yüeh* [Influence of Ch'u Tz'u on Lyric Poetry, Dramatic Poetry and Music], and his *Ch'u Tz'u*

shu-lu [Bibliography]. Also see Cheng Chen-to, "Ch'ü Yüan tso p'in tsai Chung-kuo wen-hsüeh shang te ying-hsiang" [Influence of Ch'ü Yüan's works on Chinese literature]; and *Ch'u Tz'u yen-chiu lun-wen chi* [Anthology of *Ch'u Tz'u* studies, hereafter *CTYCL*], 1:309–317.

10. Yoshikawa Kōjirō, *An Introduction to Sung Poetry*, p. 88. See James J. Y. Liu, *The Art of Chinese Poetry*, pp. 128–129, for a discussion of flower symbolism and a contrasting translation of this poem.

11. Translated in Sherman Lee and Ho Wai-kam, *Chinese Art Under the Mongols*, plate 236.

12. Wen Fong, *Sung and Yuan Paintings*, p. 71.

13. Ibid. The symbolism of the narcissis is relevant to the lore of Ch'ü Yüan. This flower is called the *shui hsien* (water goddess)—or the *ling-po hsien-tzu* (goddess who stands above the waves)—and it is associated poetically with the two main goddesses of the Hsiang River. Wen Fong says these associations linked the flower with Ch'ü Yüan. The narcissis became a popular symbol for poets only after Huang T'ing-chien (1045–1105) used it extensively. For a detailed analysis of the use of flower symbols in the *Li Sao*, see Wang Ching-hsien, "Sartorial Emblems and the Quest."

14. Lee and Ho, *Chinese Art Under the Mongols*, p. 101.

15. See Frederick Mote, "Confucian Eremitism in the Yüan Period," pp. 202–240. Also see William S. Atwell, "From Education to Politics: The Fu She," p. 334.

16. Translated in James R. Hightower, *The Poetry of T'ao Ch'ien*, pp. 259–263.

17. Translated in Irving Y. Lo, *Hsin Ch'i-chi*, p. 51. Compare the sentiments expressed by the poet Lu Yu (1125–1210), who ordinarily empathized closely with Ch'ü Yüan. "Lu preferred T'ao's course of philosophical resistance to Ch'ü's useless self destruction." Michael S. Duke, *Lu You*, p. 58.

18. Arthur Waley, *The Poetry and Career of Li Po*, p. 101.

19. Ibid., p. 100.

20. See Li Po's poem "Lu shan yao" [Song of Lu Mountain], in Obata, *The Works of Li Po*, pp. 162–163. Tu Fu, the great T'ang poet, once elaborated on this by characterizing Li Po as "feigning madness." Ibid., p. 194.

21. Waley, p. 100. Also see the biographical literature on Li Po in Obata, *Works of Li Po*, pp. 199–209. These are the data that established Li Po as a banished immortal.

22. Waley, *A Hundred and Seventy Chinese Poems*, pp. 19–20.

23. Ibid.

24. The image seems to have originated in the fifth century A.D. in the context of the first great waves of nomadic invasions of the imperium. For other illustrations see my "National Essence and the New Intelligentsia," p. 370, n. 95. Mao Tse-tung used this image in his poem "Swimming" (Yu yung, c. 1956).

25. My translation from Maspero, *La Chine antique*, pp. 496, 498. For challenges to this barbarian notion see Noel Barnard, ed., *Early Chinese Art and Its Possible Influence in the Pacific Basin*, vol. 1: *Ch'u and the Silk Manuscript*, especially the essays by Chang Kwang-chih (pp. 26–40), Jao Tsung-i (pp. 121–122), and William Watson, passim.

26. Edward Schafer, *The Vermilion Bird: T'ang Images of the South*, p. 135.

27. Translated in William Hung, *Tu Fu, China's Greatest Poet*, p. 149.

28. Yü Hsin's family had fled Honan in the early fourth century and settled in Chiang-ling, Hupei, the site of Ying. After the destruction of the Liang state by the Wei state (of nomadic origins), Yü Hsin went on to serve the Wei government. In later times he was criticized for "serving two dynasties." For Yü Hsin's identification with Ch'ü Yüan, see W. T. Graham, "Yü Hsin and the 'Lament for the South' [Ai Chiang-nan]," pp. 82–88.

Lu Yu's exile to Szechwan from the court of the Southern Sung came in 1170 because of his challenge to the appeasement policy. En route, he wrote his "Ai Ying." His identification with Ch'ü Yüan is nicely detailed in Duke, *Lu You*, pp. 46–49.

29. See biography in Nienhauser, *Liu Tsung-yuan*, especially pp. 18, 36–37, 105, 132.

30. See Liu Tsung-yuan, *T'ien wen t'ien tui chu*. Liu has been in favor among PRC literary critics, and Futan University has reprinted this special edition of his work.

31. Liu Tsung-yuan, "Mi-lo yü feng."

32. I use the editions of "Lament for Ch'ü Yüan" (Tiao Ch'ü Yüan) and commentaries in Liu Tsung-yuan, *Ho-tung hsien-sheng chi*, vol. 5; idem, *Liu Ho-tung chi*, pp. 3a–6a; and idem, *Liu Ho-tung ch'uan chi, ts'e* 1, *chüan* 19, pp. 2b–3b.

33. Cited in Steven Owens, *The Poetry of Meng Chiao and Han Yü*, p. 101.

34. Nienhauser, *Liu Tsung-yuan*, p. 15.

35. Ibid., p. 44.

36. J. D. Frodsham, trans., *The Poems of Li Ho (791–817)*, p. xvii.

37. Nienhauser, *Liu Tsung-yuan*, p. 107.

38. Ibid.

39. See G. W. Baxter, "Metrical Origins of the Tz'u," pp. 217–221.

40. Translated in ibid., p. 220.

41. Translated in Schafer, *The Vermilion Bird*, p. 47.

42. See Frodsham, *The Poems of Li Ho*, introduction.

43. See Wei-ming Tu, *Neo Confucian Thought in Action: Wang Yang-ming's Youth (1472–1509)*, pp. 16–17.

44. See Wang Yang-ming, "Tiao Ch'ü P'ing fu." And compare these earlier illustrations of the "Southern" in which no reference is made to

Ch'ü Yüan: (1) Po Chu-i, "On Being Removed from Hsün-yang and Sent to Chung-chou," in Waley, *A Hundred and Seventy Chinese Poems,* p. 219; (2) the poem written by Ou-yang Hsiu (1036–1101) on the occasion of his own "exile" to the Chung-chou area and in commemoration of Po Chu-i's experience three hundred years earlier, in Yoshikawa, *Sung Poetry,* p. 66.

45. For my observations on these two works I use the Taiwan I-wen editions.

46. See Cyril Drummond le Gros Clark, *The Prose Poetry of Su Tung-p'o,* p. 102.

47. Ibid., pp. 99–100.

48. See "Shu lao yu miao li fu" (Mysterious are the eternal verities that lie in thick wine), ibid., pp. 191–193; also see "Chung shan sung lao fu" (Pine wine), ibid., pp. 169–171.

49. "Ming chün k'o yü wei chung yen fu," ibid., pp. 70–73.

50. "Chia I lun," pp. 1000–1004.

51. See Hung Hsing-tsu, "Fan fan Li Sao," pp. 88–90; reprinted in Chu Hsi, *Ch'u Tz'u chi chu,* pp. 483–488.

52. Chu Hsi, *Ch'u Tz'u chi chu,* pp. 488–490. Professor James T. C. Liu suggests: "Chu Hsi considered Ch'ü Yüan to be excessive, chiefly because by Sung times it was possible for a demoted or exiled official to turn his main attention to local educational activities and, next to it, social welfare activities." Personal communication to author, 13 April 1978.

53. James T. C. Liu, "Yüeh Fei (1103–1141) and China's Heritage of Loyalty."

54. Ibid., p. 297. Professor Liu suggests that the object of Sung loyalism was expanded. If punished by one emperor, one could retreat and wait for the next, for one should be loyal to the whole dynastic line. "In this sense, Yüeh Fei's case is regrettable. He should have been allowed to serve the next emperor and see what happened then." Personal communication to author, 13 April 1978.

55. Cited in A. W. Sariti, "Monarchy, Bureaucracy, and Absolutism," p. 61.

56. Ibid.

57. Cited in Julia Ching, "Neo Confucian Utopian Theories and Political Ethics," p. 43. Also see Wang Gung-wu, "Feng Tao: An Essay on Confucian Loyalty."

58. See Ching "Neo Confucian Utopian Theories," for a description of the forged "Classic of Loyalty" (Chung ching).

59. For example, see Chiang Chi, *Shan tai ko chu Ch'u Tz'u,* preface. This was one of the most popular editions of the *Ch'u Tz'u* down through the 1920s.

60. The play is reprinted in Cheng Chen-to, ed., *Ch'ing jen tsa-chü ch'u-chi,* vol. 3.

61. Frodsham, *The Poems of Li Ho*, p. 211.

62. In his commentary on the *Ch'u Tz'u*, Wang Fu-chih suggests a similar filiation of motifs. See his 1709 *Ch'u Tz'u t'ung shih*.

63. Cheng Yü's play is found in Chou Wu-chin, ed., *Tsa-chü hsin pien* (1661 preface by Wu Wei-yeh).

64. The quartet is in Cheng Chen-to, *Ch'ing jen tsa-chü*, vol. 2.

65. *Ch'u Tz'u t'ung shih*, p. 174.

66. See Ian McMorran, "Wang Fu-chih and the Neo Confucian Tradition," pp. 422–423; also the editorial introduction to the Shanghai edition of *Ch'u Tz'u t'ung shih*, pp. 7–12. Wang Fu-chih himself composed a *tsa chü* entitled "Lung chou hui" (Dragon boat society). See Cheng Chen-to, *Ch'ing jen tsa-chü*, vol. 4. Ch'ü Yüan is only alluded to in passing. The subject of the play is a T'ang heroine who disguised herself as a man and risked her life to save her kin from bandits.

Chapter 3 (Pages 87–124)

1. The point of departure for challenging the historicity of Ch'ü Yüan was provided by the classical scholar Liao P'ing (1852–1932), who claimed that the *Li Sao* was written in the third century B.C. by the First Emperor of Ch'in and his academicians. Liao also said that all of the other poetry attributed to Ch'ü Yüan was written by various other poets. I believe that an approximation of Liao's original essay, which is not extant, is reprinted in *CTSM*, pp. 251–252. In one form or another, Liao's essay enjoyed great notoriety. Hsieh Wu-liang, sometime before 1913, saw the original manuscript and published a summary of it (*Ch'u Tz'u kai-lun*, p. 12). Later critics of Liao P'ing apparently saw only Hsieh's summary, or someone's summary of it. For example, see Kuo Mo-jo's refutation of the Liao P'ing thesis, "Ch'ü Yüan yen-chiu." Also see Wen I-to's reaction, "Liao P'ing lun *Li Sao*," in *Wen I-to ch'uan-chi*, 1:335–338.

Even more successful at drawing the fire of Ch'ü Yüan worshippers was Hu Shih's 1922 essay "Tu *Ch'u Tz'u*" (Reading the *Ch'u Tz'u*). This piece raised a series of questions about (1) the reliability of biographical data on Ch'ü Yüan, (2) the authenticity of various poems attributed to Ch'ü Yüan, and (3) the propriety of using Ch'ü Yüan as an exemplar for moderns. Hu Shih did not deny that there had been a Ch'ü Yüan, but rather was concerned that the "real" person and his authentic poetry were distorted by mythology. The result was a "textbook model for a loyal minister." In the past fifty years, almost every Ch'ü Yüan and *Ch'u Tz'u* scholar, including some in Taiwan, has felt obliged to refute Hu Shih's critique, often with ritualized fervor. The most elaborate exercise in doubting Ch'ü Yüan is Ho T'ien-hsing's *Ch'u Tz'u tso yü Han tai k'ao* [*Ch'u Tz'u* was written during the Han dynasty]. Ho T'ien-hsing drew upon all available skeptical scholarship from K'ang Yu-wei to Ku Chieh-kang in order to prove that Ch'ü

Yüan was really Liu An (180?–122 B.C.), the second king of Huai-nan, a Taoist adept and philosopher.

The following general works routinely lay out the populist and radical themes analyzed in this chapter, and they consistently affirm the historicity of Ch'ü Yüan and his authorship of almost all of the *Ch'u Tz'u* poetry conventionally attributed to him before the twentieth century: (1) Hsieh Wu-liang, "Ch'ü Yüan tsai wen-hsüeh shang chih chia-chih" [The value of Ch'ü Yüan in literature]; (2) Hu Huai-sha, *Chung-kuo pa ta shih-jen* [Eight great Chinese poets], pp. 1–124; (3) Lu K'an-ju, *Ch'ü Yüan yü Sung Yü* [Ch'ü Yüan and Sung Yü]; (4) Cheng Chen-to, *Chung-kuo wen-hsüeh shih* [History of Chinese literature], 1:74–83; (5) T'an Cheng-pi, *Chung-kuo wen-hsüeh shih* [History of Chinese literature], pp. 37–49.

2. See my essays: "Politics, Poetry and Death: The Southern Society, 1900–1917," paper prepared for the Conference on Chinese Intellectuals and the Problem of Conservatism in Republican China, (Dedham, Massachusetts, 1972), xerox; and "National Essence and the New Intelligentsia."

Analogies were made as well with Western figures. For example, Ch'ü Yüan's frustrations and suicidal tendencies were compared with those of Saint Simon by Ma Chün-wu, a member of the Southern Society, in "Sheng Hsi-men chih sheng-huo chi ch'i hsüeh-shuo" [Life and scholarship of Saint Simon].

3. Translation from Hellmut Wilhelm, "The Poems from the Hall of Obscured Brightness," p. 327. K'ang Yu-wei's friend was T'an Ssu-t'ung.

4. Leo Ou-fan Lee, "Genesis of a Writer: Notes on Lu Hsün's Educational Experience, 1881–1909," pp. 163, 173.

5. Harriet Mills, "Lu Hsün: Literature and Revolution—From Mara to Marx," pp. 191–192.

6. Ibid. The key source here is Lu Hsün's 1907 essay "Ma-lo shih li shuo" [The power of Mara poetry]. Professor Mills draws generally on the essays from 1906–1909, and I thank her for bringing this extraordinary literature to my attention. Also see discussions of Lu Hsün's use of Ch'ü Yüan in P. H. Chen, *Social Thought of Lu Hsün*, pp. 89, 323.

7. Maurice Meisner, *Li Ta-chao and the Origins of Chinese Marxism*, p. 2.

8. Ibid., p. 7. Also see the similar feelings expressed by Ku Chieh-kang, an eminent historian, in his preface to *Ku shih pien*, 1:12.

9. See for example, Ernest Young, "Problems of a Late Ch'ing Revolutionary: Ch'en T'ien-hua," p. 245. For further discussion of political suicides during this period, see: the opposition to Ch'ü Yüan's suicide by the Ch'ing loyalist Wang K'ai-yun (1883–1916), CTSM, p. 247; Harold Schiffrin, *Sun Yat-sen*, pp. 258, 298; Mary B. Rankin, *Early Chinese Revolutionaries*, pp. 11, 113–114, 199. For further examples from the 1920s, see Lin Yu-sheng, "The Suicide of Liang Chi: An Ambiguous Case

of Moral Conservatism"; and regarding Tai Chi-t'ao's abortive drowning suicide see *Tai Chi-t'ao hsien-sheng wen-ts'un* [Collected works of Tai Chi-t'ao] (Taipei, 1959), 4:1462.

10. Translated in Meisner, *Li Ta-chao*, p. 21.

11. Roxane Witke, "Mao Tse-tung, Women, and Suicide in the May Fourth Era," p. 142.

12. Yang Hsing-fo, "Fan tzu-sha" [Against suicide].

13. See my discussion in *Ku Chieh-kang*, pp.115–120.

14. Liu Shih-p'ei, "Nan pei hsüeh p'ai pu t'ung lun" [Northern and southern schools of scholarship are of separate origin]. Essay dated 1905.

15. For Liu, "national essence" thought and the Southern Society, see essays by Charlotte Furth, Martin Bernal, and myself in Furth, *Limits of Change*. On the relation of modern Chinese regional politics to cultural revivals and intellectual fashions, see Tu Wei-ming, "Yen Yüan: From Inner Experience to Lived Concreteness." Tu Wei-ming points out the special interest shown in various thinkers (e.g. Yen Yüan, Wang Yang-ming, Wang Fu-chih) by modern intellectuals who come from the respective regions of China associated with the thinker in question. He concludes: "It may be farfetched to correlate intellectual attachment to great personalities in the past with the politics of regionalism, but the emotional subtlety in regional pride is so important a factor in modern China that any serious study of the formulation of modern Chinese political ideologies must take into consideration the territorial origins of the leaders. Of course, in most cases, intellectual ideas were used merely to justify political aims. Frequently, the very use of a specific kind of justification, however, shaped the directions of the political aims themselves" (p. 512).

16. In addition to the materials cited below in chapter three, for a brief example of the north/south approach to literary criticism see Chang T'ai-yen, "Shih ching shih lun" [On the Odes]. Chang emphasized continuity of developments in literature from north to south, from the *Odes* to the *Ch'u Tz'u*. Also see the essay by Liu Shih-p'ei's disciple, Ch'en Chung-fan, "Chou tai nan pei wen-hsüeh chih pi-chiao" [Comparison of northern and southern literature from Chou times]. Liu Shih-p'ei's thesis was still being cited, if only to be rejected, in Liu Ta-chieh's well circulated *Chung-kuo wen-hsüeh fa-chan shih*, vol. 1.

17. Wang Kuo-wei, "Ch'ü-tzu wen-hsüeh chih ching-shen" [Spirit of Ch'ü Yüan's literature].

18. Wang Kuo-wei's use of the English word "humorous" is quite accurate according to the *Oxford Etymological Dictionary*, 2 vols. (Oxford, 1971), s.v. "humorous," 2:1347–1348.

19. Hsieh Wu-liang, *Ch'u Tz'u hsin lun*.

20. Ibid., pp. 45–46. For the growth of the populist argument, see my *Ku Chieh-kang*, chapters 4, 5.

21. Hsieh Wu-liang, *Ch'u Tz'u hsin lun*, pp. 57, 60–61, 64–65, 69–71.

22. Ibid., pp. 10–11.

23. For examples of this treatment of the *Odes*, see Schneider, *Ku Chieh-kang*, pp. 174–181. For a novel formulation of the problem, see the study by the poet and critic Ch'en Ch'ü-ping (b. 1873), *Tz'u fu hsüeh kang-yao* [Basics of tz'u and fu poetry]. Ch'en Ch'ü-ping sees the "Feng," "Ya," and "Sung" sections of the *Odes* as both the warp (*ching*) and the essential structure (*t'i*) of Chinese poetry. The rhapsody (*fu*) tradition, which encompasses the *Ch'u Tz'u*, he sees as the woof (*wei*) and the functional or contingent (*yung*) element of Chinese poetry.

24. Liang Ch'i-ch'ao, "Ch'ü Yüan yen-chiu," dated 1922.

25. Ibid., p. 52.

26. Ibid., p. 67.

27. Kuo Mo-jo, "Ch'ü Yüan yen-chiu."

28. Ibid., pp. 55, 60–61.

29. Ibid., pp. 98–99. See chapter five for Kuo's alterations of this position in the 1970s.

30. Ibid., pp. 70, 83–91, 142–143.

31. Ibid., p. 122.

32. Ibid., pp. 72–73, 76, 126, 131–132.

33. Ibid., pp. 47–48, 61, 65, 67–68.

34. Ibid., p. 92.

35. Ibid., p. 124.

36. Ibid., p. 105. According to Kuo Mo-jo, this is a summary of Hou Wai-lu's argument "Ch'ü Yüan ssu-hsiang te mi-mi" [Secret of Ch'ü Yüan's thought]. Hou Wai-lu's original essay is not available to me.

37. Kuo Mo-jo, "Ch'ü Yüan yen-chiu," p. 144.

38. Ibid., p. 71.

39. See Leo Ou-fan Lee, *The Romantic Generation of Modern Chinese Writers*.

40. Lim Boon Keng, trans. and intro., *The Li Sao: An Elegy on Encountering Sorrows*, by Ch'ü Yüan, pp. 50–51. Lim (1869–1957) studied medicine at Edinburgh and Cambridge. He was a strong supporter of Sun Yat-sen and the 1911 revolution. In 1921, after developing a lucrative medical practice in Singapore, he became the president of Amoy University. When that university came under the auspices of the Nationalist Government in 1937, Lim resigned his post.

41. Ibid., pp. 40, 41.

42. Kuo Yin-t'ien, *Ch'ü Yüan te ssu-hsiang chi ch'i i-shu* [Thought and art of Ch'ü Yüan].

43. Ibid., p. 280.

44. Ibid., pp. 49–53, 91, 160–162.

45. Ibid., p. 91.

46. Ibid., pp. 173, 183, 284.

47. Ibid., pp. 164, 165.

48. This is my translation from the Chinese. I have checked it against Creighton Gilbert's unwieldly translation from the original: *Complete*

Poems and Selected Letters of Michaelangelo (New York: Random House, 1965), pp. 139–140. The sonnet is dated c. 1546.

49. Kuo Yin-t'ien, *Ch'ü Yüan te ssu-hsiang*, p. 1.

50. Ibid., p. 277. For brief but illuminating comparisons of the *Li Sao* and the *Divine Comedy*, see Wang Ching-hsien, "Sartorial Emblems and the Quest," and Chen Shih-hsiang, "The Genesis of Poetic Time."

51. Kuo Yin-t'ien, *Ch'ü Yüan te ssu-hsiang*, p. 277.

52. Ibid., pp. 288–289.

53. See Kuo's poem translated as "Morning Snow: On Reading Carlyle's 'The Hero as Poet,'" in Kuo Mo-jo, *Selected Poems from the Goddesses*, p. 33.

54. Kuo Mo-jo, "Hsiang lei," *Kuo Mo-jo shih chi* [Collected poems], pp. 20–34. Dated 1920.

55. See Hawkes, *Ch'u Tz'u*, p. 26.

56. Kuo Mo-jo, "Po Yi che-yang ko-ch'ang" [Po Yi sang this song], *Kuo Mo-jo shih chi*, pp. 148–156. Dated 1922.

57. See Liang Pai-tchin's preface to *K'iu Yuan* (Paris: Gallimard, 1957), pp. 13–14. *K'iu Yuan* is a French translation of Kuo Mo-jo's 1942 drama "Ch'ü Yüan."

58. Kuo Mo-jo, "Ch'ü Yüan shih-tai." This comprises the first segment of the *Ch'ü Yüan yen-chiu*.

59. Kuo Mo-jo, "Ch'u Pa Wang tzu-sha" [Suicide of the tyrant of Ch'u], *Kuo Mo-jo hsuan-chi* [Selected writings], 1:208–255. Dated 1936.

60. I follow the translation of "Ch'ü Yüan" by Yang Hsien-yi and Gladys Yang, *Ch'ü Yüan*.

61. Jean Anouilh, *Antigone*, p. 87. There is more similarity here than space permits me to explore. For example, Kuo has focused the heroic action of the play in a young woman who sacrifices her life for Ch'ü Yüan and the ideals he represents.

62. I agree on this point with Kikuchi Saburō in his *Chugoku kakumei bungaku undō-shi* [History of the Chinese revolutionary literature movement], especially pp. 205–208. Kikuchi may well be correct in saying that Kuo's identity with Ch'ü Yüan was never more apparent than in this play. Kikuchi argues that the play is significant evidence for the distance remaining between major Chinese intellectuals and "the people." For all of Kuo's populism, says Kikuchi, he is still an "aristocrat"—detached, condescending, and related to the masses via feelings of noblesse oblige. Kikuchi differentiates Kuo's literature and social attitudes from the more mature populism "up north," that is, in Yenan among the communists. As for the limitations Kuo imposes on his Ch'ü Yüan, Kikuchi says this is an expression of the frustration felt by Kuo himself, as an artist.

63. Kuo Mo-jo, "Lun Wen I-to hsüeh-wen te t'ai-tu"[Wen I-to's attitude toward literature], in Kuo Mo-jo, *Li-shih jen-wu* [Historical figures], p. 195. In 1951, Kuo paid a similar compliment to the poet friend of Mao Tse-tung, Liu Ya-tzu. See Kuo's preface to *Liu Ya-tzu shih tz'u hsuan* [Selected poetry of Liu Ya-tzu]. Note that Kuo's description of Wen I-to's

intellectual "progress" closely matches his own, as he describes it in his 1921 essay on Wang Yang-ming, in *Li-shih jen-wu*, pp. 76–77.

64. Wen I-to, "Ch'ü Yüan wen-t'i," *Wen I-to ch'uan-chi* [Collected works], 1:245–258.

65. "Jen-min te shih-jen Ch'ü Yüan," *Wen I-to ch'uan-chi*, 1:259–261.

66. For examples, see Ku Chieh-kang, et al., "Mo-tzu hsing-shih pien" [Symposium on the name Mo-tzu]. Initially, Wen's essay was a response to a piece by Sun Tzu-t'an not available to me. Sun apparently challenged the historicity of the conventional Ch'ü Yüan. He intimated that the Ch'ü Yüan of the standard lore was, if anything, a miserable slave who had to affect effeminate characteristics in order to please the perverted whims of the king. Wen I-to does not simply reject Sun's arguments out of hand, but rather he chooses to salvage the notion of "slave" and to turn it in a very different direction.

67. Wen I-to, *Wen I-to ch'uan-chi*, pp. 250–251.

68. Ibid., p. 251.

69. Ibid., pp. 253–255.

Chapter 4 (Pages 125–157)

1. This festival is known by a number of names. *Tuan wu* is the most common. This may be translated as "correct" or "exact middle," reflecting its occurrence at the mid-point of the solar calendar, the summer solstice, which most often takes place in the fifth lunar month. Göran Aijmer concludes "the Correct Middle was probably regarded as the middle of the solar year placed in the lunar calendar, i.e. the day of the solstice projected on the lunar calendar." See *The Dragon Boat Festival on the Hupeh Hunan Plain, Central China: A Study in the Ceremonialism of the Transplantation of Rice*, pp. 26–27. Another name for the festival is *Tuan yang*, "sun's extremity." The Five Elements cosmology perhaps plays a role in a third designation, *T'ien chung*, "middle of the heavens." In the Five Elements system, the number five is associated with the center, as opposed to the four points of the compass.

2. See Lu K'an-ju, "Wu yüeh wu jih" [The fifth of the fifth], pp. 73–75; Yu Kuo-en, *Ch'u Tz'u kai-lun* [Summary of *Ch'u Tz'u*], p. 106.

3. Wolfram Eberhard, *The Local Cultures of South and East China*, p. 161.

4. Ibid., p. 153; Wang Ch'ung, *Lun Heng*, 1:161. Also see C. S. Wong, *A Cycle of Chinese Festivals*, pp. 125–127.

5. For a general discussion of the many customs associated with this day, see Ou-yang Fei-yün, "Tuan wu o-jih k'ao" [Study of Tuan Wu as an evil day]; Derk Bodde, *Festivals in Classical China: New Year and Other Annual Observances During the Han Dynasty*, chapter 13. The most comprehensive study is Huang Shih, *Tuan wu li su shih* [History of the Tuan Wu festival].

6. Eberhard, *Local Cultures*, p. 157.

7. Ibid., p. 159. Cp. Bodde, *Festivals in Classical China*, pp. 299–301. See another translation of this passage in Jacques Gernet, *Daily Life in China on the Eve of the Mongol Invasion 1250–1276*, pp. 193–194. The source cited by Gernet is a thirteenth-century description of the city of Hangchow. This source also describes the day of Tuan Wu as a bad one for taking the civil service examination.

8. The *Ch'ü Yüan wai chuan* is reprinted in Chiang Chi, *Shan tai ko chu Ch'u Tz'u*. It is reprinted and punctuated in Lü T'ien-ming, *Ch'ü Yüan, Li Sao chin i* [Modern commentary on *Li Sao*], pp. 66–67, where it is called *Ch'ü Yüan pieh chuan*. Parts of *Ch'ü Yüan wai chuan* are cited and glossed in Chan An-t'ai, *Ch'ü Yüan*, pp. 3–4. Some of the anecdotes in the *Ch'ü Yüan wai chuan* seem to be derived from the *Shih i chi* (Forgotten tales), attributed to Wang Chia of the Tsin period (265–420). It was edited by Hsiao Ch'i of the Liang period (520–557). The epigraph to my chapter four is taken from book four of the *Shih i chi* and was translated in Lu Hsün, *A Brief History of Chinese Fiction* (Peking: Foreign Languages Press, 1959), pp. 69–70.

9. Arthur Waley, *The Nine Songs: A Study of Shamanism in Ancient China*, p. 49. This passage collates materials respectively from the *Shih chi*, 126.14a; *Shui ching chu*, 10; and *Shih chi*, 15.10b. Cp. Sir James G. Frazer, *The Golden Bough: A Study in Magic and Religion*, p. 430: "[Egyptian] tradition runs that the old custom was to deck a young virgin in gay apparel and throw her into the river as a sacrifice to obtain a plentiful inundation. Whether that was so or not, the intention of the practice appears to have been to marry the river, conceived as a male power, to his bride the cornland, which was so soon to be fertilised by his water." Frazer notes that in his day a straw doll surrogate was used, or money was thrown into the canal on such occasions.

10. Eberhard, *Local Cultures*, pp. 37–38.

11. Ibid., p. 38. Also see CTYCL, 1:30–33, for discussion of the *Nine Songs*, the drowned river goddess Erh Fei, and her relationship to the sage-king and river god Shun.

12. Eberhard, *Local Cultures*, p. 393.

13. Edward Schafer, *The Divine Woman: Dragon Ladies and Rain Maidens in T'ang Literature*, pp. 46, 116.

14. Ibid., p. 6.

15. See summary of dragon symbolism and dragon's relationship to rain and water in Henri Maspero, "The Mythology of Modern China," pp. 276–277.

16. See Huang Shih, *Tuan wu li su shih*, p. 131. This is one example of a Kwangtung custom associated with Ch'ü Yüan: the dragon king's temple is visited; incense is burned to the dragon and he is draped in red banners. This dragon apparently is not considered malevolent.

17. Schafer, *Divine Woman*, pp. 28–29.

18. Lu K'an-ju collated materials on this subject at an early date in *Ch'ü Yüan yü Sung Yü*. Also see Ou-yang Fei-yün, "Tuan wu o-jih k'ao."

19. Translated in Hawkes, "Quest of the Goddess," pp. 46–47. Hawkes cites Pan Ku, *Hou Han shu* [History of the Latter Han], chapter 84 (Lieh nü chuan). I use this translation rather than Arthur Waley's, with which Hawkes takes issue. See Waley, *The Nine Songs*, p. 31. Also see discussion of this passage in Chan Ping-leung, "Ch'u Tz'u and Shamanism in Ancient China," p. 132. Cf. Hayashi Minao's comments on the term "shen wu" (divine shaman), which appears in Wang I's commentary on the *Li Sao*. Wang I wrote that "Wu Hsien in ancient times was a divine shaman." Hayashi cites a passage from a later text to illuminate the obscure term: "In the eastern [i.e. lower] stretches of the Yangtze, the place called Wu-tsang is the abode of the descendents of the divine shaman Wu Tu of Yüeh. When he died, Kou-chien had him buried in the centre of the river—the shamans and the gods wanted to take advantage of this to overturn the boats of the Wu people." Hayashi Minao, "The Twelve Gods of the Chan-kuo Period Silk Manuscript Excavated at Ch'ang-sha," p. 135. I discuss Kou-chien in chapter four below.

20. Cited in Hsu Chung-yü, "Tuan wu min-su k'ao" [Study of Tuan Wu folklore], p. 34. Part of this same story is found in Herbert Giles, *A Chinese Biographical Dictionary*, 2:759.

21. Eberhard, *Local Cultures*, pp. 38, 393.

22. Huang Shih, *Tuan wu li su shih*, p. 122.

23. Wang Ch'ung, *Lun Heng*, 2:247–251.

24. Eberhard, *Local Cultures*, p. 391.

25. See note 2 above. Also see Arthur Waley's translation of the folktale "Wu Tzu-hsü," in *Ballads and Stories from Tunhuang*, pp. 25–52. The tale is full of motifs from the river goddess lore and the post-Han lore of Ch'ü Yüan.

26. The two continue to be confused with each other and with other figures. For example, Wolfram Eberhard reports that "in Tainan [Taiwan] there is a temple for a Shui-hsien tsun-wang (water-saint honored king) which has been a cult center for merchants, sailors, and fishermen since 1715. Nobody there knows who he is although some say the name refers to three dieties: Yü, Wu Tzu-hsü and San-lü ta-fu [Ch'ü Yüan]. Others add to these Wang Po and Li Po." Other sources associate other names with the saint, but Wu Tzu-hsü and Ch'ü Yüan appear most frequently. See Eberhard, *Local Cultures*, p. 402. Cornelius Osgood's study of Hong Kong shows that the Dragon Boat Festival is very popular, but his informants either do not know who is being celebrated or offer suggestions such as this: the commemoration is for "a Sung dynasty minister of court who drowned himself in a river in protest against abuses which were being perpetrated on the people." Cornelius Osgood, *The Chinese: A Study of a Hong Kong Community*, p. 910.

27. W:RGH, 1:226, 2:479, 481. HSWC, p. 336. Also see Wen Ch'ung-i "Chiu ko chung te shui-shen yü Hua-nan te lung-chou sai-shen" [English subtitle: Water Gods and Dragon Boats in South China], p.73ff.

28. Wang Ch'ung, *Lun Heng*, 2:327.

29. Schafer, *Divine Woman*, p. 58.

30. Huang Shih, *Tuan wu li su shih*, pp. 110–112. This draws upon Yang Ssu-ch'ang, *Wu-ling ching-tu lüeh*, a basic reference for the festival. See chapter four and notes below.

31. Watson, *Chuang Tzu*, p. 329.

32. Ku Yen-wu, *Jih chih lu*, ts'e 4, pp. 83–84. Also see Lu K'an-ju, "Wu yüeh wu jih," and Ou-yang Fei-yün, "Tuan wu o-jih k'ao."

33. Chien T'ang, "Tuan wu k'ao" [Study of Tuan Wu]; E. T. C. Werner, *Myths and Legends of China*, pp. 106, 248–250; *Tz'u Hai* [dictionary], s.v. "Chung K'uei," p. 1389; Morohashi Tetsuji, *Dai kan-wa jiten* [Chinese encyclopedic dictionary], s.v. "Chung K'uei," 2:601; Lu Hsün, *A Brief History of Chinese Fiction*, pp. 288, 379; M. L. C. Bogan, *Manchu Customs and Superstitions*, p. 33.

34. Tun Li-ch'en, *Annual Customs and Festivals in Peking as Recorded in the Yen-ching sui-shih-chi*, p. 44.

35. Wen I-to, "Tuan wu k'ao" [A study of Tuan Wu], *Wen i-to ch'uan-chi*, 1:221–228.

36. Wen I-to, "Tuan chieh te li-shih chiao-yü" [Historical lessons of Tuan Wu], in *Wen I-to ch'uan-chi*, 1:239–242.

37. Wen I-to, *Wen I-to ch'uan-chi*, pp. 228–231.

38. Bodde, *Festivals in Classical China*, p. 315.

39. Eberhard, *Local Cultures*, p. 34.

40. Chao Wei-pang, trans. and ed., "The Dragon Boat Race in Wu-ling, Hunan—by Yang Ssu-ch'ang," p. 10. Chao cites this evidence: "When a Hei-miao has died, a coloured thread is tied up on the top of a bamboo stick which is erected in front of the tomb; men and women made offerings to it. When a Kuo-ch'uan Ch'i-lao is sick, a five-coloured thread is bound up on a tiger's bone, which is put in a winnowing fan, and a sorcerer is invited to pray for him."

41. See Hawkes, *Ch'u Tz'u*, "Chao Hun," p. 105:

> The priests are there who call you, walking
> backwards to lead you in.
> Ch'in basket-work, silk cords of Ch'i, and
> silken banners of Cheng:
> All things are there proper for your recall;
> and with long-drawn, piercing cries they
> summon the wandering soul.

42. Mircea Eliade, *Shamanism: Archaic Techniques of Ecstasy*, pp. 111, 117. On these pages Eliade is specifically discussing the rituals of the Manchurian shamans.

43. Eberhard, *Local Cultures*, p. 197.

44. See Wu Chün, *Hsü ch'i chieh-chi*. This sixth-century text is cited and discussed in Yu Kuo-en, "Wei-ta shih-jen Ch'ü Yüan chi ch'i wen-hsüeh" [Great poet Ch'ü Yüan and his writings], *Kung-jen jih-pao* [Daily

worker] (13 June 1953), reprinted in Yu Kuo-en, *Ch'u Tz'u lun wen chi* [Anthology of writings on *Ch'u Tz'u*], pp. 273–274. Also see Chan An-t'ai, *Ch'ü Yüan*, p. 4, and Chao Wei-pang, "The Dragon Boat Race in Wuling," p. 11. Cf. Huang Shih, *Tuan wu li su shih*, p. 21, for variant of this tale.

45. James Legge, "The Li Sao Poem and Its Author," p. 79. Cf. Rev. Justus Doolittle, *Social Life of the Chinese*, 2:56.

46. Eberhard, *Local Cultures*, p. 395. There is strong concensus by scholars on this. It is the conclusion, for example, of the contemporary research of Yu Kuo-en and Lu K'an-ju. It was also the opinion of Yang Ssu-ch'ang, in the Ming dynasty.

47. Eberhard, *Local Cultures*, p. 396.

48. Ibid.

49. Yang Ssu-ch'ang was a native of Wu-ling, Hunan (present-day Ch'ang-te, just northwest of Changsha). He received his *chin shih* degree in 1610 and was president of the Ministry of War in 1637. See C. Goodrich and C. Y. Fang, eds., *Dictionary of Ming Biography*, 2:1538–1542. Yang is the reputed author of the invaluable *Wu-ling ching-tu lüeh* (Dragon Boat Races in Wu-ling), the main source for this subject. It describes in great detail the contemporary festival and collates data going back to the sixth century. The entire text is translated in Chao Wei-pang, "The Dragon Boat Race in Wu-ling." The text is analyzed in detail in Aijmer, *Dragon Boat Festival*.

50. Translated in Chao Wei-pang, "The Dragon Boat Race in Wuling," pp. 7–8.

51. Ibid., p. 5.

52. Ibid., p. 8.

53. Ibid., p. 9. For the Dragon Boat Festival celebrations in the Sung dynasty, see Chang Ch'i-yün, "Nan Sung tu-ch'eng Hang-chou" [Hangchow, the Southern Sung capital], p. 88.

54. Aijmer, *Dragon Boat Festival*, pp. 24–25. 73–77.

55. For example, see Wen Ch'ung-i, "Chiu ko chung te shui-shen," pp. 73–77.

56. Aijmer, *Dragon Boat Festival*, p. 104. Also see Carl W. Bishop, "Long Houses and Dragon Boats," p. 417. Bishop compares searching for Ch'ü Yüan's body and recalling his soul to the ancient Egyptian ritual search for the drowned corpse of Osiris as described by Plutarch. Bishop concludes that the Dragon Boat Festival "appears to be [a rite] of rainmaking in connection with agriculture, and it is pretty certainly of preChinese origin. Not improbably it once centered about a human sacrifice by drowning, and embodied the very widespread notion of a 'dying god' and the return of the growing season."

57. Aijmer, *Dragon Boat Festival*, pp. 105, 113.

58. Frazer, *Golden Bough*, pp. 481–488.

59. Eliade, *Shamanism*, p. 442.

60. Cited in Lü T'ien-ming, *Ch'ü Yüan, Li Sao chin i*, p. 66. Cp. vernacular transcription of text in Chan An-t'ai, *Ch'ü Yüan*, pp. 3–4.

61. Huang Shih, *Tuan wu li su shih*, passim, and Eberhard, *Local Cultures*, p. 197.

62. Wen Ch'ung-i, "Chiu ko chung te shui-shen," pp. 94–104.

63. Eberhard says "Aijmer (in his *The Dragon Boat Festival*) studied the aspect of the festival which is called 'ching tu' (wading through, in competition). He has defined this festival as a festival of rice planting, and I think he is correct. I doubt, however, that the dragon boat race is a 'crossing' of a water course. A boat festival does not make much sense in a rice planting ceremony. His 'Study of the Ceremonialism in the Transplantation of Rice' as he calls the book, refers to customs in Hunan and Hupei. The boat race, however, seems to be connected with the lower Yangtze area, Anhui, Kiangsu, Kiangsi, Chekiang, Fukien and the Yüeh area, where rice transplantation does not seem to be a part of the festival" (*Local Cultures*, p. 405).

64. Huang Shih, *Tuan wu li su shih*, p. 132. Unfortunately, Huang Shih gives no dates for this custom—a typical flaw with his book, and a characteristic problem with data gathered on Tuan Wu by other Chinese scholars.

65. For Yang Ssu-ch'ang's conclusions, see Chao Wei-pang, "The Dragon Boat Festival in Wu-ling," pp. 8–9, 11–12; and Wen Ch'ung-i, "*Chiu ko* chung te shui-shen," pp. 73–77.

Chapter 5 (Pages 158–199)

1. Yang Yu, "The People Commemorate Ch'ü Yüan," pp. 30–31.

2. See British Peace Committee, *We Can Save Peace*. This publication contains details about the formation of the World Peace Congress and, in appendices, rosters of membership, committees, etc.

3. See illustration in text for postage stamps and *Postage Stamps of the People's Republic of China*, p. 36. I have not been able to locate a copy of the booklet. It is entitled *Commemoration of Ch'ü Yüan, Nicolaus Copernicus, Francois Rabelais, José Marti* (Peking, 1953). It might be a translation of *Wen-i pao* 11 (1953).

4. For a discussion of the reevaluation of Ts'ao Ts'ao, see Albert Feuerwerker, "China's History in Marxian Dress," pp. 39–43.

5. See Huang Yao-mien, "P'ing 'Shih-chien k'ai-shih le' " [Critique of the poem "Time begins"], in Huang Yao-mien, *Ch'en-ssu chi* [Reflections], pp. 168–210; and "Lun Ch'ü Yüan tso-p'in chih ssu-hsiang hsing ho i-shu hsing" [Spirit of Ch'ü Yüan's thought and art] in ibid., pp. 1–44. Dated May 1953. The "Kuo shang" is translated by Hawkes, *Ch'u Tz'u*, p. 43.

Huang Yao-mien was a professor of Chinese literature at Peking Teachers Training College during the 1950s. He was an expert in

Marxist-Leninist literary theory and editor of *Wen-i pao* and *Wen-hsüeh yen-chiu*. Until 1957, when he was attacked as a "rightist," he was one of a group of writers acclaimed for their contributions to literary criticism. He was "influenced by Western ideas and well acquainted with European [and] Soviet literature." In 1957 he was charged with "doubting the wisdom of party control of literary affairs." See D. W. Fokkema, *Literary Doctrine in China and Soviet Influence, 1956–1960*, pp. 180–181.

6. See Lao Meng-yüan, *Li-shih jen-wu te p'ing-chia wen-t'i* [Evaluating historical personages], pp. 30–31. Lao cites the Chinese translation of the *History of the Communist Party of the USSR, Bolshevik* (Peking, 1949).

7. Lao Meng-yüan, "Ko-jen tsai li-shih shang te tso-yung" [Role of the individual in history], pp. 14–29.

8. For example, Ho Ch'i-fang's "Ch'ü Yüan ho t'a te tso-p'in" [Works of Ch'ü Yüan], partially translated in *People's China* 14 (1953). Ho Ch'i-fang urges the reader to consider Ch'ü Yüan's often "naive and utopian" thought in relation to his times. Contextualism is also the mode of Ch'en Hsu-lin, *Lun li-shih jen-wu p'ing-chia wen-t'i* [Problem of evaluating historical personages].

9. Ho Ch'i-fang, "Ch'ü Yüan ho t'a te tso-p'in," from the *People's China* translation, p. 8.

10. Chou Yang, *A Great Debate on the Literary Front*, p. 12. Original speech given to Chinese Writers' Union, September 1957.

11. Ma Mao-yüan, *Ch'u Tz'u hsuan*, p. 63.

12. Yen Hsüeh-k'ung, "Tui-yü ku-tai tso-chia tso-p'in p'ing-chia te chi-tien jen-shih" [Acquaintance with criticism of ancient writers], pp. 13–14.

13. See James Pusey, *Wu Han: Attacking the Present Through the Past*, p. 46, citing Wang Ssu-chih in 1964.

14. Hu Shih, "Tu *Ch'u Tz'u*," p. 94. Also see Lu K'an-ju, "Shen-mo shih Chiu Ko?" [What are the *Nine Songs?*], pp. 79–89; Chung Ching-wen, ed., *Ch'u Tz'u chung te shen-hua ho ch'uan-shuo* [Myth and legend in the *Ch'u Tz'u*].

15. Yu Kuo-en, *Ch'ü Yüan*, pp. 76–78.

16. Cheng Chen-to, "Ch'ü Yüan: Poet-Patriot," pp. 16–17.

17. For a stronger defense of Ch'ü Yüan's authorship and a refutation of Yu Kuo-en's position, see *CTYCL*, 2:12–29; Wen Huai-sha, *Ch'ü Yüan Chiu ko chin i* [Modern commentary on the *Nine Songs*], especially the 1951 preface. Cp. Chan Ping-leung, "Ch'u Tz'u and Shamanism," pp. 170–171. For a translation and discussion of Wang I's interpretation of the *Nine Songs*, see Hawkes, "The Quest of the Goddess," pp. 43–44.

18. For a scholar who remained skeptical of Ch'ü Yüan's authorship, see Lu K'an-ju, *Ch'u Tz'u hsuan* [Collected writings on *Ch'u Tz'u*], pp. 4–5. A summary of arguments contending that Ch'ü Yüan's poetry had folk derivation is to be found in T'an Pi-mo, *Chung-kuo wen-hsüeh shih kang* [Concise history of Chinese literature], 1:49. Futan University's *Chung-kuo wen-hsüeh shih* also emphasizes the *Nine Songs* and the populist connection.

19. Cheng Chen-to, "Mi-lo chiang" [Milo River]. Dated 1957.

20. For example, see Cheng Chen-to, "Ch'ü Yüan: Poet-Patriot," p. 13.

21. *Ch'ü Yüan te ku-shih* [Legend of Ch'ü Yüan], pp. 49–50.

22. Fu Wen-lin, *Tuan wu chieh te ku-shih*. For confirmation that the Fifth of the Fifth was indeed used as a day for settling financial accounts, like New Year's Day, see Rev. Justus Doolittle, *Social Life of the Chinese*, 2:60.

23. Kuo Mo-jo published a vernacular rendition of the *Li Sao* in *Ch'ü Yüan fu chin i* [New interpretation of Ch'ü Yüan's poetry]. Tung Tse-wei and Liu Tan-tse collaborated as illustrator and writer to produce a Ch'ü Yüan comic book, *Ch'ü Yüan* (Shanghai, 1955). There is an English language edition of the comic book published by Foreign Languages Press in 1957. Chang Tsung-i published a higher middle-school textbook entitled *Ch'ü Yüan yü Ch'u Tz'u.*

24. See the T'ang dynasty *Ch'ü Yüan wai chuan.* Also see Clark, *Su Tung-p'o*, p. 102, n. 4; and Yu Kuo-en, *Ch'ü Yüan*, pp. 14–16.

25. Kuo Mo-jo and Yu Kuo-en, for example. Cp. Chan An-t'ai, *Ch'ü Yüan*, pp. 38–39.

26. See photos in *Magnificent China*, pp. 224–225. Some of these photos are reproduced in the Taiwan magazine *Beautiful China* 85 (1975):15.

27. Su Tung-p'o, "Ch'ü Yüan t'a" [Ch'ü Yüan memorial].

28. *Ch'ü Yüan te ku-shih*, p. 56. Also see Cheng Chen-to, "Ch'ü Yüan: Poet-Patriot," p. 17, for photo of memorial mound and stele.

29. Cited in *Magnificent China*, p. 225.

30. *Ch'ü Yüan te ku-shih*, pp. 51–52.

31. Ibid., pp. 52–53. Also see Rewei Alley, *In the Spirit of Hunghu: A Story of Hupeh Today*, p. 31: "On my last day in Wuhan, I drove out to East Lake again, and spent some time in the Ch'ü Yüan Memorial Hall there." Alley provides a photo of an open air statue, larger than life size, of Ch'ü Yüan in East Lake Park. See photos grouped after p. 30, ibid.

32. Ross Terrill, *Flowers on an Iron Tree*, p. 281.

33. Kuo Chia-lin, *Ch'ü Yüan, Ch'u Tz'u*, p. 68. Also see *CTYCL*, 1:96.

34. Huang Yao-mien, *Ch'en-ssu chi*, p. 36.

35. *CTYCL*, 2:41–45.

36. Ho Ch'i-fang, "Ch'ü Yüan ho t'a tso-p'in." Hou Wai-lu's "Ch'ü Yüan ssu-hsiang te mi-mi" [Secret of Ch'ü Yüan's thought] is discussed by Kuo Mo-jo, "Ch'ü Yüan yen-chiu," p. 105.

37. *CTYCL*, 1:26.

38. Kuo Mo-jo, "Ch'ü Yüan: Great Patriotic Poet," p. 5. Also see *Ch'ü Yüan te ku-shih*, pp. 8–9; Lin Keng, *Chung-kuo wen-hsüeh chien-shih* [Short history of Chinese literature], 1:105. Lin Keng refers to Ch'ü Yüan

as one of those "han shih," poor scholars, who were "within" the ranks of the common people.

39. Yu Kuo-en, "Chi-nien tsu-kuo wei-ta te shih-jen Ch'ü Yüan" [Commemorate our nation's great poet]. Reprinted in Yu Kuo-en, *Ch'u Tz'u lun-wen chi* [Anthology of Ch'u Tz'u studies], pp. 256–257, 259, 271.

40. *CTYCL*, 1:204–205, 222. Ch'ü Yüan's populist sentiments were sometimes demonstrated with philological arguments which have tried to arrive at the meaning in the *Li Sao* of the words "min" (generically: people) and "chung" (generically: a group or collectivity of people). These words in contemporary usage are found in vernacular "binoms" meaning the common people (*jen-min, min-chung*). In 1948, Lin Keng rejected claims that "min" in the *Li Sao* meant the commoners or peasants of Ch'u. See Lin Keng, *Shih-jen Ch'ü Yüan chi ch'i tso-p'in yen-chiu* [Study of Chü Yüan and his works], pp. 42–51. For similar arguments see Chao Sheng-p'ing, *Ch'ü Yüan chi ch'i tso-p'in yen-chiu*, pp. 6, 79–80. Scholarship on this subject during the 1950s could not come to any consensus, and it kept open the possibility that Chü Yüan had indeed been speaking in populist terminology directly about the common people. For examples see *CTYCL*, 1:177–179, 2:41–45. More recently, this possibility was rejected altogether. See Wang Yun-hsi, et al., "Shih-lun Ch'ü Yüan te tsun Fa, fan Ju ssu-hsiang" [Ch'ü Yüan's pro-Legalist, anti-Confucian thought], p. 58.

41. Fokkema, *Literary Doctrine in China*, p. 194.

42. Translated in ibid.

43. Cited in ibid., pp. 201–202.

44. Ibid.

45. Ibid., p. 199.

46. Chou Yang, *Hung ch'i* [Red flag] 1 (1958), and translated in Fokkema, *Literary Doctrine in China*, pp. 33–39.

47. Kuo Mo-jo, "Lang-man chu-i yü hsien-shih chu-i," pp. 6–7.

48. Ibid. Cp. Kuo Mo-jo, *Li Po yü Tu Fu*, p. 87. Here Kuo expresses doubts about Li Po's ability to measure up to Ch'ü Yüan. Li Po was superstitious and believed in what Ch'ü Yüan only used for rhetorical purposes. The same position on Li Po and other "imitators" of Ch'ü Yüan is taken by Jen Fang-ch'iu, ed., *Chung-kuo ku-tien wen-hsüeh yen-chiu lun-chi* [Materials for the study of classical Chinese literature], p. 16.

49. Chou Yang, *The Path of Socialist Literature and Art in China*.

50. Ibid.

51. Ibid.

52. Feng Hsüeh-feng, "Hui-ta kuan-yü 'Shui-hu' chi-ke wen-t'i" [Response to the essay—several questions on the novel *Shui-hu chuan*], p. 32.

53. Ibid., p. 34.

54. Ho Ch'i-fang, "Ch'ü Yüan ho t'a te tso-p'in," *People's China* translation, p. 7.

55. For examples see: (1) the high school textbook by the Literature Department of Peking University, *Chung-kuo wen-hsüeh shih* (Peking, 1955; 1959), 1: 111–115. (2) *CTYCL*, 2:113–125. (3) Kuo Chia-lin, *Ch'ü Yüan, Ch'u Tz'u*, p. 39. (4) Lu Ch'in-li, *Ch'ü Yüan Li Sao chien-lun* [Short discussion of Ch'ü Yüan's *Li Sao*], p. 55.

56. Ma Mao-yüan, *Ch'u Tz'u hsuan*, pp. 14–15, 22–23, 52.

57. For examples, see Lu K'an-ju, *Ch'ü Yüan*, pp. 91, 94; Yu Kuo-en, "T'ien wen yen-chiu," p. 111.

58. For summary of authenticity problems, see *CTYCL*, 2:12–29.

59. Kuo Mo-jo, "Ch'ü Yüan: Great Patriotic Poet," p. 10.

60. Kuo Mo-jo, "Ch'ü Yüan, Ancient China's Patriot Poet," p. 15.

61. *CTYCL*, 3:128. Also see Kuo Chia-lin, *Ch'ü Yüan, Ch'u Tz'u*, p. 50.

62. *CTYCL*, 1:154–155.

63. Kuo Mo-jo, ed., *Chung-kuo shih-kao* [History of China], 2:42–44. Also see Wang Yun-hsi, "Shih-lun Ch'ü Yüan te tsun Fa, fan Ju ssu-hsiang," pp. 56–57.

64. The Taiwan consensus is that Ch'ü Yüan was Confucian and not Legalist. For examples, see: Liu Wei-ch'ung, *Ch'ü Yüan p'ing-chuan* [A critical biography of Ch'ü Yüan], p. 66; Yang Yung-tsung, "Ch'ü Yüan wei Ju-chia k'ao" [Ch'ü Yüan was a Confucian]; Lü T'ien-ming, *Ch'ü Yüan Li Sao chin i* [Modern commentary on the *Li Sao*].
Anthologies of translated materials central to the debates on Legalism in the PRC are to be found in two excellent volumes edited by Li Yu-ning: *The First Emperor of China: The Politics of Historiography*, and *Shang Yang's Reforms and State Control in China*.

65. See chapter three above.

66. Lin Keng, *Shih-jen Ch'ü Yüan chi ch'i tso-p'in*, p. 45. Cp. T'ao Kuang, "Ch'ü Yüan chih szu" [Death of Ch'ü Yüan]. This article rejects the Confucian and Taoist categories for Ch'ü Yüan. For a discussion of periodic interest in "Confucianism" during the 1950s and 1960s, see Merle Goldman, "The Chinese Communist Party's Cultural Revolution of 1962–1964."

67. Kuo Mo-jo, "Ch'ü Yüan: Great Patriotic Poet," p. 7.

68. For example see Yu Kuo-en, "Chi-nien tsu-kuo wei-ta te shih-jen Ch'ü Yüan." During the Hundred Flowers movement, Yu Kuo-en was attacked for this position. See for example the anthology *Wen-hsüeh yen-chiu yü p'i-p'an* [Literary research and criticism]. Also see *CTYCL*, 3:162–171.

69. *CTYCL*, 2:1–7.

70. *CTYCL*, 1:177–179.

71. *CTYCL*, 2: 8–11.

72. See H. G. Creel, "The Beginnings of Bureaucracy in China: The Origins of the Hsien."

73. Lu Ch'in-li, *Ch'ü Yüan Li Sao chien-lun*, pp. 10, 24, 35; and also Chan An-t'ai, *Ch'ü Yüan*, pp. 6–9, 45–48, 62–69.

74. Chang Tsung-i, *Ch'ü Yüan yü Ch'u Tz'u*.

75. R. Clark and A. Sowerby, *Through Shen-Kan*, p. 45. Cited in Edward Friedman, *Backward Toward Revolution*, p. 156.

76. *Nu li chih shih-tai* [Age of slavery] (Peking, 1954; 1973), p. 157.

77. *Ch'ü Yüan te ku-shih*, pp. 39, 46.

78. Cheng Chen-to, "Mi-lo chiang," pp. 563–564.

79. This argument goes back to Hsieh Wu-liang's *Ch'u Tz'u hsin lun*, and to Yu Kuo-en's own "Wei-ta te shih-jen Ch'ü Yüan chi ch'i wen-hsüeh." Yu Kuo-en was criticized for this argument during the Hundred Flowers campaign because of its "idealist" implications. See the broadsides of the Mao Tse-tung Literary Club of Peking University in *Wen-hsüeh yen-chiu yü p'i-p'an*, 1:124–130, 2:14.

80. See the following: (1) Lin Keng, *Shih-jen Ch'ü Yüan*, p. 4. (2) Fang Shih-ming, *Jen-min te shih-jen Ch'ü Yüan*, p. 5. (3) Introductory essay to special Ch'ü Yüan issue of *Wen-i pao* 11 (June 1953). (4) Huang Yao-mien, *Ch'en-ssu chi*, pp. 4–5. (5) Ch'en Hsu-lin, *Lun li-shih jen-wu p'ing-chia wen-t'i*, p. 14. (6) Chan An-t'ai, *Ch'ü Yüan*, pp. 6–7, 12–13. (7) Chang Tsung-i, *Ch'ü Yüan yü Ch'u Tz'u*, pp. 19–20.

81. Pusey, *Wu Han*, p. 20.

82. For a lucid summary of the changing public models and heroes of the CCP, see Frederic Wakeman Jr., *History and Will: Philosophical Perspectives of Mao Tse-tung's Thought*, pp. 23–24.

83. Cp. Joseph R. Levenson's analysis of this problem for the 1950s and 1960s, "The Place of Confucius in Communist China," *Confucian China and Its Modern Fate*, 3:61–84.

84. See Li Yu-ning, *The First Emperor of China*, and Wang Gung-wu, "Juxtaposing Past and Present in China Today."

85. Li Yu-ning, *The First Emperor of China*, p. 52.

86. Wang Yun-hsi, "Shih-lun Ch'ü Yüan te tsun Fa, fan Ju ssu-hsiang," pp. 53, 55–56, 58; and Liu Ta-chieh, *Chung-kuo wen-hsüeh fa-chan shih*, 1:111–112, 122–123.

87. For an extended analysis of this point within the context of the historicist vs. class viewpoint controversy, see Arif Dirlik, "The Problem of Class Viewpoint Versus Historicism in Chinese Historiography," and Arif Dirlik and Laurence Schneider, "China: Recent Historiographical Issues."

88. In 1973, at the outset of the reevaluation of the First Emperor, and as part of the anti-Confucian campaign, Kuo Mo-jo changed his long-held periodization of ancient Chinese history. From the 1920s up to this time, he had argued that the transition from the slave to the feudal period came in the Spring and Autumn-Warring States era. Now he claimed it took place later, in the late Warring States-Ch'in era. Confucius and the Confucians could be considered "revolutionary" by Kuo in the 1930s because

he considered them to be heralds of the feudal stage of history and enemies of the slave society which he claimed was coming to an end around the time of Confucius. In the new scheme, Confucianism develops within and reflects the values of an ongoing slave society. Thus, the Legalists and the First Emperor, representatives and spokesmen for the newly evolved landlord class, were in direct conflict with the Confucians in the third century B.C., and related to them as progressives to reactionaries.

Conclusion (Pages 200–211)

1. Metzger, *Escape from Predicament*, p. 76. In this section I have adopted some of Metzger's terminology and formulations, revolving around the idea of "predicament," because some of the conclusions in his book are quite relevant to my study of Ch'ü Yüan and consonant with my findings.

2. See Chen Shih-hsiang, "The Genesis of Poetic Time." Professor Chen draws upon the work of George Poulet for this theory of the relationship of time and self.

3. See J. H. Elliott, *The Old World and the New, 1492–1650*, pp. 24–25, 41–44. Elliott suggests "Fifteenth-century Christendom's own sense of self-dissatisfaction found expression in the longing for a return to a better state of things. The return might be to the lost Christian paradise, or to the Golden Age of the ancients, or to some elusive combination of both these imagined worlds. With the discovery of the Indies and their inhabitants, who went around naked and yet—in defiance of the Biblical tradition—mysteriously unashamed, it was all too easy to transpose the ideal world from a world remote in time to a world remote in space. Arcadia and Eden could now be located on the far shores of the Atlantic" (p. 25). Cp. Fiedler, *Return of the Vanishing American*, chapter 1.

4. One of the common alternate names of Ch'ü Yüan, in addition to Ling chün, is Ch'ü P'ing. I interpret this as "Ch'ü the Straight," in the same sense as "Ch'ü Yüan the sober one." The word "p'ing" additionally implies level or balanced—further anomalies for a persona often characterized as excessive. The reference of course is to Ch'ü Yüan's morality. One thinks of Wang I's description of Ch'ü Yüan's character (his loyalty and moral purity) as "smooth as a whetstone and straight as a dart."

Notes and Credits
for Illustrations

Plate 1. "Lord of the Clouds." Album leaf painting from *Chiu-ko shu-hua ts'e* [Nine Songs illustrated], after Chao Meng-fu (1254–1322). Dated 1305. Album of sixteen double leaves: 11 paintings with facing leaves of text. Ink on paper. Total dimensions: H. 12½". W. 15⅝". By permission: The Metropolitan Museum of Art, Fletcher Fund, 1973.

Plate 2. A Good Official Is Pickled by an Evil King. Ch'en Hung-shou and Hsiao Yun-ts'ung, *Ch'u Tz'u t'u chu* [Ch'u Tz'u with illustrations and commentary], seventeenth-century woodblock. Harvard-Yenching Library collection.

Plate 3. Fourteenth-century portrait of Ch'ü Yüan. From "Chiu-ko t'u" [The Nine Songs], by Chang Wu, active 1335–1365. Ink on paper. Handscroll, 11" x 172½". By permission: The Cleveland Museum of Art, purchase from the J. H. Wade Fund.

Plate 4. Fourteenth-century album leaf portrait of Ch'ü Yüan. From *Chiu-ko shu-hua ts'e*. By permission: The Metropolitan Museum of Art, Fletcher Fund, 1973.

Plate 5. Portraits of Ch'ü Yüan. Reproduced in Cheng Chen-to, ed., *Ch'u Tz'u t'u* [Illustrations of the Ch'u Tz'u], 2 *ts'e*. Peking, 1963.

Plate 6. "Kutsugen" by Taikan Yokoyama. Sumi and color on silk. 52½" x 114". Itsukushima Shrine collection, Miyajima. My reproduction is taken from *Yu-shih wen-i* 30 (Taipei, July 1969). According to John M.

Rosenfield, this painting was intended to be an allegorical portrait of Oka-kura Kakuzo, leader of the movement in Japan to retain Classical Japanese and Chinese elements in the arts. Rosenfield says that Taikan's portrait is a classic example of early Nihon-ga, a style of "Japanese painting" Okakura and his colleagues had devised for government sponsored activities, using traditional Asian subject matter and materials. However, Rosenfield sees many Western elements in this portrait: an "overriding sense of melo-drama, of individualism, of theatrical self-consciousness in the face of Ch'ü Yüan and in the landscape setting. These were traits never found in the impassive, reserved visages of traditional portraiture in Japan." He sees a "mood of romantic egoism; a highly personal style of painting, which would shock [Taikan's] audience." See John M. Rosenfield, "Western-Style Painting in the Early Meiji Period and Its Critics," in *Tradition and Mod-ernization in Japanese Culture*, ed. Donald Shively (Princeton: Princeton University Press, 1971) pp. 181, 203. Okakura himself described the paint-ing in this way: "Taikan brings into the field his wild imagery and tempes-tuous conceptions, as shown in his 'Kutsugen Wandering on the Barren Hills' amongst wind-blown narcissus—the flower of silent purity—feeling the raging storm that gathers in his soul." Cited in Rosenfield, "Western-Style Painting," p. 203. Also see Yoshizawa Chu, *Taikan, Modern Master of Oriental-Style Painting, 1868–1958* (Tokyo: Kodansha, 1962).

Plate 7. "The Lady of the Hsiang River." Album leaf from fourteenth-century *Chiu-ko shu-hua ts'e*. By permission: The Metropolitan Museum of Art, Fletcher Fund, 1973.

Plate 8. "The God of the Yellow River" (Ho Po). From Chang Wu, "Chiu-ko t'u." By permission: The Cleveland Museum of Art, purchase from the J.H. Wade Fund.

Plate 9. "Lady of the Hsiang River" and "Lord of the Hsiang River." From Chang Wu, "Chiu-ko t'u." By permission: The Cleveland Museum of Art, purchase from the J.H. Wade Fund.

Plate 10. "Lord and Lady of the Hsiang River." Seventeenth-century woodblock from Ch'en and Hsiao, *Ch'u Tz'u t'u chu*.

Plate 11. "Searching for Ch'ü Yüan" is an illustration from the nine-teenth-century periodical *T'ien shih ch'ai hua pao*. My thanks to Ralph Croizier for the photograph. The Chinese caption begins: "On Lake Wu [Anhwei province], during the Tuan Wu festival, Dragon Boat racing takes place. [The contestants] compete to get ahead, each displaying his special skill." It then tells the story of a group of Hunan coal barge sailors who drowned while celebrating Tuan Wu. They had got drunk on festival wine and pretended they were Dragon Boat racers and upset their craft in the river. The story seems to be a warning about the hazards of Tuan Wu water festivals and/or carelessness around water.

Plate 12. "Four Giants of World Culture." 1953 issue, People's Repub-lic of China commemorative postage stamps. From author's collection.

Plate 13. "Spirits of the Fallen" (Kuo shang). From Chang Wu,

"Chiu-ko t'u." By permission: The Cleveland Museum of Art, purchase from the J.H. Wade Fund.

Plate 14. Ch'ü Yüan comic book. From Tung Tse-wei, *Ch'ü Yüan* (Shanghai, 1955).

Plate 15. "The Archer Yi." Ch'en and Hsiao, *Ch'u Tz'u t'u chu*.

Plate 16. Astrological chart, Ch'en and Hsiao, *Ch'u Tz'u t'u chu*. Translations from *Heavenly Questions* after David Hawkes, trans., *Ch'u Tz'u: The Songs of the South* (London: Oxford University Press, 1959; Boston, 1962) pp. 46–51.

Glossary of Selected Terms and Names

"Ai Chiang-nan" 哀江南
"Ai shih ming" 哀時命
"Ai Ying" 哀郢

Chang Chiu-ling 張九齡
ch'ang-ming-lü 長命縷
Ch'ang-te 常德
Chao Ch'ü T'ing 招屈亭
chao-hun 招魂
Chao Meng-chien 趙孟堅
Chao Meng-fu 趙孟頫
chen-shih 眞實
Ch'en Tu-hsiu 陳獨秀
cheng-chün 徵君
Cheng Yü 鄭瑜
Chi-tzu 箕子
Chi Yung-jen 稽永仁
Chia I (Chia Yi) 賈誼
Chiang-ling 江陵

Chiang-nan 江南
chiao lung 蛟龍
Chieh Tzu-t'ui 介子推
Chieh Yü 接輿
ch'ih 癡
"Ch'ih pi fu" 赤壁賦
ching 經
Ching Ch'u sui shih chi
　荊楚歲時記
ching tu 競渡
"Chiu Chao" 九昭
Chiu-chen 九眞
"Chiu Huai" 九懷
"Chiu ko shu-hua ts'e"
　九歌書畫冊
"Chiu ko t'u" 九歌圖
Chou 周
Ch'u Tz'u hou yü 楚辭後語
Ch'ü P'ing 屈平

245

Ch'ü Yüan　屈原
Ch'ü Yüan pieh chuan
　屈原別傳
Chuang-tzu　莊子
chün-tzu　君子
chung　眾
chung, chen　忠貞
Chung ching　忠經
Chung-hua min-tsu　中華民族
Chung Hung　鍾嶸
Chung K'uei　鍾馗
Chung Shan-fu　仲山甫
Chung yuan　中原

Erh Fei　二妃

fa-chih　法制
Fan Li　范蠡
"Fan sao"　反騷
fan shen　翻身
fei ch'i shih　非其時
"Feng"　風
Feng-su t'ung-i　風俗通義
Fu She　復社

han shih　寒士
Han shih wai chuan　韓詩外傳
Han shu　漢書
Han Ying　韓嬰
Han Yü　韓愈
"Han-yun fu"　旱雲賦
Hei Miao　黑苗
Ho Po　河伯
Hou Han shu　後漢書
hsia-fang　下方
Hsiang　湘
Hsiang-yin　湘陰
Hsiang Yü　項羽
Hsieh Yeh　泄冶
hsien　縣
Hsiling　西陵

hsin-chih　心制
Hsü Ch'i chieh-chi　續齊諧記
"Hsü Li Sao"　續離騷
Hsü Yu　許由
Hsün-tzu　荀子
Huai (King of Ch'u)　懷
huan-hsiang　幻想
Huang T'ing-chien　黃庭堅
hun　魂

i szu wu chün　以死悟君

jen cheng　仁政
jen-min　人民

Kou Chien　勾踐
Kuan Han-ch'ing　關汗卿
Kuan Lung-feng　關龍逢
k'uang　狂
k'uang Ch'an　狂禪
k'uang-sheng　狂生
k'un, ch'ien　坤乾
Kuo-ch'uan Ch'i-lao　鍋圈犵狫
"Kuo shang"　國殤

Lao-tzu　老子
lei　累
Li Ho　李賀
Li Po　李白
Li Sao　離騷
li-shih chu-i　歷史主義
Li Ta-chao　李大釗
Liang Sung　梁竦
Liang Wu-chün　梁吳均
Liao P'ing　廖平
"Lieh nü chuan"　列女傳
Lieh Tzu　列子
Lin Wen-ch'ing (Lim Boon Keng)
　林文慶
Ling-chün　靈均
ling-po hsien-tzu　凌波仙子

Liu An 劉安

Liu Hsia-huei 柳下惠

Liu Hsieh 劉勰

Liu Yü-hsi 劉禹錫

Lo-p'ing Li 樂平里

Lu Yu (Lu You) 陸游

Lun Heng 論衡

Lung-chou-chieh 龍舟節

Meng Chiao 孟郊

Mi-lo (Milo) 汨羅

min-chung 民衆

Nü Hsü 女嬃

O Hui 歐回

pai hua 白話

Pan Ku 班固

P'eng Hsien 彭咸

Pi Kan 比干

Pien Sui 卞随

p'ing min 平民

Po Yi (Po-i) 伯夷

San Jen 三仁

San lü ta-fu 三閭大夫

San lü tz'u 三閭祠

sao 騷

Shang 商

Shang Ti 上帝

Shang-yü 上虞

Shen O-chih 沈亞之

Shen-t'u Ti 申徒狄

Shen wu 神巫

shih 時

Shih chi 史記

shih ming 時命

Shih p'in 詩品

shih pu yü fu 士不遇賦

Shu Ch'i 卞齊

Shui ching chu 水經注

shui-hsien 水仙

shui-hsien tsun-wang 水仙尊王

Shun 舜

ssu-hsiang (szu-hsiang) 思想

Ssu-ma Ch'ien 司馬遷

Ssu-ma Kuang 司馬光

su 俗

Su Shih (Su Tung-p'o) 蘇軾

"Sung" 頌

ta-chung-hua 大衆化

Tai Chi-t'ao 戴季陶

Taikan Yokoyama 大觀橫山

T'an Ssu-t'ung 譚嗣同

T'ao Ch'ien 陶潛

t'i 體

"Tiao sao fu" 弔騷賦

T'ien chung chieh 天中節

t'ien ts'ai 天才

tsa-chü 雜劇

Ts'ao Hsüeh-ch'in 曹雪芹

Ts'ao O 曹娥

Ts'ao Yü 曹玉

Ts'ui Chia 崔嘉

tsung-tzu 粽子

Tu Fu 杜甫

Tuan Wu 端午（端五）

Tuan yang chieh 端陽節

Tung-t'ing 洞庭

Tzu-chih t'ung-chien 資治通鑑

Tzu-kuei 秭歸

Wang An-shih 王安石

Wang Ch'ung 王充

Wang K'ai-yün 王閩運

Wang Pao 王褒

wei 緯

Wei-tzu 微子

Wu Ch'i 吳起

Wu-ling 武陵

Wu-ling ching-tu lüeh
武陵競渡略
Wu Tzu-hsü　吳子胥
wu-wei　無爲

"Ya"　雅
Yang Hsiung　揚雄
Yang Ssu-ch'ang　楊嗣昌
Yen Chi　嚴忌
yin-yang　陰陽
Ying　郢

Yu T'ung　尤侗
"Yu yung"　游泳
Yü　禹
Yü Hsin　庾信
Yü-hsün　玉荀
yuan-jen　原人
"Yuan Yu"　遠遊
Yüeh　越
Yüeh Fei　岳飛
yung　用
Yung-chou　永州

Bibliography

Aeschylus. *Prometheus Bound*. Translated by Philip Vellacott. Baltimore: Penguin, 1961.

Aijmer, Göran. *The Dragon Boat Festival on the Hupeh Hunan Plain, Central China: A Study in the Ceremonialism of the Transplantation of Rice*. Stockholm, 1964.

Allan, Sarah. "The Identities of Taigong Wang in Zhou and Han Literature." *Monumenta Serica* 30 (1972–1973): 57–99.

———. "The Heir and the Sage: A Structural Analysis of Ancient Chinese Dynastic Legends." Ph.D. dissertation draft, University of California, Berkeley, October, 1973.

Alley, Rewei. *In the Spirit of Hunghu: A Story of Hupeh Today*. Peking: New World Press, 1966.

Anouilh, Jean. *Antigone*. Translated and adapted by Lewis Galanterie. New York: Random House, 1946.

Atwell, William S. "From Education to Politics: The Fu She." In *The Unfolding of Neo Confucianism*, edited by W. T. de Bary, pp. 333–368. New York: Columbia University Press, 1975.

Balazs, Etienne. *Chinese Civilization and Bureaucracy*. New Haven: Yale University Press, 1964.

Barnard, Noel, ed. *Early Chinese Art and Its Possible Influence in the Pacific Basin, vol. 1: Ch'u and the Silk Manuscript*. New York: Intercultural Arts Press, 1972.

Baxter, G. W. "Metrical Origins of the Tz'u." In *Studies in Chinese Litera-*

ture, edited by J. L. Bishop, pp. 186–225. Cambridge, Mass.: Harvard University Press, 1966.

Bishop, Carl W. "Long Houses and Dragon Boats." *Antiquity* 12 (December 1938): 411–424.

Bodde, Derk. *Festivals in Classical China: New Year and Other Annual Observances During the Han Dynasty.* Princeton: Princeton University Press, and the Chinese University of Hong Kong, 1975.

Bogan, M. L. C. *Manchu Customs and Superstitions.* Peking, 1928.

British Peace Committee. *We Can Save Peace.* London, 1950.

Brooks, E. B. "A Geometry of the Shīr pǐn." In *Wen lin–Studies in Chinese Humanities*, edited by T. T. Chow. Madison: University of Wisconsin Press, 1968.

Chan An-t'ai 詹安泰 . *Ch'ü Yüan.* Shanghai, 1957.

Chan Ping-leung. "The *Ch'u Tz'u* and Shamanism in Ancient China." Ph.D. dissertation, Ohio State University, 1972.

Chang Ch'i-yün 張其昀 . "Nan Sung tu-ch'eng Hang-chou" 南宋都城杭州 [Hangchow, the Southern Sung capital]. *Shih ti hsüeh-pao* 史地學報 [History and geography] 3 (May 1925).

Chang T'ai-yen 章太炎 . "Shih ching shih lun" 詩經始論 [On the Odes]. In *Chang T'ai-yen wen-hsuan* 章太炎文選 [Collected works], pp. 64–66. Shanghai, 1937.

Chang Tsung-i 張縱逸 . *Ch'ü Yüan yü Ch'u Tz'u.* Ch'ang-chün, 1957.

Chao Sheng-p'ing 趙昇平 . *Ch'ü Yüan chi ch'i tso-p'in yen-chiu* 屈原及其作品研究 [Ch'ü Yüan and his works]. Taipei, 1968.

Chao Wei-pang, trans. and ed. "The Dragon Boat Race in Wu-ling, Hunan—by Yang Ssu-ch'ang." *Folklore Studies* 2 (1943): 1–18.

Chen, P. H. *Social Thought of Lu Hsün.* New York: Vantage, 1976.

Chen Shih-hsiang, trans. *Essay on Literature, Written by the Third Century Chinese Poet Lu Chi.* Portland Me.: Anthoensen, 1953.

———. "The Genesis of Poetic Time: The Greatness of Ch'ü Yüan, Studied With a New Critical Approach." *Tsinghua Journal of Chinese Studies* (n.s., June 1975): 1–43.

Ch'en Ch'ü-ping 陳去病 . *Tz'u fu hsüeh kang-yao* 辭賦學綱要 [Basics of *tz'u* and *fu* poetry]. 1927; Taipei, 1971.

Ch'en Chung-fan 陳鐘凡 . "Chou tai nan pei wen-hsüeh chih pi-chiao" 周代南北文學之比較 [Comparison of northern and southern literature from Chou times]. *Kuo-hsüeh ts'ung-k'an* 國學叢刊 [National studies], no. 3 (1923): 11–26.

Ch'en Hsu-lin 陳旭麓 . *Lun li-shih jen-wu p'ing-chia wen-t'i* 論歷史人物評價問題 [Problem of evaluating historical personages]. Shanghai, 1955.

Ch'en Hung-shou 陳洪綬 and Hsiao Yun-ts'ung 蕭雲從 . *Ch'u Tz'u t'u chu* 楚辭圖注 [*Ch'u Tz'u* with illustrations and commentary]. Taipei: Chunghua, 1971.

Cheng Chen-to 鄭振鐸 , ed. *Ch'ing jen tsa-chü ch'u chi* 清人雜
劇初集 [First collection of *tsa-chü* dramas from Ch'ing times]. 10
vols. Shanghai, 1931–1934.

———. *Chung-kuo wen-hsüeh shih* 中國文學史 [History of Chinese
literature]. 4 vols. Peking, 1932.

———. "Ch'ü Yüan tso-p'in tsai Chung-kuo wen-hsüeh shang te ying-
hsiang" 屈原作品在中國文學上的影響 [Influence
of Ch'ü Yüan's works on Chinese literature]. *Wen-i pao* 文藝報
[Literary arts] 17 (1953).

———. "Ch'ü Yüan: Poet Patriot." *China Reconstructs* 5 (1953).

———. "Mi-lo chiang" 汨羅江 [Milo River]. In *Cheng Chen-to
wen-chi* 鄭振鐸文集 [Collected works of Cheng Chen-to]. 2 vols.
Peking, 1959. 1:554–571.

———. *Ch'u Tz'u t'u* 楚辭圖 [Illustrations of *Ch'u Tz'u*]. 2 ts'e.
Peking, 1963. Preface dated 1953.

Cheng Yü 鄭瑜 . "Mi-lo chiang" 汨羅江 [Milo River]. In
Tsa-chü hsin pien 雜劇新編 [New collection of *tsa-chü*
dramas], edited by Chou Wu-chin 鄒武金 . 1661.

Chi Yung-jen 稽永仁 . "Hsü Li Sao" 續離騷 [*Li Sao*
continued]. In Cheng Chen-to, ed., *Ch'ing jen tsa-chü ch'u chi*.
Vol. 2.

Chiang Chi 蔣驥 . *Shan tai ko chu Ch'u Tz'u* 山帶閣注楚辭
[Commentary on *Ch'u Tz'u*]. 1727; reprint Taipei: Kuang Wen,
1962.

Chiang Liang-fu 姜亮夫 . *Ch'u Tz'u shu-mu wu-chung* 楚辭書目五
種 [Five-fold bibliography of *Ch'u Tz'u*]. Shanghai, 1961.

Chiang Shan-kuo 蔣善國 , ed. *Ch'u Tz'u*. Shanghai, 1924.

Chien T'ang 間堂 . "Tuan wu k'ao" 端午考 [Study of Tuan Wu].
Lun yü 論語 [Analects] 114 (June 1937): 826–829.

Ching, Julia. "Wang Yang-ming: A Study in Mad Ardour." *Papers on Far
Eastern History* 3 (March 1971): 85–130.

———. "Neo Confucian Utopian Theories and Political Ethics." *Monumenta Serica* 30 (1972–1973): 1–56.

———. *To Acquire Wisdom*. New York: Columbia University Press,
1976.

Chou Yang. *The Path of Socialist Literature and Art in China*. Report to the
Third Congress of Chinese Literary and Art Workers. Peking: Foreign
Languages Press, 1960.

———. *A Great Debate on the Literary Front*. 3d ed. Peking: Foreign
Languages Press, 1965.

Chou Wu-chin 鄒武金 , ed. *Tsa-chü hsin pien* 雜劇新編 [New
collection of *tsa-chü* dramas]. 1661.

Chu Hsi 朱熹 . *Ch'u Tz'u chi chu* 楚辭集注 [Collected writings on
Ch'u Tz'u]. Taipei: I-wen, 1967.

Ch'u Tz'u yen-chiu lun-wen chi 楚辭研究論文集 [Anthology of *Ch'u Tz'u* studies]. 3 vols. Peking, 1957–70.

Ch'ü Yüan. By the Language and Literature Department, 11th Women's Middle School of Peking. Peking, 1959.

Ch'ü Yüan te ku-shih 屈原的故事 [Legend of Ch'ü Yüan]. Wuhan, 1956.

"Ch'ü Yüan wai chuan" 屈原外傳 [Unofficial biography]. In Lü T'ien-ming, *Ch'ü Yüan, Li Sao chin i.* Taipei, 1969.

Ch'ü Yüan yen-chiu tzu-liao hui-pien 屈原研究資料彙編 [Research materials on Ch'ü Yüan]. 2 vols. xerox. n.p. Gest Oriental Library, Princeton University, n.d.

Chung Ching-wen 鍾敬文 , ed. *Ch'u Tz'u chung te shen-hua ho ch'uan-shuo* 楚辭中的神話和傳說 [Myth and legend in the *Ch'u Tz'u*]. Canton: Chung-shan University, 1929; Taipei, 1970.

Clark, Cyril Drummond le Gros, trans. *The Prose Poetry of Su Tung-p'o.* Shanghai, 1945; New York, 1964.

Clark, R. and Sowerby, A. *Through Shen-Kan.* London, 1912.

Commemoration of Ch'ü Yüan, Nicholaus Copernicus, Francois Rabelais, José Marti. Peking, 1953.

Couvreur, F. S. *Dictionnaire classique de la langue Chinoise.* Taipei: Book World, 1963.

Cox, Richard H. "Ideology, History and Political Philosophy: Camus' *L'Homme Revolté.*" *Social Research* 32 (Spring 1965): 69–97.

Creel, H. G. "The Beginnings of Bureaucracy in China: The Origins of the Hsien." *Journal of Asian Studies* 23 (February 1964): 155–184.

————. *Shen Pu-hai: A Chinese Political Philosopher of the Fourth Century BC.* Chicago: University of Chicago Press, 1974.

Croizier, Ralph. *Koxinga and Chinese Nationalism: History, Myth, and the Hero.* Cambridge, Mass.: Harvard University Press, 1977.

Crump, J. I. *Intrigues—Studies of the Chan-kuo ts'e.* Ann Arbor: University of Michigan Press, 1964.

de Bary, W. T., ed. *Self and Society in Ming Thought.* New York: Columbia University Press, 1970.

————, ed. *The Unfolding of Neo Confucianism.* New York: Columbia University Press, 1975.

Dirlik, Arif. "The Problem of Class Viewpoint Versus Historicism in Chinese Historiography." *Modern China* 3 (1977): 465–489.

————, and Schneider, Laurence. "China: Recent Historiographical Issues." In *International Handbook of Historiography,* edited by Georg Iggers. Westport: Greenwood Press, 1979.

Doolittle, Rev. Justus. *Social Life of the Chinese.* 2 vols. New York: Harper, 1865.

Dubs, Homer, trans. *The Works of Hsuntze.* London, 1928; Taipei, 1966.

Duke, Michael S. *Lu You*. Boston: Twayne, 1977.

Eberhard, Wolfram. *The Local Cultures of South and East China*. Leiden: Brill, 1968.

Eliade, Mircea. *Shamanism: Archaic Techniques of Ecstasy*. Rev. ed. Translated by W. R. Trask. New York: Pantheon, 1964.

Elliott, J. H. *The Old World and the New, 1492–1650*. Cambridge: Cambridge University Press, 1970.

Fang Shih-ming 方詩銘 . *Jen-min te shih-jen Ch'ü Yüan* 人民的詩人屈原 [People's poet Ch'ü Yüan]. Shanghai, 1953.

Feng Hsüeh-feng 馮雪峯 . "Hui-ta kuan-yü 'Shui-hu' chi-ke wen-t'i" 回答關於水滸 幾個問題 [Response to the essay "Several questions on the novel *Shui-hu chuan*"]. *Wen-i pao* 文藝報 [Literary arts] 6 (March 1954): 32–38.

Feuerwerker, Albert. "China's History in Marxian Dress." In *History in Communist China*, edited by Albert Feuerwerker, pp. 14–44. Cambridge, Mass.: MIT Press, 1968.

Fiedler, Leslie. *Return of the Vanishing American*. New York: Stein and Day, 1968.

Fokkema, D. W. *Literary Doctrine in China and Soviet Influence, 1956–1960*. The Hague: Mouton, 1965.

Fong, Wen. *Sung and Yuan Paintings*. New York: Metropolitan Museum of Art, 1973.

Frazer, Sir James G. *The Golden Bough: A Study in Magic and Religion*. Rev. ed. in 1 vol. New York: Macmillan, 1960.

Friedman, Edward. *Backward Toward Revolution*. Berkeley and Los Angeles: University of California Press, 1974.

Frodsham, J. D., trans. and intro. *The Poems of Li Ho (791–817)*. Oxford: Clarendon, 1970.

Fu Ssu-nien 傅斯年 . *Fu Meng-chen hsien-sheng chi* 傅孟眞先生集 [Fu Ssu-nien's collected works]. 6 vols. Taipei, 1952.

Fu Wen-lin 傅文琳 . *Tuan wu chieh te ku-shih* 端午節的故事 [Story of the Tuan Wu festival]. Wuhan, 1958.

Fung Yu-lan. *A History of Chinese Philosophy*. 2 vols. Translated by Derk Bodde. Princeton: Princeton University Press, 1953.

Furth, Charlotte, ed. *Limits of Change: Essays on Conservative Alternatives in Republican China*. Cambridge, Mass.: Harvard University Press, 1976.

Futan University. *Chung-kuo wen-hsüeh shih* 中國文學史 [History of Chinese literature]. Shanghai, 1958.

Gernet, Jacques. *Daily Life in China on the Eve of the Mongol Invasion 1250–1276*. Stanford: Stanford University Press, 1970.

Giles, Herbert. *A Chinese Biographical Dictionary*. 2 vols. Taipei, 1962.

Goldman, Merle. "The Chinese Communist Party's Cultural Revolution of 1962–1964." In *Ideology and Politics in Contemporary China,* edited by Chalmers Johnson, pp. 219–254. Seattle: University of Washington Press, 1973.

Goodrich, C. and Fang C. Y., eds. *Dictionary of Ming Biography.* 2 vols. New York: Columbia University Press, 1976.

Graham, W. T. "Yü Hsin and 'The Lament for the South' [*Ai Chiang-nan*]," *Harvard Journal of Asiatic Studies* 36 (1976):82–113.

Granet, Marcel. *Danses et légendes de la Chine ancienne.* 2 vols. Paris, 1926.

Hawkes, David, trans. *Ch'u Tz'u: The Songs of the South.* London: Oxford University Press, 1959; Boston, 1962.

———. "The Supernatural in Chinese Poetry." *The Far East: China and Japan (University of Toronto Quarterly,* supp. no. 5, 1961): 311–324.

———. "The Quest of the Goddess." In *Studies in Chinese Literary Genres,* edited by Cyril Birch, pp. 42–68. Berkeley and Los Angeles: University of California Press, 1974.

Hayashi Minao. "The Twelve Gods of the Chan-kuo Period Silk Manuscript Excavated at Ch'ang-sha." In *Early Chinese Art and Its Possible Influence in the Pacific Basin, vol. 1: Ch'u and the Silk Manuscript,* edited by Noel Barnard. New York: Intercultural Arts Press, 1972.

Heesterman, J. C. "India and the Inner Conflict of Tradition." *Daedalus* (Winter 1973): 97–114.

Hermassi, Karen. *Polity and Theatre in Historical Perspective.* Berkeley and Los Angeles: University of California Press, 1977.

Hightower, James R., trans. *Han shih wai chuan: Han Ying's Illustrations of the Didactic Application of the Classic of Songs.* Cambridge, Mass.: Harvard University Press, 1952.

———. "Ch'ü Yüan Studies." In *Silver Jubilee Volume of the Zinbun-kagaku-kenkyusyo Kyoto University,* pp. 192–223. Kyoto, 1954.

———. "The Fu of T'ao Ch'ien." *Harvard Journal of Asiatic Studies* 17 (1954): 169–254.

———. *The Poetry of T'ao Ch'ien.* Oxford: Clarendon, 1970.

Ho Ch'i-fang 何其方. "Ch'ü Yüan ho t'a te tso-p'in" 屈原和他的作品[Works of Ch'ü Yüan]. *Jen-min wen-hsüeh* 人民文學 [People's literature] 6 (1953).

———. "The Works of Ch'ü Yüan." *People's China* 14 (1953):5–9.

Ho T'ien-hsing 何天行. *Ch'u Tz'u tso yü Han tai k'ao* 楚辭作於漢代考 [*Ch'u Tz'u* was written during the Han dynasty]. Shanghai, 1948.

Hsieh Wu-liang 謝无量. "Ch'ü Yüan tsai wen-hsüeh shang chih chia-chih" 屈原在文學上之價值 [The value of Ch'ü Yüan in literature]. In Hsieh Wu-liang, *Chung-kuo liu ta wen-hao* 中國六大文豪 [Six great Chinese literary heroes]. pp. 6–55. Shanghai, 1916.

————. *Ch'u Tz'u kai-lun* 楚辭概論 [Summary of *Ch'u Tz'u*]. Shanghai, 1923.

————. *Ch'u Tz'u hsin lun* 楚辭新論 [New study of *Ch'u Tz'u*]. Shanghai, 1923.

Hsu Chung-yü 徐中玉 . "Tuan wu min-su k'ao" 端午民俗考 [Study of Tuan Wu folklore]. *Kuo wen chou-pao* 國聞週報 [National news], no. 15 (1936): 31–34.

Hu Huai-sha 胡懷琛 . *Chung-kuo pa ta shih-jen* 中國八大詩人 [Eight great Chinese poets]. Shanghai, 1925.

Hu Shih 胡適 . "Tu *Ch'u Tz'u*" 讀楚辭 [Reading the *Ch'u Tz'u*]. In *Hu Shih wen-ts'un* 胡適文存 [Collected works]. 6 vols. Taipei, 1953. 2:91–98.

Huang Shih 黃石 . *Tuan wu li su shih* 端午禮俗史 [History of the Tuan Wu festival]. Hong Kong, 1963.

Huang Yao-mien 黃藥眠 . *Ch'en-ssu chi* 沈思集 [Reflections]. Shanghai, 1953.

Hung Hsing-tsu 洪興祖 . "Fan fan Li Sao" 反反離騷 [Contre contre *Li Sao*]. In Hung Hsing-tsu, *Ch'u Tz'u pu chu* 楚辭補註 [Commentary on *Ch'u Tz'u*], pp. 88–89. Taipei: I-wen, 1968.

Hung, William. *Tu Fu, China's Greatest Poet.* Cambridge, Mass.: Harvard University Press, 1952.

Jao Tsung-i 饒宗頤 . *Ch'u Tz'u shu-lu* 楚辭書録 [*Ch'u Tz'u* bibliography]. Hong Kong, 1956.

————. *Ch'u Tz'u yü tz'u ch'ü yin yüeh* 楚辭與詞曲音樂 [Influence of *Ch'u Tz'u* on lyric poetry, dramatic poetry, and music]. Hong Kong, 1958.

————. "Ching Ch'u wen-hua" 荊楚文化 [Culture of Ch'u]. *Chung-yang yen-chiu yuan li-shih yu-yen yen-chiu so chi-k'an* [Academia Sinica, Taipei] 41 (1969): 273–315.

Jen Fang-ch'iu 任訪秋 , ed. *Chung-kuo ku-tien wen-hsüeh yen-chiu lun-chi* 中國古典文學研究論集 [Materials for the study of classical Chinese literature]. Wuhan, 1956.

Kammen, Michael. *People of Paradox: An Inquiry Concerning the Origins of American Civilization.* New York: Knopf, 1972.

Kikuchi Saburō 菊地三郎 . *Chugoku kakumei bungaku undō-shi* 中國革命文學運動史 [History of the Chinese revolutionary literature movement]. Tokyo, 1953; 1973.

Knechtges, David R. "Two Han Dynasty *Fu* on Ch'ü Yüan: Chia I's *Tiao Ch'ü Yüan* and Yang Hsiung's *Fan-sao.*" *Parerga* 1 (Seattle: Far Eastern and Russian Institute, 1968).

————. *The Han Rhapsody: A Study of the Fu of Yang Hsiung (53 B.C.–A.D. 18).* Cambridge: Cambridge University Press, 1976.

Ku Chieh-kang 顧頡剛 , ed. *Ku-shih pien* 古史辨 [Critiques of ancient history]. 7 vols. Shanghai, 1926–1941.

————, ed. *Meng-chiang ku-shih: yen-chiu chi* 孟姜故事研究集 [Legend of Lady Meng-chiang: anthology of studies]. Canton: National Sun Yat-sen University, 1929.

————, et al. "Mo-tzu hsing-shih pien" 墨子姓氏辨 [Symposium on the name Mo-tzu]. *Shih-hsüeh chi-k'an* 史學集刊 [Historical studies] 1 (1936): 151–175.

Ku Yen-wu 顧炎武. *Jih chih lu* 日知録. 6 *ts'e.* Taipei, 1956.

Kuo Chia-lin 郭嘉林. *Ch'ü Yüan, Ch'u Tz'u.* Peking, 1959.

————. *Ch'ü Yüan.* Peking, 1962.

Kuo Mo-jo 郭沫若. *Kuo Mo-jo shih chi* 郭沫若詩集 [Poetry anthology]. Shanghai, 1931.

————. "Ch'ü Yüan shih-tai" 屈原時代 [Age of Ch'ü Yüan]. *Wen hsüeh* 文學 [Literature], no. 2 (1936): 242–251.

————. "Ch'ü Yüan yen-chiu" 屈原研究 [Ch'ü Yüan studies], in Kuo Mo-jo, *Mo-jo wen-chi* 沫若文集 [Collected works]. Shanghai, 1946. 1: 1–147.

————. *Li-shih jen-wu* 歷史人物 [Historical figures]. Shanghai, 1947; 2d ed., Shanghai, 1951.

————. *Kuo Mo-jo hsuan-chi* 郭沫若選集 [Selected writings]. 2 vols. Peking, 1951.

————. *Ch'ü Yüan.* Translated by Yang Hsien-yi and Gladys Yang. Peking: Foreign Languages Press, 1953.

————. "Ch'ü Yüan, Ancient China's Patriot Poet." *People's China* 11 (1953): 12–17.

————. "Ch'ü Yüan: Great Patriotic Poet." *Chinese Literature* 2 (1953): 5–11.

————. *Ch'ü Yüan fu chin i* 屈原賦今譯 [New interpretation of Ch'ü Yüan's poetry]. Peking, 1954.

————. *Ch'ü Yüan wu mu chü* 屈原五幕劇 [Ch'ü Yüan, five act play]. Peking, 1954.

————. *Nu li chih shih-tai* 奴隷制時代 [Age of slavery]. Peking, 1954.

————. *K'iu Yuan.* Translated by Liang Pai-tchin. Paris: Gallimard, 1957.

————. *Selected Poems from the Goddesses.* Translated by John Lester and A. C. Barnes. Peking: Foreign Languages Press, 1958.

————. "Lang-man chu-i yü hsien-shih chu-i" 浪漫主義與現實主義 [Romanticism and realism]. *Hung ch'i* 紅旗 [Red flag] (July 1958); *Peking Review* (15 July 1958): 7–11.

————. Preface to *Liu Ya-tzu shih tz'u hsuan* 柳亞子詩詞選 [Selected poetry of Liu Ya-tzu], edited by Liu Wu-chi 柳無垢. Peking, 1959.

————. *Chung-kuo shih-kao* 中國史稿 [History of China]. 3 vols. Peking, 1964–.

———. *Li Po yü Tu Fu* 李白與杜甫 . Peking, 1971.

Kuo Yin-t'ien 郭銀田 . *Ch'ü Yüan te ssu-hsiang chi ch'i i-shu* 屈原
的思想及其藝術 [Thought and art of Ch'ü Yüan]. Chungking,
1944.

Lao Meng-yüan 榮孟源 . "Ko-jen tsai li-shih shang te tso-yung"
個人在歷史上的作用 [Role of the individual in history]. In
Li-shih chiao-hsüeh chiang-tso 歷史教學講座 [Teaching
history]. Peking, 1950–51.

———. *Li-shih jen-wu te p'ing-chia wen-t'i* 歷史人物的評價問題
[Evaluating historical personages]. Shanghai, 1954.

Lee, Leo Ou-fan. *The Romantic Generation of Modern Chinese Writers.*
Cambridge, Mass.: Harvard University Press, 1973.

———. "Genesis of a Writer: Notes on Lu Hsün's Educational Experi-
ence, 1881–1909." In *Modern Chinese Literature in the May Fourth
Era,* edited by Merle Goldman, pp. 161–188. Cambridge, Mass.:
Harvard University Press, 1977.

Lee, Sherman, and Ho Wai-kam. *Chinese Art Under the Mongols.* Cleveland: Cleveland Museum of Art, 1968.

Legge, James. "The Li Sao Poem and Its Author." *Journal of the Royal
Asiatic Society of Great Britain and Ireland* (London, 1895): 77–91;
571–599; 847–864.

———, trans. *The Chinese Classics.* 5 vols. Hong Kong: Hong Kong University Press, 1960.

Levenson, Joseph R. *Confucian China and Its Modern Fate.* 3 vols. Berkeley and Los Angeles: University of California Press, 1958–1965.

*Li-shih chiao-hsüeh chiang-tso*歷史教學講座[Teaching history]. Peking,
1950.

Li Yu-ning, ed. *The First Emperor of China: The Politics of Historiography.*
White Plains: IASP, 1975.

———, ed. *Shang Yang's Reforms and State Control in China.* White
Plains: M. E. Sharpe, 1977.

Liang Ch'i-ch'ao 梁啓超 . "Ch'ü Yüan yen-chiu"屈原研究. In Liang
Ch'i-ch'ao, *Yin-ping-shih wen-chi* 飲冰室文集 [Collected works].
67 vols. Taipei: Chunghua, 1960. 14:49–69.

Lim, Boon Keng, trans. and intro. *The Li Sao: An Elegy on Encountering
Sorrows by Ch'ü Yüan.* Shanghai: Commercial Press, 1929.

Lin Keng 林庚 . *Shih-jen Ch'ü Yüan chi ch'i tso-p'in yen-chiu* 詩人屈
原及其作品研究[Study of Ch'ü Yüan and his works]. Shanghai,
1952.

———. *Chung-kuo wen-hsüeh chien-shih* 中國文學簡史 [Short
history of Chinese literature]. Shanghai, 1957.

Lin Yu-sheng. "The Suicide of Liang Chi: An Ambiguous Case of Moral
Conservatism." In *Limits of Change: Essays on Conservative Alterna-*

tives in Republican China, edited by Charlotte Furth, pp. 151–168. Cambridge, Mass.: Harvard University Press, 1976.

Liu Hsieh. *The Literary Mind and the Carving of Dragons*. Translated by Vincent Y. C. Shih. New York: Columbia University Press, 1959.

Liu, James J. Y. *The Art of Chinese Poetry*. Chicago: University of Chicago Press, 1962.

Liu, James T. C. *Ou-yang Hsiu, An Eleventh Century Neo Confucianist*. Stanford: Stanford University Press, 1967.

————. "Yüeh Fei (1103–1141) and China's Heritage of Loyalty." *Journal of Asian Studies* 31 (February 1972): 291–298.

Liu Shih-p'ei 劉師培 . "Nan pei hsüeh p'ai pu t'ung lun" 南北學派不同論 [Northern and southern schools of scholarship are of separate origin]. In Liu Shih-p'ei, *Liu Shen-shu hsien-sheng i-shu* 劉申叔先生遺書 [Collected works]. 4 vols. Taipei, 1965. 1: 656–672.

Liu Ta-chieh 劉大杰 . *Chung-kuo wen-hsüeh fa-chan shih* 中國文學發展史 [Development of Chinese literature]. 2 vols. 2d rev. ed. Shanghai, 1973.

Liu Tsung-yüan 柳宗元 . *Ho-tung hsien-sheng chi* 河東先生集 [Collected works]. Taipei: Kuangying, n.d.

————. *Liu Ho-tung chi* 柳河東集 [Collected works]. Shanghai, 1933.

————. "Mi-lo yü feng" 汨羅遇風 [Encountering the wind at the Milo River]. In Liu Tsung-yüan, *Liu Ho-tung ch'uan chi* 柳河東全集 . Ssu-pu pei-yao ed. *ts'e* 2, *chüan* 49, p. 18b.

————. *T'ien-wen t'ien tui chu* 天問天對註 [Parody of the *Heavenly Questions*]. Shanghai: Futan University, 1973.

Liu Wei-ch'ung 劉維崇 . *Ch'ü Yüan p'ing chuan* 屈原評傳 [A critical biography of Ch'ü Yüan]. Taipei, 1962.

Lo, Irving Y. *Hsin Ch'i-chi*. New York: Twayne, 1971.

Lu Ch'in-li 逯欽立 . *Ch'ü Yüan Li Sao chien-lun* 屈原離騷簡論 [Short discussion of Ch'ü Yüan's *Li Sao*]. Shen-yang, 1957.

Lu K'an-ju 陸侃如 . *Ch'ü Yüan*. Shanghai, 1923.

————. "Shen-mo shih Chiu Ko?" 甚麼是九歌 [What are the *Nine Songs*?]. *Kuo-hsüeh yüeh-pao* 國學月報 [National studies monthly] 1 (1924): 79–89.

————. "Wu yüeh wu jih" 五月五日 [The Fifth of the Fifth]. *Kuo-hsüeh yüeh-pao* [National studies monthly] 1 (1924): 61–64.

————. *Ch'ü Yüan yü Sung Yü* 屈原與宋玉 [Ch'ü Yüan and Sung Yü]. Shanghai, 1935.

————. *Ch'u Tz'u hsuan* 楚辭選 [Collected writings on *Ch'u Tz'u*]. Shanghai, 1962.

Lu Hsün. *A Brief History of Chinese Fiction*. Peking: Foreign Languages Press, 1959.

———. 魯迅 . "Ma-lo shih li shuo" 摩羅詩力説 [The power of Mara poetry]. In *Lu Hsün san-shih nien chi* 魯迅三十年集 [Collected works of 30 years]. 31 vols. 1967. 2:53-100.

Lü T'ien-ming 呂天明 . *Ch'ü Yüan Li Sao chin i* 屈原離騷今譯 [Modern commentary on the *Li Sao*]. Taipei, 1969.

Ma Chün-wu 馬君武 . "Sheng Hsi-men chih sheng-huo chi ch'i hsüeh-shuo" 聖西門之生活及其學説 [Life and scholarship of Saint Simon]. *Hsin-min ts'ung-pao* 新民叢報 [New citizen magazine] 31 (May 1903): 2-4.

Ma Mao-yüan 馬茂元 . *Ch'u Tz'u hsuan* 楚辭選 [Collected writings on *Ch'u Tz'u*]. Peking, 1958.

Magnificent China. 2d ed. Hong Kong: Hua Hsia, 1972.

Maspero, Henri. "The Mythology of Modern China." In *Asiatic Mythology*. 2d. English ed. New York, 1963.

———. *La Chine antique*. Rev. ed. Paris: Annales du Musée Guimet, Presses Universitaires de France, 1965.

McMorran, Ian. "Wang Fu-chih and the Neo Confucian Tradition." In *The Unfolding of Neo Confucianism*, edited by W. T. de Bary, pp. 413-468. New York: Columbia University Press, 1975.

Meisner, Maurice. *Li Ta-chao and the Origins of Chinese Marxism*. Cambridge, Mass.: Harvard University Press, 1967.

Metzger, Thomas A. *Escape from Predicament. Neo-Confucianism and China's Evolving Political Culture*. New York: Columbia University Press, 1977.

Mills, Harriet. "Lu Hsün: Literature and Revolution—From Mara to Marx." In *Modern Chinese Literature in the May Fourth Era*, edited by Merle Goldman, pp. 189-220. Cambridge, Mass.: Harvard University Press, 1977.

Morohashi Tetsuji 諸橋 轍次 , ed. *Dai kan-wa jiten* 大漢和辭典 [Chinese encyclopedic dictionary]. 13 vols. Tokyo, 1957-1960.

Mote, Frederick. "Confucian Eremitism in the Yüan Period." In *The Confucian Persuasion*, edited by A. F. Wright, pp. 202-240. Stanford: Stanford University Press, 1960.

———. "A Fourteenth Century Poet: Kao Ch'i." In *Confucian Personalities*, edited by A. F. Wright and Denis Twitchett, pp. 235-259. Stanford: Stanford University Press, 1962.

Nienhauser, William H., ed. *Liu Tsung-yuan*. New York: Twayne, 1973.

Obata, Shigeyoshi, trans. and comp. *The Works of Li Po*. Reprint. New York: Paragon, 1965.

Osgood, Cornelius. *The Chinese: A Study of a Hong Kong Community*. 3 vols. Tucson: University of Arizona Press, 1971.

Ou-yang Fei-yün　　歐陽飛云　　. "Tuan wu o-jih k'ao"
端午惡日考 [Study of Tuan Wu as an evil day]. *I ching* 逸經
32 (June 1937): 488–491.

Owens, Steven. *The Poetry of Meng Chiao and Han Yü.* New Haven: Yale University Press, 1975.

Peking University Literature Department. *Chung-kuo wen-hsüeh shih*
中國文學史 [History of Chinese literature]. Peking, 1959.

Plaks, Andrew. *Archetype and Allegory in the Dream of the Red Chamber.* Princeton: Princeton University Press, 1976.

Postage Stamps of the People's Republic of China. Peking: Foreign Languages Press, 1959.

Pusey, James. *Wu Han: Attacking the Present Through the Past.* Cambridge, Mass.: Harvard University Press, 1964.

Rankin, Mary B. *Early Chinese Revolutionaries.* Cambridge, Mass.: Harvard University Press, 1971.

Rosenfield, John. "Western-style Painting in the Early Meiji Period and Its Critics." In *Tradition and Modernization in Japanese Culture,* edited by Donald Shively, pp. 181–219. Princeton: Princeton University Press, 1971.

Sariti, A. W. "Monarchy, Bureaucracy, and Absolutism." *Journal of Asian Studies* 32 (November 1972): 53–76.

Schafer, Edward. *The Vermilion Bird: T'ang Images of the South.* Berkeley and Los Angeles: University of California Press, 1967.

————. *The Divine Woman: Dragon Ladies and Rain Maidens in T'ang Literature.* Berkeley and Los Angeles: University of California Press, 1973.

Schiffrin, Harold. *Sun Yat-sen.* Berkeley and Los Angeles: University of California Press, 1968.

Schneider, Laurence A. *Ku Chieh-kang and China's New History.* Berkeley and Los Angeles: University of California Press, 1971.

————. "National Essence and the New Intelligentsia." In *Limits of Change: Essays on Conservative Alternatives in Republican China,* edited by Charlotte Furth, pp. 57–89. Cambridge, Mass.: Harvard University Press, 1976.

Ssu-ma Ch'ien. *Records of the Grand Historian of China.* Translated by Burton Watson. 2 vols. New York: Columbia University Press, 1961.

Su Tung-p'o　蘇東坡　. *Tung-p'o ch'i-chi*　東坡七集　[Collected works], Ssu-pu pei-yao ed.

————. "Chia I lun" 賈誼論 [About Chia I]. In *Ku tai Han yü*
古代漢語 [Classical Chinese], pp. 999–1004. Peking, 1964.

T'an Cheng-pi　譚正璧　　*Chung-kuo wen-hsüeh shih*
中國文學史 [History of Chinese literature]. Shanghai, 1936.

T'an Pi-mo 譚丕模 .　　　　*Chung-kuo wen-hsüeh shih kang*

中國文學史綱 [Concise history of Chinese literature]. Peking, 1958.

T'ao Kuang 陶光. "Ch'ü Yüan chih szu" 屈原之死 [Death of Ch'ü Yüan]. *Ta-lu tsa-chih* 大陸雜誌 [Mainland gazette] 8 (31 October 1950): 7–11.

Terrill, Ross. *Flowers on an Iron Tree.* Boston: Little, Brown, 1975.

Todo Akiyasu 藤堂 明保. "Kutsu Gen to Shiba Sen" 屈原と司馬遷 [Ch'ü Yüan and Ssu-ma Ch'ien]. *Tokyo Shina gakuho* 東京支那學報 [Tokyo China studies] 9 (June 1963): 85–98.

Tökei, Ferenc. *Naissance de l'elegie Chinoise: K'iu Yuan et son epoque.* Paris: Gallimard, 1967.

Tu Wei-ming. "Yen Yüan: From Inner Experience to Lived Concreteness." In *The Unfolding of Neo Confucianism,* edited by W. T. de Bary, pp. 511–542. New York: Columbia University Press, 1975.

―――. *Neo Confucian Thought in Action: Wang Yang-ming's Youth (1472–1509).* Berkeley and Los Angeles: University of California Press, 1976.

Tun Li-ch'en. *Annual Customs and Festivals in Peking as Recorded in the Yen-ching sui-shih-chi.* 2d rev. ed. Translated by Derk Bodde. Hong Kong, 1965.

Tung Tse-wei董子畏. *Ch'ü Yüan* (illustrated comic book). Shanghai, 1955; English ed., Peking: Foreign Languages Press, 1957.

Tz'u hai 辭海 [Chinese-Chinese dictionary]. 1 vol. ed. Taipei: Chunghua, 1956.

Wakeman, Frederic Jr. "The Price of Autonomy: Intellectuals in Ming and Ch'ing Politics." *Daedalus* (Spring 1972): 35–70.

―――. *History and Will: Philosophical Perspectives of Mao Tse-tung's Thought.* Berkeley and Los Angeles: University of California Press, 1973.

Waley, Arthur, trans. *A Hundred and Seventy Chinese Poems.* New York: Knopf, 1919.

―――, trans. *The Temple and Other Poems.* New York: Knopf, 1923.

―――, trans. *The Analects of Confucius.* London: Allen and Unwin, 1938.

―――. *The Poetry and Career of Li Po.* London: Macmillan, 1950.

―――, trans. *The Nine Songs: A Study of Shamanism in Ancient China.* London: Allen and Unwin, 1955.

―――, trans. *Ballads and Stories from Tunhuang.* New York: Macmillan, 1960.

―――, trans. *The Book of Songs.* New York: Grove Press, 1960.

Wang Chia 王嘉. *Shih i chi* 拾遺記 [Forgotten tales]. Edited by Hsiao Ch'i 蕭綺 (fl. 502–557).

Wang Ching-hsien. "Sartorial Emblems and the Quest: A Comparative

Study of the *Li Sao* and the Faerie Queene." *Tamkang Review* 2:2/3:1 (October 1971/April 1972): 309–328.

Wang Ch'ung. *Lun Heng.* Translated by Alfred Forke. 2 vols. New York: Paragon, 1962.

Wang Fu-chih 王夫之 . "Lung chou hui" 龍舟會 [Dragon boat society]. In Cheng Chen-to, ed. *Ch'ing jen tsa-chü ch'u chi.* Shanghai, 1934. Vol. 4.

———. *Ch'u Tz'u t'ung shih* 楚辭通釋 [Commentary on *Ch'u Tz'u*]. 1709; Shanghai, 1959; Taipei, 1966.

Wang I 王逸 . *Ch'u Tz'u chang chü* 楚辭章句 [*Ch'u Tz'u* edition]. Taipei: I-wen, 1967.

Wang, Gung-wu. "Feng Tao: An Essay on Confucian Loyalty." In *Confucian Personalities,* edited by A. F. Wright, pp. 123–145. Stanford: Stanford University Press, 1962.

———. "Juxtaposing Past and Present in China Today." *China Quarterly* 61 (1975): 1–24.

Wang Kuo-wei 王國維 . "Ch'ü-tzu wen-hsüeh chih ching-shen" 屈子文學之精神 [Spirit of Ch'ü Yüan's literature]. In Wang Kuo-wei, *Wang Kuan-t'ang hsien-sheng ch'uan-chi* 王觀堂先生全集 [Collected works]. 16 vols. Taipei, 1968. 5:1848-1855.

Wang Yang-ming 王陽明 . "Tiao Ch'ü P'ing fu" 弔屈平賦 [Lament for Ch'ü Yüan]. In Wang Yang-ming, *Wang Yang-ming ch'uan-shu* 王陽明全書 [Collected works]. 4 vols. Taipei: Chengchung, 1953. 2:119–120.

Wang Yun-hsi 王運熙 , et al. "Shih-lun Ch'ü Yüan te tsun Fa, fan Ju ssu-hsiang" 識論屈原的尊法反儒思想 [Ch'ü Yüan's pro-Legalist, anti-Confucian thought]. *Hsüeh-hsi yü p'i-p'an* 學習與批判 [Study and criticism] 1 (September 1973): 53–58.

Watson, Burton, trans. *Records of the Historian.* New York: Columbia University Press, 1958.

———. *Ssu-ma Ch'ien, Grand Historian of China.* New York: Columbia University Press, 1958.

———, trans. *The Complete Works of Chuang Tzu.* New York: Columbia University Press, 1968.

———. *Chinese Rhyme-Prose.* New York: Columbia University Press, 1971.

Wen Ch'ung-i 文崇一 . "Chiu ko chung te shui-shen yü Hua-nan te lung-chou sai-shen" 九歌中的水神與華南的龍舟賽神 [English subtitle: Water Gods and Dragon Boats in South China]. *Chung-yang yen-chiu yuan. Min-tsu hsüeh yen-chiu so chi-k'an* [Academia Sinica, Taipei] 11 (1961): 51–124.

———. *Ch'u wen-hua yen-chiu* 楚文化研究 [Culture of Ch'u]. Nan kang: Academia Sinica, 1967.

Wen-hsüeh yen-chiu yü p'i-p'an 文學研究與批判 [Literary research and criticism]. 2 vols. Peking, 1958.

Wen Huai-sha 文懷沙 . *Ch'ü Yüan Li Sao chin i* 屈原離騒今繹 [Modern commentary on *Li Sao*]. Shanghai, 1954.

———. *Ch'ü Yüan Chiu ko chin i* 屈原九歌今繹 [Modern commentary on *Nine Songs*]. Shanghai, 1956.

Wen I-to 聞一多 . *Wen I-to ch'uan-chi* 聞一多全集 [Collected works]. 4 vols. Shanghai, 1938; Hong Kong, 1968.

Werner, E. T. C. *Myths and Legends of China*. New York: Farrar and Rhinehart, 1922.

Wilhelm, Hellmut. "The Scholar's Frustration: Notes on a Type of *Fu*." In *Chinese Thought and Institutions*, edited by J. K. Fairbank, pp. 310–319. Chicago: University of Chicago Press, 1957.

———. "The Poems from the Hall of Obscured Brightness." In *K'ang Yu-wei*, edited by J. P. Lo, pp. 319–340. Tucson: University of Arizona Press, 1967.

Wilhelm, Richard, trans. *The I Ching or Book of Changes*. 2 vols. New York: Pantheon, 1950.

Witke, Roxane. "Mao Tse-tung, Women, and Suicide in the May Fourth Era." *China Quarterly* 31 (1967): 128–147.

Wong, C. S. *A Cycle of Chinese Festivals*. Singapore: Malaysia Publishing House, 1967.

Yang Hsing-fo 楊杏佛 . "Fan tzu-sha" 反自殺 [Against suicide]. In *Yang Hsing-fo wen ts'un* 楊杏佛文存 [Collected writings], pp. 229–230. Shanghai, 1929.

Yang Yu. "The People Commemorate Ch'ü Yüan." *People's China* 14 (1953): 30–31.

Yang Yung-tsung 楊胤宗 . "Ch'ü Yüan wei Ju-chia k'ao" 屈原爲儒家考 [Ch'ü Yüan was a Confucian]. *K'ung Meng yüeh-k'an* 孔孟月刊 [Confucius, Mencius monthly] 3 (Taipei, July 1965): 10–15.

Yen Hsüeh-k'ung 顏學孔 . "Tui ku-tai tso-chia tso-p'in p'ing-chia te chi-tien jen-shih" 對古代作家作品評價的几點認識 [Acquaintance with criticism of ancient writers]. *Wen shih che* 文史哲 [Literature, history, philosophy] 95 (1964): 8–18.

Yoshikawa Chu. *Taikan—Modern Master of Oriental Style Painting 1868–1958*. Tokyo: Kodansha, 1962.

Yoshikawa Kōjirō. *An Introduction to Sung Poetry*. Translated by Burton Watson. Cambridge, Mass.: Harvard University Press, 1967.

Young, Ernest. "Problems of a Late Ch'ing Revolutionary: Ch'en T'ien-hua." In *Revolutionary Leaders of Modern China*, edited by C. T. Hsueh, pp. 210–247. New York: Oxford, 1971.

Yu Kuo-en 游國恩 . "T'ien wen yen-chiu" 天問研究 [Study of *Heavenly Questions*]. *Kuo-hsüeh yüeh-pao* 國學月報 [National studies monthly] 1 (1924): 102–112.

————. *Ch'ü Yüan*. Shanghai, 1946; Hong Kong, 1957.

————. "Chi-nien tsu-kuo wei-ta te shih-jen Ch'ü Yüan" 紀念祖國 偉大的詩人屈原 [Commemorate our nation's great poet, Ch'ü Yüan]. *Jen-min jih-pao* 人民日報 [People's daily] (16 June 1953).

————. "Wei-ta te shih-jen Ch'ü Yüan chi ch'i wen-hsüeh" 偉大 的詩人屈原及其文學 [Great poet Ch'ü Yüan and his writing]. *Kung-jen jih-pao* 工人日報 [Daily worker] (15 June 1953).

————. *Ch'u Tz'u lun-wen chi* 楚辭論文集 [Anthology of *Ch'u Tz'u* studies]. Shanghai, 1955; Hong Kong, 1969.

————. *Chung-kuo wen-hsüeh shih* 中國文學史 [History of Chinese literature]. 4 vols. Peking, 1964.

————. *Ch'u Tz'u kai-lun* 楚辭概論 [Summary of *Ch'u Tz'u*]. Taipei, 1968.

Yu shih wen-i 幼獅文藝 [Young lions' literary arts.]. 30 (Taipei; July 1969).

Yu T'ung 尤同. "Tu Li Sao" 讀離騷 [Reading the *Li Sao*]. In Cheng Chen-to, ed., *Ch'ing jen tsa-chü ch'u chi*. Vol. 3.

Yü Ying-shih. "Life and Immortality in the Mind of Han China." *Harvard Journal of Asiatic Studies* 25 (1964–1965): 80–122.

Index

Designer: Dave Comstock
Compositor: Viking Typographics
Printer: Thomson-Shore, Inc.
Binder: John H. Dekker & Sons, Inc.
Text: VIP Electra
Display: Typositor Windsor Elongated
Cloth: Holliston Kingston 3543 Natural
Paper: 55lb. P&S offset regular

3